An Ideology of Revolt

JOHN'S CHRISTOLOGY
IN SOCIAL-SCIENCE PERSPECTIVE

An Ideology of Revolt

Jerome H. Neyrey, S.J.

FORTRESS PRESS   PHILADELPHIA

Chapter 6, "A Basic Model: Christology and Revolt," is a revised version of "Johannine Christology," in *Christ Is Community* (Wilmington: Michael Glazier, 1985). It is used by permission of the publisher.

The chart on pp. 120–21 is from Bruce Malina, *Christian Origins and Cultural Anthropology* (Atlanta: John Knox Press, 1986).

Biblical quotations, unless otherwise noted, are from the Revised Standard Version of the Bible, copyright 1946, 1952, © 1971, 1973 by the Division of Christian Education of the National Council of the Churches of Christ in the U.S.A., and are used by permission.

Library of Congress Cataloging-in-Publication Data

Neyrey, Jerome H. 1940–
An ideology of revolt.

  Bibliography: p.
  Includes indexes.
  1. Jesus Christ—History of doctrines—Early church,
ca. 30–600. 2. Bible. N.T. John—Criticism, interpretation, etc. 3. Sociology, Biblical. I. Title.
BTI98.N49 1988   232'.09'015   88–45334
ISBN 0–8006–0895–X

3464D88 Printed in the United States of America 1–895

CONTENTS

PART TWO.
NOT OF THIS WORLD:
CHRISTOLOGY IN SOCIAL-SCIENCE PERSPECTIVE

CONTENTS

LIST OF FIGURES

PREFACE

We are all familiar with the Prologue of the Fourth Gospel where the great affirmation is made that "the Word was God . . . And the Word became flesh." But what did it mean for Christians to acclaim Jesus as God? How could such a belief emerge from the unrelentingly monotheistic Judaism in which Christianity was cradled? And how can this same Gospel later insist that "the flesh is of no avail" and that Jesus is decidedly "not of this world"? The Gospel contains clues that its confession of Jesus as God and its devaluation of flesh brought it into extreme conflict both with synagogue Jews and other Christians.

This book first examines the content of the confession that Jesus is "equal to God," and then investigates the implications of the assertion that he is a heavenly figure who is emphatically "not of this world." No explanation of this Christology is complete without inquiry into the social dynamics of the community which authored it. The double assertion that Jesus is "equal to God" and yet "not of this world" describes an ideology of revolt against both synagogue Judaism and other forms of Christian confession. This book, then, is about the ideological implications of the confession of Jesus who is "equal to God," but "not of this world." To explain the social implications of John's distinctive Christology we will employ social-science modeling as well as more traditional exegetical questions.

The perspective of this book was shaped many years ago when I was a student of Wayne Meeks. He had just published his celebrated article on Johannine sectarianism, and was even then encouraging students to read biblical texts from social-science perspectives. Later involvement with Bruce Malina and the seminar in the Catholic Biblical Association on the use of the social sciences for biblical interpretation provided me with further experience in social-science modeling. My basic insight into the development of the Johannine community was first sketched in "The Christologies of John's Gospel," the fifth chapter of *Christ is Community*, which is reprinted here with the permission of Michael Glazier, Inc. The generous grant in 1984–85 of a Bannan Fellowship at Santa Clara University allowed me finally to write the book. And it is to the Jesuit Community of Santa Clara University, whose support and fellowship I richly enjoyed, that this project is dedicated.

JEROME H. NEYREY, S.J.
February 20, 1988

INTRODUCTION

BEYOND THE PROLOGUE

From start to finish, this investigation focuses on the high christological confession in the Fourth Gospel. It will not, however, concentrate on those classic places in the Gospel, such as John 1:1-2 and 20:28, where Jesus is acclaimed as "God" and "Lord and God." Rather, it will examine the Gospel's more pervasive discussion of Jesus as "equal to God" (5:18; 10:31-33). This focus does not imply a judgment that John's Prologue (1:1-18) has been exhausted by biblical criticism or that consensus has now been reached on its interpretation. I have decided that strategically it is more fruitful to concentrate on a systematic exposition of what I perceive as the real focus of the Gospel's high Christology: Jesus' status and powers as a figure equal to God.

We have a large body of scholarly literature on the Prologue. Studies of it have been primarily interested in its sources[1] or redaction.[2] Some scholarship also treats thematic issues implied in it: monotheism, preexistence,[3] or incarnation.[4] But little can be found on the precise contents of the Johannine confession of Jesus as a divine, heavenly figure. An attempt to specify what the author of the Gospel was arguing when he insisted that Jesus is equal to God will, I suggest, clarify more precisely what is contained in naming Jesus "God" (1:1-2) and "Lord" (20:28).

Inasmuch as confession of Jesus as equal to God is not common in the New Testament,[5] the Fourth Gospel's insistence that Jesus is equal to God is all the more striking. But what does it mean to call him equal to God? Of course, traditional methods of exegesis are helpful in this task. From a history-of-religions perspective, for example, we will discern how Jesus is equal to God because he enjoys God's two basic powers. He is rightly called God because of his creative power

1

and Lord because of his eschatological power. Jesus may also be con-sidered a divine figure because he functions as the appearing deity of Israel's past and because he enjoys God's eternity and imperishability, the formal content of "I AM" (Exod. 3:14). Much of my investigation will be accomplished by further study of Jewish midrashic materials and comparable arguments in Philo and Hellenistic literature, which are standard features of biblical scholarship.

The content of the high christological confession, however, did not emerge as a scholastic exercise. It developed and came to articu-lation in controversy. The social context, meaning, and function of the acclamation of Jesus as equal to God, therefore, must also be taken into account. This new focus requires techniques and ques-tions not traditionally employed in biblical interpretation—in this case, models from cultural anthropology. Thus this study consists of two parts. In part 1, using traditional exegetical procedures, I examine in detail the traditional issue of the content of the confes-sion of Jesus as equal to God. In part 2, with the aid of social-science models and perspectives, the ideological or symbolic meaning and function of that same confession is addressed. I demonstrate how Jesus, who is equal to God, is emphatically not of this world, a value statement that implies a distinctive social relationship to the world. Hence, the plan of this book is necessarily complex, reflecting the two parts of the inquiry: "Equal to God" but "Not of This World."

CHRISTOLOGY IN SOCIAL CONTEXT

Confession of Jesus as equal to God came to be understood as a state-ment that Jesus is radically from above and not of this world—John 1:14 notwithstanding. In fact, the Gospel indicates that confession of Jesus as a heavenly being from above was eventually understood as a negative judgment on the value and importance of his early deeds as well as on all things material of "this world . . . from below" (8:23). At a certain point, a judgment of value was made, "The spirit is what gives life; the flesh is of no avail" (6:63). That judgment celebrated what is from above while totally devaluing all that is from below. Such spatial metaphors and value statements have a direct bearing on the way the high christological confession should be understood. They are clues to the social context and social strategy of the Johannine community. In the case of the Fourth Gospel, they enable an investiga-tion of the ideological implications of the confession.

In part 2, therefore, I attempt to develop a series of overlapping models from cultural anthropology to study the context, structure, and strategy represented by the confession of Jesus, who is at one point described primarily as a divine figure. The work of Mary Douglas, as refined and expanded by biblical scholars,[6] can serve adequately as a basic cross-cultural model for our task. Her writings, moreover, allow for further refinement concerning the spirit/flesh dichotomy and the cultural implications of "spirit." They have a direct bearing on our appreciation of the Fourth Gospel, especially in the light of 6:63. After all, the high christological confession of Jesus as equal to God was phrased dichotomously, contrasting heaven with earth (8:23) and spirit with matter (6:63). Jesus, the divine figure, is preeminently from above, not from below; he belongs to another world, not this world; he is linked with spirit not flesh. Christology replicates cosmology, such that Jesus is an alien here below, this place of obtuseness, hostility, and evil. Douglas's work, "The Social Pre-Conditions of Enthusiasm and Heterodoxy,"[7] offers important further material for interpreting how such a high Christology can serve as a cipher for the Johannine community's alienation from the synagogue and its revolt against certain apostolic Christians of inadequate faith.

Finally, the Fourth Gospel came to place all value on the side of spirit over against flesh (6:63), a strategic move that implies that the heavenly, divine Jesus is linked with the symbolic meaning of spirit. What is needed, then, is a model of how spirit can function as a code word or symbol for a strategy of revolt. Douglas's basic model, her analysis of the spirit/flesh dichotomy, and her anthropological suggestions on how spirit is perceived offer a fresh, cogent, coherent, and testable way of examining the social implications of a confession that Jesus is radically from above, that he is equal to God but not of this world.

A CONTINUING CONVERSATION

If critical scholarship is best understood as a continuing conversation, the conversation most influential for understanding this study can be found in the works of J. Louis Martyn, Raymond Brown, Ernst Käsemann, and Wayne Meeks. Martyn[8] popularized in Johannine scholarship a model of the Gospel's historical development in terms of a shift from low to high Christology. At an early stage Jesus is called Christ, King, and Prophet, titles that still mean that Jesus is a human figure. Later, however, a high Christology developed in which he was acclaimed God and Lord and God. The Gospel, then, underwent a process of development, of which

Christology is a valid indicator. Brown,[9] while resistant to calling the Johannine community a sect, nevertheless showed how that group was fractured into competing and conflicting factions, which can be seen quite clearly in the polarized positions of 1 John 4:1–3 and 5:6–8. Again, Christology becomes the place where ideological positions are compared and contrasted.

In his interpretation of John 17, Käsemann argued that the incarnate Jesus is perceived there as a docetic figure whose glory and heavenliness so dominate the presentation of him as to diminish the value of his earthly existence.[10] While Käsemann's proposal lacks a certain exactness, he presents a perspective on the Gospel that I will define more precisely in part 2.

Finally, in his initial foray into the use of the social sciences for New Testament interpretation, Meeks[11] discussed the origin and function of the motif of the descending/ascending Son of man as an ideology for a group experiencing radical alienation. For Johannine Christians, the heavenly Jesus was an alien who was out of place here below in a hostile, evil world. This view of Jesus replicates the experience of the Johannine group, who were excommunicated from the synagogue and found themselves in conflict with their neighbors.

All of these scholars have urged that further conversation on the Fourth Gospel take into account development in the Gospel, which is reflected in the Gospel's Christology. This in turn comes to function as an ideology for the social location and strategy of the Johannine community. This book represents one more voice[12] in that conversation.

IDEOLOGY AND CONFESSION

Throughout this introduction I have alluded to an ideology encoded in the christological confession of the Fourth Gospel. In this I am refining several of the key ideas advanced by Käsemann and Meeks. Each argued that certain Johannine christological confessions imply much about the shape of the community that formulated them, the community's social dynamics, and its relationship to its neighbors. Although Käsemann did not allude to the sociology of knowledge, Meeks[13] modestly employed the work of Peter Berger and Thomas Luckmann.[14] While not relying strictly on the sociology of knowledge as described by Berger, I am pursuing the same question by using a more exact model.[15]

What is meant by "ideology" or the "ideological implications" of a theological statement? Feminist thinkers in our time offer a good example of attention to ideology, for they are keenly aware of what they would describe as a value system or ideology encoded in the way God and God's people are described in the Scriptures. Their impetus to develop nonsexist language is based on a perceived system in the Scriptures of values and structures that they find reprehensible.[16] For example, instead of constantly referring to "men of Israel" when an inclusive audience is implied, we should speak of "people of Israel," thus ensuring that the phrase does not carry the false idea that women are to be excluded from legitimate roles and status in society. Some also claim that reference to God as "Father" implies an ideology of patriarchalism, which leads to the subordination of women.

It is beyond our scope here to enter fully the discussion of ideology as it is found in the social sciences.[17] In one sense I am using the term in the same way as those who study the sociology of perception or meaning.[18] They describe the general way in which people need to impose order on the world and so develop coherent world views. Verbal communications, such as confessions, can indeed imply a system of cognitive and moral maps of the universe and urge a social behavior in keeping with this world view.

The confession of Jesus as "equal to God" was perceived in a way that associated him exclusively with the heavenly world of spirit, not the earthly world of flesh. This understanding must be seen in light of the confessing group's social experience of hostility from their neighbors and their own rejection of the world in which they were living. Their experience led them to an acute sense of superiority over the world. Such a perception places value only in the world above; it implies a posture of disdain for all that is from below. They identified as "from below" certain apostolic churches and even Jesus' own flesh, rituals, and death on the cross. The confession that emphasizes Jesus' heavenliness embodies the same ideology or cultural system as is found in cosmological statements such as John 8:23 and 6:63. In short, equal to God was understood as a value statement (not of this world). It implied both a coherent, systematic view of the world divided into above and below and a social attitude of superiority over all things fleshly, material, and earthly.

In one sense, I am not pursuing a new goal when I ask about the relationship of confession and social context and experience. It has been implicit in the longstanding scholarly search for the correct setting in life of a document, which is the legacy of form criticism. What is new here is the explicit appeal to formal social-science models and concepts to tease out the full structural implications of a confessional statement: What kind of group is reflected? What are its values? How does it structure the world? In other words, our interest lies in the cultural system[19] or perception of the cosmos[20] reflected in the christological statements of the Fourth Gospel. It is the hypothesis of this study that equal to God has ideological implications that correlate with a spatial map of the universe (heaven/earth, 8:23) as well as an anthropological map (spirit/flesh, 6:63).

PART ONE

Equal to God

EXEGESIS
AND EXPOSITION

1

JESUS,
EQUAL TO GOD:
JOHN 5

The initial half of this investigation focuses on the debate surrounding the claim that Jesus is equal to God. As I hope to show, this claim serves as a summary statement of the high Christology in the Fourth Gospel. Naturally, the place to begin is John 5:18, the first time in the Fourth Gospel that Jesus' equality with God is formally introduced and discussed.

This claim about Jesus' "equality with God" is embedded in a story that is narrated deep into the course of his ministry; the context in one sense presupposes that we are familiar with Jesus' sign-miracles and his conflicts in Jerusalem, for which the reader has been amply prepared. But, little if any preparation has been given to the reader for the novel claim of Jesus' "equality with God" (5:18) and the particular discussion of it (5:19–29), which seem to be new materials embedded in an older, traditional narrative in which a healing on the Sabbath leads to a forensic inquiry, such as are described in John 7 and 9. At first glance, it appears that there are two stories being told in John 5: (1) a controversy over alleged violations of the Sabbath (5:16, 30–47), which seems to be the older part of John 5; and (2) a charge and defense of Jesus as "equal with God" (5:18, 19–29). As we seek to understand the content of this claim on Jesus' behalf, we must take into account the history of this material to discover how a traditional healing narrative has been redacted into a controversy and confession of Jesus' equality with God.

My hypothesis about John 5 takes seriously the two narratives that make up this text segment. (1) An early narrative of a *miracle* (5:1–9) was redacted into a *controversy* over Sabbath observance (vv. 10–15), issuing in a *formal charge* that Jesus violates the Sabbath (v. 16), and precipitating a *defense* of Jesus' actions on the Sabbath (vv. 30–47).[1]

9

Centering around christological claims for the human Jesus, this redaction appears to be relatively early in the community's history. (2) But evidence in the text suggests another narrative, a shift in the charges against Jesus in 5:17–18, from a charge of Sabbath violation to blasphemy, in that "he makes himself equal to God." This new charge indicates a later development in the community's history when Jesus was in fact acclaimed as a divine figure. This is the period of high Christology. The defense of this new charge/claim occurs in 5:19–29, in which Jesus is shown to be equal to God by virtue of having God's two powers, creative and judgmental. The different redactions, which reflect different Christologies, occur at different periods of Johannine history. Let us, then, examine John 5, focusing on the different charges made against Jesus and the different apologies to those charges.

THE EARLY STRATUM:
SIGN, CONTROVERSY, DEFENSE

Scholars generally agree that the author of the Fourth Gospel had access to a source for the account of the healing in 5:2–9.[2] Four features indicate a form-critical similarity with typical healings found in the Synoptic Gospels: (1) the acute seriousness of the illness mentioned in 5:5 (cf. Luke 13:16; Mark 5:25); (2) the short conversation between Jesus and the sick person before the healing in 5:6–7 (cf. Mark 1:40; 9:23–24); (3) the healing word (5:8), which is identical with Jesus' word in Mark 2:11; (4) demonstration of the cure by carrying the pallet in 5:9 (see Mark 2:12).[3]

In incorporating this traditional healing story into the Fourth Gospel, the evangelist redacted it in several important ways. First, he added the note in 5:9c that Jesus had healed on the Sabbath, thus shifting the focus from a healing sign to a controversy. The addition of 5:10–16, which exhibits numerous characteristic elements of Johannine style and themes,[4] introduces the reader to the preliminary steps in a forensic process, not unlike the forensic processes found in John 7–10:

1. A crime is discovered: "It is the Sabbath. It is not lawful for you to carry your pallet" (5:10)
2. Responsibility is denied: "The man who healed me said to me: 'Take up your pallet, and walk'" (5:11)
3. Agent's identity is unknown: "'Who is the man who said to you, "Take up your pallet, and walk"?' Now the man who had been healed did not know who it was" (5:12–13)

4. Identity is reported: "The man went away and told the Jews that it was Jesus who had healed him" (5:15)

At this point, completion of a preliminary inquiry leads directly to a formal forensic process against Jesus. Now that the agent of the unlawful act has been properly identified, formal charges can be leveled against him personally.

Although a longstanding tradition exists about Jesus' alleged violation of the Sabbath, we should not lightly overlook the seriousness of this action as a symbolic challenge to the system of Jewish religion. Judaism in the first century paid special attention to three particularistic customs that served to distinguish and define members of God's chosen people: (1) kosher diet, (2) circumcision, and (3) strict Sabbath observance.[5] It is no accident that the controversy in John 5 takes place over Sabbath observance, a key indicator of authentic covenant membership. As I have shown elsewhere,[6] Jesus is engaged in a comprehensive campaign of contesting and replacing Jewish feasts, cult, and revelation. His challenge to the Sabbath should be seen as part of this general pattern of replacement.

In a book on the forensic character of John's Gospel, A. E. Harvey described the legal process reflected in John 5, calling attention to the charges lodged, the defense offered, and the role of witnesses in the defense.[7] In general, the judges were probably the leading men of the city or the synagogue, the ones who administered justice "in the gate" (Amos 5:15; Deut. 19:12). As Harvey points out, their function was not primarily the investigation of facts[8] but a decision on the admissibility and competence of the witnesses who spoke on behalf of or against the accused. In short, the essence of the forensic process lay in the battery of impressive witnesses who could be summoned to testify. As Harvey noted, the person with the more impressive array of witnesses normally won.[9] Clearly, John 5 knows of a charge (5:16), a defense (5:30–47), and a marshaling of competent and admissible witnesses on Jesus' behalf (5:31–39). No verdict is recorded.

Spelling out the forensic character of the passage, we note that John records a formal charge against Jesus in 5:16 ("He did these things on the Sabbath"), implying that Jesus had done something evil and is disobedient to God (see 7:23; 9:16, 24). The defense, which begins in 5:30, alleges that the charge itself is false. The action of Jesus is not the presumptive action of an evil and disobedient man. What he did was to heal, and healing is an act of God, not man ("I am not able to do anything of myself," 5:30a). His

11

action is not disobedient to God ("As I hear, I judge," 5:30b); nor is it a rebellious act of independence from God ("My judgment is just because I do not seek my own will but the will of him who sent me," 5:30c). The charge, then, is totally false. Jesus has done nothing disobedient; on the contrary, he has acted obediently and in accord with God's will.

Following the defendant's rejection of the charge (5:30), he calls on his defense witnesses to testify that he is a God-fearing person. Admitting the legal fact that his testimony alone is not valid (5:31; see 8:13, 17)[10] he calls upon a series of four witnesses acceptable to these judges.[11] The first witness, John the Baptizer (5:33–35),[12] is eminently acceptable to them, for they themselves formerly sent to him for testimony (5:33, see 1:19, 25) and "rejoiced in the light" of his testimony (5:35), for he is acknowledged as one who witnesses to the truth (5:33b). He enjoys, then, an unimpeachable standing in this court. Furthermore, the exclusive function of the Baptizer in this Gospel has been that of a forensic witness.[13] He came for testimony, to bear witness to the light (*eis martyrian* . . . *hina martyrēsei*, 1:7–8); he testified concerning the "one coming after me" (*martyrei*, 1:15). His testimony (*hautē hē martyria*, 1:19), which is a confession about the worthiness of the "one coming after" him, affirms Jesus' fundamental holiness when he claims that he saw the Spirit of God on Jesus (*emartyrēsen*, 1:32). John, then, has been a consistent witness to Jesus' sinlessness; for, according to him, Jesus is not a sinner who is hostile to God, but rather the "Son of God" (1:34). Far from being sinful, Jesus is the Lamb of God who takes away the sin of the world (1:29, 36). This body of testimony to Jesus' sinlessness is evoked in summoning John to witness in Jesus' defense in 5:33–35.

The works of Jesus constitute a second and better witness (5:36).[14] This kind of testimony has already been admitted into court by the Jewish leader Nicodemus, who acknowledged Jesus as a "teacher from God," because "nobody could do the signs you do unless God were with him" (3:2). Other Jews have accepted this testimony when they exclaim, "The Christ, when he comes, will he do more signs than this man does?" (7:31). Jesus' working on the Sabbath, however, can produce diverse judgments among Jews. Confronted with the man born blind, the Pharisees judge negatively, "This man is not of God, for he does not keep the Sabbath" (9:16a). But others judge differently, "How can a sinner do such signs?" (9:16b). This dual judgment is repeated at the end of John 9 when the Pharisees render their final judgment: "We know that this man is a sinner" (9:24). But the man born blind renders the better judgment: "We know that God does not listen to sinners, but if any one is a worshiper of God and does his will, God listens to him. Never since the world began has it been heard that any one opened the eyes of a man born blind. *If this man were not from God, he could do nothing*" (9:31–33). The works of Jesus, therefore, are an acceptable witness to many, and they testify "that the Father sent me" (5:36). Jesus, then, has done nothing evil nor is he a sinner, hostile to God. He has, in fact, healed, which he could never do were he not from God.

The third witness is God (5:37–38), whose testimony is difficult to obtain.[15] The text insists that God has already given testimony (*memartyrēken*, 5:37; cf. 8:18). Since in John, God did not speak "You are my beloved son" at Jesus' baptism or transfiguration, we must look elsewhere for God's testimony. "No one," moreover, "has ever seen God" (1:18; 6:46); nor has "anyone ever gone up to heaven" (3:13) to receive God's revelations. In fact, the text asserts that no one has ever heard God's voice or seen his image (5:37–38), so no appeal can be made to a revelatory tradition, such as Sinai.[16] Where, then, can we find God's testimony to Jesus? The works the Father gave Jesus to do are God's testimony (see 10:25, 36); these works are done in public for all to see (7:31; 18:20); they testify that he does nothing evil or hostile to God (on the contrary, see 9:31–33). God's other testimony can be found in the Scriptures.[17] It has been suggested that God's testimony in 5:37–38 is God's word to the world, which Jesus was commissioned to speak.[18] If the issue were one of revelation or Torah, this suggestion would be persuasive. But the issue here is a forensic defense, and the witnessing here must be construed in terms of Jesus' forensic defense. The function of witnessing, then, is not revelation but forensic defense.[19]

The fourth witness to testify on Jesus' behalf is the Scriptures (5:39–40), a witness whose testimony is readily accessible to all.[20] The early testimony about Jesus was based in part on searching the Scriptures, which witness to "the one of whom Moses in the Law and also the Prophets wrote" (1:45).[21] This scriptural testimony of Moses is evoked again in 5:46, where Jesus claims that "Moses wrote about me." Like Jesus' works, this testimony is subject to differing judgments. In John 7 a schism occurs over the use of Scripture in testifying to Jesus: some accept the apostolic interpretation of the Scriptures, but others search the Scriptures to prove that Jesus *cannot* be the Christ (7:40–43, 52). The Scriptures, one way or another, testify about the claims of Jesus.

Jesus' defense, then, consists of a rejection of the charge itself (5:30) and the summoning of a battery of witnesses on his behalf (5:31–39). Inasmuch as the weight of forensic proceedings rested on the admissibility and competence of the witnesses summoned, Jesus' list of witnesses (John the Baptizer, miracles, God, and Scripture) is admissible, impressive, and persuasive.

In forensic proceedings it was possible that a defendant's case might be argued so convincingly that his accusers were shown to have been at fault in charging him in the first place; and so they bring down judgment upon themselves.[22] In Jewish trials, it was not always clear who was judging whom, for the tables might actually be turned as the case progressed. The accusers would become the accused and the judges find themselves judged. This seems to be the case in the trial of Jesus in 5:41–47. The tables are turned and the judges are judged.[23] A countercharge is made against the judges of Jesus: it is not Jesus who is a disobedient sinner but the judges themselves ("I know that you do not have the love of God in you," 5:42). The proof of the charge lies in their failure to accept God's emissary ("I have come in the name of my Father, and you do not receive me," 5:43). In form this resembles the reversal of charges in John 3, where Nicodemus was charged with failing to accept the testimony of Jesus (3:11) and is judged for rejecting the one whom God sent (3:16–19).[24]

The inverted trial continues. The judges of Jesus acquire a special prosecuting witness, Moses. Ironically, Moses was Israel's repeated defender and paraclete (Exod. 32:11–14; Num. 14:13–19). Wayne A. Meeks has collected numerous instances of this tradition in Philo, Josephus, Qumran, and the midrashim.[25] They all attest to the obvious expectation of Moses as Israel's defender and hence to the extraordinary irony of the Johannine claim that Moses will be witness for the prosecution, not the defense. The judges, it is charged, do not believe Moses; if they did, they would believe Jesus, "for Moses wrote about me" (5:46).

The tables are turned; the judges are themselves judged; the defender becomes the prosecutor. The charges of evildoing and disobedience are ultimately turned back on the accusers. And Jesus is not just innocent of evil, but vindicated in his claim to be God's apostle and revealer.

The form-critical analysis of John 5:10–16, 30–47 indicates the extent of this first Johannine redaction of a simple healing story (5:2–9) into a report of a formal forensic proceeding against Jesus.

14

Yet this Johannine redaction raises another issue: At what point in the Johannine history was this miracle story made into a forensic inquiry? Or to rephrase this in the light of J. Louis Martyn's suggestions, what elements of the community history are reflected in the story of Jesus' controversy with the Jews? These verses, 5:10–16 and 30–47, reflect a situation later than the missionary propaganda of the first disciples, the proclamation of Jesus' signs. The issue no longer appears to be mission but defense: the appropriate form is no longer preaching but forensic apology. The noncombative relations between Nicodemus and Jesus have given way to a highly aggressive situation in which Jesus is formally persecuted, charges are levied, and a defense is required. The missionary propaganda converted some, but not others. Yet the dynamic in 5:10–16 reveals not simply the reaction of people who were not persuaded, but rather aggressive charges against Jesus that he does what is unlawful, that he is a sinner (9:16, 24), that he has a demon (7:20; 10:20), and that he is leading the people astray (7:13, 47). This is the stuff of formal controversy.

This redaction of John 5:2–9 belongs to a larger pattern of redaction in the Johannine narrative in which formal forensic processes against Jesus begin to be described in full. Martyn has suggested that the story of Jesus serves as a cipher for the story of the Johannine church. He describes the forensic material in John 5 in terms of the attempt by the synagogue to erect a wall of separation between it and the followers of Jesus. Once Jesus and his preachers were heard and their message evaluated, it became evident to some that they were outside the pale of synagogue orthodoxy. A wall of separation arose.[26] Efforts were made to identify Christians and, when found, to charge them with evil and error, and expel them. This portrays the Johannine Christians in a rather defensive stance; the optimistic propaganda of its missionary posture yields to apologetic responses in the context of forensic proceedings. The Christology here is most definitely not high, for it deals with Jesus as reforming prophet, an authorized agent from God. It suggests an early stage of the Gospel's development.

A SECOND REDACTION

Yet John 5 appears to have undergone another redaction, for we have not only two different charges (5:16, 18) but different defenses (5:30–47, 19–29). What is immediately striking is the difference in the two charges leveled against Jesus in the controversy that results from his healing on the Sabbath.

5:16	5:18
This was why the Jews *persecuted* Jesus because he did this on *the Sabbath*	This was why the Jews *sought all the more* to kill Jesus because he not only broke *the Sabbath,* but also called God his own Father, making himself equal with God

First, the content of the charges is quite different: violating the Sabbath is *not* the same thing as claiming to be equal to God. The consequences of the charges are likewise different: persecuting Jesus is simply not comparable with seeking to kill him. The charge in 5:18 that he "makes himself equal to God" is not a natural extension of the charge of Sabbath violation in 5:16. Certainly the Synoptic Gospels show no trace of concluding to Jesus' divinity on the basis of his healing on the Sabbath. John 5:16 and 18, moreover, are not the only time in John that these two charges are distinguished. Although the Jews are portrayed as mightily disturbed about Jesus' works, especially his healings on the Sabbath (see 9:16; 10:21), when they seek to stone Jesus, their charge is formally blasphemy (*peri blasphēmias*): he, a man, makes himself equal to God (10:33). The evangelist distinguishes between Sabbath violation and blasphemy. If we compare the charges in 5:18 and 10:33 we find striking similarities: (1) in both it is charged that Jesus "makes himself God," (2) as a result, in both 5:18 and 10:31 the Jews seek to kill Jesus, the appropriate penalty for blasphemy, but not for Sabbath violation. John 10:31–33, then, has a direct bearing on how we are to read 5:16–18. Two persistent but distinct charges are leveled against Jesus: Sabbath violation and blasphemy. The distinction, moreover, between Sabbath violation and blasphemy indicates a second, later charge, which stems from a situation different from Jesus' Sabbath controversy.

The Fourth Gospel, second, records two different defenses in response to the two different charges. At the risk of anticipating the later analysis of these passages, it should be noted that 5:19–29 yields a coherent defense, but only in response to the charge in 5:18, not to that in 5:16. It argues clearly in favor of Jesus' equality with God by showing how God gave him his two comprehensive powers: to create and to judge. The defense in 5:30–47, however, has nothing to do with the charge of blasphemy in 5:18; it argues rather in response to the charge of Sabbath violation in 5:16, that

Jesus was sinful and disobedient for healing on the Sabbath. Instead of spelling out in detail how Jesus is "equal to God" in honor and creative and judgmental powers, as is the case in 5:19–29, the defense in 5:30–47 consists merely of testimony to Jesus' sinlessness, his obedience, and his authorization as God's emissary. The different defenses, then, respond to radically different charges.

Third, certain elements found in one defense are appropriate to it, but they are not found in the other defense. For example, a block of material in 5:21–29 deals with eschatological matters, while eschatological material is totally missing in 5:30–47. This is not surprising for it is difficult to see what having life in oneself and raising the dead have to do with Sabbath violation.[27] But this very eschatological material is appropriate in 5:21–29 for showing that Jesus is "equal to God"; for God has given him all judgment (v. 22), to have life in himself just as God has (v. 26), to be honored just as God is (v. 23). Because God has given Jesus his judgmental power, Jesus is truly equal to God. A second example consists of the matter of witnesses. In 5:31–39 witnesses are summoned to testify to Jesus' sinlessness and to the fact that he is God's emissary, and so they argue that his actions on the Sabbath are not sinful acts disobedient to God's law. But no witnesses occur in the defense in 5:19–29 for no witnesses can be summoned to testify that Jesus is equal with God. What is appropriate in one defense, then, is not appropriate in the other.

Fourth, even specific themes are treated differently in 5:19–29 and 30–47. (1) For example, Jesus' "works" in 5:30–47 testify that God sent him; they are his credentials. But in 5:19–20 Jesus' "works" are God's creative actions, which God gave to Jesus, so that Jesus is equal to God because he has God's creative power. (2) The judgment material is treated differently in 5:21–29 and 41–47. In the latter passage self-judgment occurs because the Jews reject Jesus as God's emissary (see 3:19–21). But in 5:21–23 and 26–29 God has given all judgment to Jesus so that Jesus judges. Having God's judgmental power to the full, Jesus is therefore equal to God. (3) The judgment materials, moreover, function differently in 5:21–29 and 41–47. In the former instance, they function as apologetic clarifications of the claim that Jesus is equal to God, whereas in 5:41–47, they are polemically directed against those who reject Jesus as God's emissary.

Preliminary investigation of 5:17–18, 19–29 suggests that it records a totally different forensic process against Jesus than that found in 5:10–16, 30–47, as the following summary indicates.

5:10–16, 30–47	5:17–18, 19–29
1. *charge:* Sabbath violation	1. *charge:* blasphemy
2. *defense:* witnesses testify to Jesus' sin- lessness and God's authoriza- tion of him	2. *defense:* exposition of how Jesus really is equal to God, because he has God's powers
3. *judge:* Jews judge Jesus	3. *judge:* Jesus judges all people
4. *witnesses:* John, Jesus' works, God, the Scriptures	4. *witnesses:* no witnesses summoned
5. *judgment:* judges are judged for rejecting Jesus	5. *judgment:* unbelievers judged for not honoring Jesus

The issue may be summarized. (1) There is a sharp difference between the charges in 5:16 and 18—Sabbath violation is not blasphemy. (2) The apologies in 5:19–29 and 30–47 argue totally different defenses. (3) Even the common topics within the two apologies are given radically different treatments in their arguments. (4) Two different Christologies are reflected in the two forensic processes: John 5:10–16, 30–47 argues that Jesus is the sinless agent of God, whereas 5:17–18, 19–29 maintains that Jesus is "equal with God." Thus it can no longer be maintained that 5:16–47 is a seamless, homogeneous text. New suggestions are necessary and welcome to account for the shift in charges, defenses, and Christologies.

A NEW CHARGE, A NEW DEFENSE:
5:17–29

According to my hypothesis, 5:1–16, 30–47 underwent another redaction at a later period of the Johannine history. The form of the narrative continues to be that of a forensic process: (1) Jesus makes a new claim (5:17), (2) which leads to a new charge against him (5:18), and (3) issues in a new defense (5:19–29).

Regarding the new claim, Rudolf Bultmann observed that 5:17 "stands out from the rest of the scene."[28] In it the justification for Jesus' healing on the Sabbath is raised to a level not found in the Gospel traditions, a level consonant only with John's high Christology. In short, Jesus' "justification" is a bold, new claim on his behalf. When we compare Jesus' defense in John with defenses in the Synoptic Gospels for "violating" the Sabbath, the explanations tend to fall

18

into two categories: (1) Jesus claims special prophetic authority to reform and correct Sabbath observance: "The Son of man is Lord even of the Sabbath" (Mark 2:28; Matt. 12:8); (2) Jesus does what he does on the Sabbath for humanitarian reasons:[29]

> The Sabbath was made for man, not man for the Sabbath. (Mark 2:27)

> Is it lawful on the Sabbath to do good or to do harm, to save life or to kill? (Mark 3:4)

> I desire mercy, and not sacrifice. (Matt. 12:7)

> Does not each of you on the Sabbath untie his ox or his ass from the manger and lead it away to water it? And ought not this woman, a daughter of Abraham whom Satan bound for eighteen years, be loosed from this bond on the Sabbath? (Luke 13:15–16)

Even in the evangelist's apology in John 7 for Jesus' behavior on the Sabbath, Jesus argues in ways similar to those in the Synoptic Gospels: "I did one deed, and you all marvel at it. Moses gave you circumcision . . . and you circumcise a man upon the Sabbath. If on the Sabbath a man receives circumcision, so that the law of Moses may not be broken, are you angry with me because on the Sabbath I made a man's whole body well?" (7:21–23). In this apology, Jesus presents a halachic argument proving that he did not violate the Sabbath, which implies a low level of authorization. A humanitarian motive likewise figures in the response, "I made a man's whole body well." This type of apology is consonant with the defensive apology offered in 5:30–47, where Jesus argues that he is not sinner but God's designated agent.

It is precisely on this point that 5:17 differs from typical synoptic apologies for Jesus' Sabbath behavior. The issue rests neither on humanitarian concerns, nor on prophetic authority, but in the claim: "My father is working even now, and I am working." John's Gospel considerably aids our interpretation of 5:17, for it gives an adequate contemporary reading of the passage in the next verse. Jews in Jesus' time would hear in 5:17 two claims, both dealing with John's high Christology: (1) he called God his own Father; (2) making himself equal with God (5:18). In 5:17, Jesus' remark functions differently from comparable apologetic remarks in the synoptic Sabbath controversies. First, it is more of a claim than an apology, comparable to other claims of Jesus in John's Gospel that provoke either misunderstanding or hostility (see 3:3; 4:10; 6:35–40; 8:21; 10:25–30). There are considerable parallels to Jesus' remark in

Philo and rabbinic writings which serve as apologies for the notion of a changeless deity *not* resting on the Sabbath.[30] But in 5:17, the evangelist is not interested in the technical explanation of how God can work and "rest" and yet be unchanging, but in Jesus' parity with God.[31] Yet, the issue of work/rest on the Sabbath introduces into the discussion the motif of creation and God's "resting" on the seventh day, thus putting the subsequent remarks in the context of a discussion of God's creative activity. If, as Jesus claims, God "is working still," then God continues to exercise creative power, even on the Sabbath. Accordingly, as God works on the Sabbath, Jesus works also, " . . . and I am working." And Jesus' action on the Sabbath takes on the same coloring as God's action: both are creative actions or exercises of God's creative power.

The quality of Jesus' action is now formally described not as a sign or a healing, but as a "creative action." His authorization to do creative actions rests on God's uniquely being his Father, and not on Jesus' being the Son of man (Mark 2:28). Jesus' purpose in doing this action is precisely to be like God and to act equally with God. The Johannine Jesus makes a new christological claim, far superior to the Christology of the earlier redaction. The new claim results in another forensic process, which begins with a new charge against Jesus. The charge in 5:18 is no mere doublet of 5:16, as was noted earlier. Verse 5:18 correctly understands the new christological claim made in 5:17, a claim that was interpreted as blasphemy, not Sabbath illegality. Hence the new charge!

Turning to 5:18, we note that the charge against Jesus contains two elements: (1) he makes himself and (2) equal to God.[32] Although Jesus' defense in 5:30 simply denies the charge, that is not the case in 5:19–29. The evangelist makes a careful distinction between two items in the new charge in 5:18: "He makes himself" is a false charge, which the defense roundly denies, whereas "equality with God" is not denied but firmly defended and explained.

Regarding the first element of the charge ("he makes himself"), it is explained in 5:19 that Jesus is certainly not acting independently of God, for "of himself he can do nothing."[33] Rather, he does "what he sees the Father doing," which does not mean that he spies on God or steals heavenly secrets. On the contrary, "the Father loves the Son and shows him all that he does" (v. 20). Inasmuch as no one has ever seen God (1:18) nor ascended to receive heavenly secrets honestly or otherwise (3:13), Jesus is placed in a unique position vis-à-vis God by these claims. He is not a mere human—for such

20

have never seen God; rather he has been shown these special works by God, surely in the heavenly realm in eternity, where God shows him all that he does.[34] Jesus, then, does not make himself anything; it is God who makes him equal to God by showing him and empowering him to do *all* that God does.

If the first part of the charge is dismissed, the second part (equal to God) is defended as true. The equality of Father and Son is argued in 5:19, where Jesus' deeds are judged not as sinful acts but as God's own deeds: "Whatever he does, that the Son does likewise" (5:20). These deeds are not simply prophetic signs and wonders such as are attributed to Moses, Elijah, Elisha, or any charismatic figure. Nor are these deeds presented, as they are in 5:36, as credentials proving that God sent him. Rather, the point is emphatically made that Jesus' deeds are God's own deeds, clearly asserting Jesus' equality with God.

Verses 5:19–20, together with 5:17–18, indicate that Jesus is credited with a special power of God.[35] The initial criticism of Jesus implied that as God rested on the Sabbath after creation, so should God's creatures. But John's Gospel asks whether God truly rested on the Sabbath. Did not God's creative/providential power continue? John and Jesus say that it did (5:17). Therefore, what Jesus is really mirroring in 5:19–20 is God's continuing creative/providential power: "My Father is working still, and I am working" (v. 17). As we noted above, the background of 5:17 is properly a discussion of God's creative activity, which continues after creation. Philo, for example, insists that God continues to work as a creator: "He never ceases to work all that is best and most beautiful" (*Cher.* 88–89), and "God never leaves off making, but even as it is the property of fire to burn and snow to chill, so it is the property of God to make" (*Leg. All.* I.5). The rabbis and the midrash agree as well that God indeed kept "working" even on the Sabbath.[36] Hence the appeal in John 5:17 to God's continued activity is a formal reference to his creative power. Thus when Jesus remarks that "The Father is working still and I am working," the activity of Jesus in 5:2–9 is made parallel to God's creative activity. The earlier miracle, therefore, has been reinterpreted as an act of creative power. The charge in 5:18 makes it clear that Jesus' activity is to be interpreted in this light, as a claim that Jesus does God's creative works. Inasmuch as the Gospel has already confessed that Jesus made the cosmos, and that without him nothing was made (1:1–3), the argument in 5:17, 19–20 can be seen to continue the proclamation of Jesus' continued exercise of the creative power of God.

21

The reader is reminded how this interpretation of Jesus' "working" differs from that in the other apology (5:36). In that latter passage, the evangelist labels the works of Jesus as an official *witness*, "testifying about me that God sent me." But in 5:19–20, the evangelist construes Jesus' works not as the credentials of an emissary, but as the creative work of God that Jesus does because he is equal to God. The different treatments are clearly in response to different christological claims.

In summary, 5:19–20 argues that Jesus is "equal to God" for God gave him his creative power. The remainder of the apology (vv. 21–29) deals with the second of God's powers given to Jesus, his eschatological power to raise the dead and judge them.

The defense, then, does not relax after showing how Jesus is equal to God in regard to his creative works. Even to show that was in itself a tour de force which should adequately answer the charge in 5:18 and put to rest the controversy over working on the Sabbath. But the defense boldly presses on to explain fully how Jesus is "equal to God"—equal in terms of having not only God's creative power but also God's judgmental power. This further discussion of Jesus' having God's judgmental power is not strictly necessary to answer the charge in 5:18. But in the interest of showing that Jesus is unequivocally equal to God, the evangelist further argued that he has God's judgmental power. Hence the discussion of eschatological material in 5:21–29 functions in the text as part of the apology to the charge in 5:18 by showing that indeed Jesus is "equal to God" because he has to the full God's two powers—creative and judgmental.

Again the strategy of the defense consists in denying part of the charge ("he makes himself"), while affirming another part of the charge ("equal to God"). The apology states emphatically that all that Jesus claims is God's *gift* to him:

The Father . . . has given all judgment to the Son. (5:22)

. . . so he has granted the Son to have life in himself. (5:26)

. . . and has given him authority to execute judgment. (5:27)

One part of the charge is false: Jesus never makes himself anything nor steals anything from God. All that he is and has, God has *given* him. And surely God is free to do whatever God wants.

John 5:17 labeled Jesus' Sabbath healing as a creative action, demonstrating his possession of God's creative power. "Creation," then, serves as a code word for God's power not only to make the

22

world but to continue it in existence and to act providentially on its behalf. Comparably, when we speak of eschatological power in 5:21–29, this is likewise a code summary for God's executive power to attend, not to the beginning of the world, but to its conclusion. God's fundamental authority over creation will be concluded in the eschaton by an interrelated series of acts:

Creative Power	*Eschatological Power*
1. to make the world	1. to raise the dead and give them life
2. to sustain creation	2. to judge the good and the wicked
3. to act providentially on behalf of creation	3. to be honored as Lord and Lawgiver
	4. to have life in himself (imperishability)

Regarding the apology for the second part of the charge in 5:21–29, the evangelist explains that Jesus is "equal to God" not only in creative power but now also in eschatological power. As the following indicates, Jesus has these four aspects of eschatological power:

God	*Jesus*
RESURRECTION	
"As the Father raises the dead and gives them life . . . "	" . . . so the Son gives life to whom he wills" (5:21). "The dead will hear the voice of the Son of God, and those who hear will live" (5:25). "All who are in the tombs will hear his voice and come forth" (5:28)
JUDGMENT	
"The Father judges no one . . . "	" . . . but has given all judgment to the Son" (5:22); " . . . and has given him authority to execute judgment because he is the Son of man" (5:27). "All who are in the tombs . . . will come forth, those who have done good, to the resurrection of life, and those who have done evil, to the resurrection of judgment" (5:28–29)

God	*Jesus*
HONOR	
"The Father has given all judgment to the Son, that even as they honor the Father . . . "	" . . . all may honor the Son. Who does not honor the Son does not honor the Father" (5:22–23)
IMPERISHABILITY	
"As the Father has life in himself . . . "	" . . . so he has given the Son also to have life in himself" (5:26)

Resurrection. "As the Father raises the dead and makes alive, so the Son makes alive those whom he wishes" (v. 21). John 5:25 and 28–29 describe how those in the tombs will hear Jesus' command and be resurrected (v. 28); and they will come forth to judgment, either a resurrection of life or a resurrection of judgment (v. 29). *Judgment.* Jesus not only raises the dead, he judges them as well; "[the Father] has given all judgment to the Son" (v. 22). *Honor.* These eschatological powers, moreover, have been given to Jesus for the expressed purpose that "all should honor the Son just as they honor the Father" (v. 23). His equality with God extends even to equal reverence; and it is God's will that this be so, not Jesus' vain self-extension. *Imperishability.* Finally, 5:26 takes up another aspect of eschatological power given to Jesus. The evangelist articulates anew the equality of Father and Son in terms of "having life in oneself." "As the Father has life in himself, so he has given the Son to have life in himself," which in this Gospel is related to Jesus' power over death, his imperishability, and his own resurrection (see 8:24, 28, 58; 10:17–18; 11:25).

The fullness of eschatological power is matched by the full extent of that power: (1) *all* judgment is given to Jesus; (2) *all* should honor the Son; and (3) *all* who are in the tombs will come forth at his voice. All power over everyone is given to Jesus! This eschatological material is of no particular help in answering the charge of Sabbath violation, but together with 5:19–20 it argues unequivocally and forcefully that Jesus is indeed "equal to God." He has God's creative and judgmental powers *to the full:*

Creative Power	*Eschatological Power*
God shows Jesus *all* that he does (5:20)	God has given *all* judgment to the Son (5:22)

24

In terms of the charge, therefore, Jesus does not make himself anything. God loves him and shows him all he does (v. 20); God has given him all judgment (v. 22). No, it is false to claim that Jesus arrogantly makes himself God. This is God's own doing. Nevertheless, he is "equal to God" in two basic but comprehensive ways. God has given him his two greatest powers: creative power (vv. 19–20) and eschatological power (vv. 21–29).

GOD'S TWO POWERS

What is the significance of arguing that Jesus was given both creative and judging powers? What do these two powers signify? I suggest that John reflects Jewish traditions about God's two powers, and so, to appreciate its importance in John 5:19–29, it is imperative that we briefly investigate the background of this material.

Philo was constantly concerned with giving the Hellenistic world a modern, rational explanation of his Deity and Scriptures. In his exposition of the mystery of God, Philo introduced a discussion of God's two powers. Humans cannot see God, who is invisible and utterly transcendent. They can only know God through the Deity's effects and operations. According to Philo, God's operations in the world may be broadly classified as creative and ruling, which Philo regularly calls God's two powers: *dynamis poiētikē, dynamis basilikē*,[37] a concept that includes of all God's powers (see *Plant.* 85–89; *Abr.* 121–22).[38]

As Philo discussed God's *dynamis poiētikē* and *dynamis basilikē*, he explained how each of these is a genus, inclusive of many diverse aspects. For example, *dynamis poiētikē* is described by the terms "goodness" (*agathotēs: Cher.* 27; *Sac.* 59), "kindness" (*euergetēs: Somn.* I.162–63; *Abr.* 124–25; *Plant.* 86–87; *Spec. Leg.* I.307), "beneficent" power (*charistikē: Heres.* 166), as well as "creative" power (*poiētikē: Fuga* 95, 100; *Mos.* II.99). It is through this power that God "creates and operates the world" (*Q.Gen.* IV.2). The *dynamis basilikē* is also a genus described by different terms, such as "sovereignty" (*archē: Sac.* 59; *Abr.* 28), "authority" (*exousia: Cher.* 27–28), "governing" power (*archikē: Abr.* 124), "punitive" power (*kolastikē: Heres.* 166; *Cong.* 171; *Q.Ex.* II.68), as well as "ruling" power (*basilikē: Abr.* 125; *Fuga* 95, 98, 100; *Mos.* II.99). By this power God "rules what has come into being" (*Q.Gen.* IV.2). These two powers, therefore, represent the complete and fundamental aspects of the Deity, creation and judgment.

At times the two powers are said to inhere in the divine Logos and to flow from that figure. In his allegorical exposition of the ark (Exod. 25:22), for example, Philo lists the various features of this object: the ark itself, the ordinances stored in it, the mercy seat upon it, the cherubim, and the presence of God. The two cherubim are identified with the two powers of God, in whose midst is the Logos. Philo then explains the relationship of the Logos and the two powers:

> And from the divine Logos as from a spring, there divide and break forth two powers. One is the creative power through which the Artificer placed and ordered all things: this is named "God." And the other is the royal power, since through it the Creator rules over created things; this is called "Lord." (*Q.Ex.* II.68; see *Fuga* 101)

The divine Logos, in consort with the Deity, exercises the two powers of God.

The two powers, moreover, are given exalted names by Philo.[39] *Dynamis poiētikē* is regularly called *theos*, whereas *dynamis basilikē* is named *kyrios*. For example, in explaining the cherubim (Exod. 25:18), Philo identifies the two powers of the Deity and names them accordingly:

> I should myself say that they [the Cherubim] are allegorically representations of the two most august and highest potencies (*dynameis*) of Him that is, the creative and the kingly. His creative potency is called God (*theos*), because through it He placed and made and ordered this universe, and the kingly is called Lord (*kyrios*), being that with which He governs what has come into being and rules it steadfastly with justice. (*Mos.* II.99)[40]

Thus, in Philo, the two powers of God include all God's actions, God's creation and ruling of the world. These two powers adhere in God's divine Logos, flow from that source, and are governed by it. They are respectively called by God's own names, *theos* and *kyrios*.

In his presentation of the two powers of God, Philo is generally considered to echo Jewish traditions about God's two "measures."[41] In the great revelation to Moses (Exod. 34:6–7), God was described as merciful and just, which two attributes were labeled in the rabbinic literature as God's two "measures" (*middoth*). God deals with the world in two ways, according to the measure of mercy or goodness and according to the measure of law and punishment. Each measure is itself generic for a host of God's actions;

for example, the measure of mercy is a creative activity; the merciful qualities of God are enumerated in the rabbinical sources as the "thirteen norms."[42] Philo also reflects older traditions when he identifies the two powers with God's two names. The rabbis likewise associate God's two measures with the two divine names, although they link the Tetragrammaton with mercy not judgment, and Elohim with justice not creation. Nevertheless, the pattern is clear that God's basic powers or measures are called by God's two names.[43]

Such a background offers many useful clues to 5:19–29. Inasmuch as it gives shape and form to the claim that the evangelist credits Jesus with God's two powers, the argument in 5:19–29 is clarified. Philo, moreover, offers a contemporary parallel for understanding the evangelist's claim that God could give exercise of these two powers to someone: according to Philo, the Logos has God's powers; in John, Jesus has them. Third, it can be shown[44] that other New Testament writers know of this doctrine of God's two powers, and so this Gospel can be said to be using easily recognized materials.

If the attribution of two powers to Jesus is clear, what about the names *Theos* and *Kyrios* in John? According to Philo and the rabbis, these names are associated with specific powers of God. Is this the case in John also? Does he indicate any correspondence between the two powers of God and God's two names? Although the data in the Gospel is meager, some evidence suggests that John distinguishes the meanings of the two names of God, associating them respectively with the two powers. Initially, the Gospel credits Jesus with creative power and in that context calls him *Theos*:[45] "In the beginning was the Word, and the Word was with God, and the Word was 'god' [*theos*]. . . . All things were made by him, and without him was not made anything that was made" (1:1–3). Surely when Jesus is called *theos* there, he is not acclaimed as Yahweh; rather, as the Jewish background suggests, he is called *Theos* in virtue of his exercise of God's creative power. *Theos* and creation—this is just the connection Philo noted so clearly.

John 5:17–20 is primarily concerned with creative power: the miracle itself (5:1–9) is interpreted in 5:17 in the context of Jesus' imitation of God's not resting on the Sabbath, that is, God's maintenance of creation. The defense in 5:19–20 asserts that Jesus sees and does all that God does, that is, God's act of creation and its maintenance. And so, when seen alongside of 1:1–2, 5:17–20 would seem to make the same connection between creative power and the name *Theos*. One must hasten to add that the association of *Theos* and creative power in John 5:17–20 remains implicit in that text and needs a clear standard such as 1:1–2 to make it explicit.

The case for *Kyrios* is more complicated. In the Fourth Gospel numerous references to Jesus as *Kyrios* are constantly open to the minimalist interpretation as "sir" or "master." But in 20:28 Thomas acclaims Jesus as "My Lord [*Kyrios*] and my God [*Theos*]." Bultmann is surely correct that here, at least, *Kyrios* is a cultic title;[46] in combination with *Theos*, Jesus is acclaimed as a heavenly being, equal to God.[47] But what does *Kyrios* mean in this context?

Jesus has already demonstrated by his miracle in John 5 that he possesses the creative power. Inasmuch as it was stated in 1:1–2 that he created the world, Jesus' action in 5:2–9 further demonstrates that he possesses the creative power of God—not only to make the world but to maintain it by his creative providence. Jesus' name of *Theos* is appropriate in 5:18—it has been demonstrated. Judgmental power, however, was credited to Jesus in 5:21–29, but it was merely an attribution that remained to be demonstrated, a demonstration forthcoming in the narrative.

The next three chapters of this study attempt to show that 5:21–29 indeed functions as a topic statement, which the evangelist will unpack and develop item by item in the subsequent narrative situations. In fact, the clue to understanding the christological claims of John 8, 10, and 11 depends on seeing them as conscious developments of each aspect of Jesus' eschatological power. The point of John 5:19–29 is that Jesus' claim to have full eschatological power is just that, a claim. Demonstration by the evangelist is necessary! By 20:28 the claim from 5:21–29 that Jesus has God's full eschatological power has been demonstrated, not only in Jesus' actions in John 6–19, but especially by Jesus' "taking his own life back" in his self-resurrection. But honor? Where is Jesus honored equally with God? Thomas's exalted confession becomes a paradigm of the Johannine community's honoring of Jesus as "equal with God." Thomas speaks for the group[48] when he gives Jesus honor equal with God: "My Lord and my God."

Like many ancient texts, the Fourth Gospel is structured according to rhetorical principles, and key rhetorical places in a text are its beginning and its ending. There a reader expects special communication of a summary or climactic nature. So it is with the Fourth Gospel: the clearest articulation of its high Christology is found in both its beginning ("The Word was 'god,'" 1:2) and its end ("My

Lord and my God," 20:28). Yet these two great confessions differ in terms of the power and the name given to Jesus.

Prologue (1:1–3)	Thomas's Confession (20:28)
1. *power:* creative power	1. *power:* eschatological power
2. *name:* God (*Theos*)	2. *name:* Lord (*Kyrios*)

If "Lord" in Thomas's confession can be said to have any content,[49] that content will be indicated from the context of the use of the title. Inasmuch as the meeting with Thomas is the Gospel's demonstration to him that Jesus is imperishable, that he has life in himself, and that he has raised himself from death, Thomas's appropriate acknowledgment of that power is contained in the new name he gives Jesus: not merely God, but also Lord.

This background yields still another point. Just as Philo and the rabbis ascribed to each of God's two powers a distinctive name, so it appears that in 1:1–3 and 20:28 the evangelist likewise associates Jesus' creative power with the name "God" (*Theos*) and his eschatological power with "Lord" (*Kyrios*). The Fourth Gospel, then, does not waffle in any way in calling Jesus equal with God. He has God's two basic powers to the full, and he is appropriately called by each of the special names corresponding to these two powers.

THE COMPOSITION AND
SITZ IM LEBEN
OF 5:17–29

Even if the background study of 5:19–29 confirmed John's argument there, a host of literary and historical questions remain concerning this second redaction of John 5. Whence the terminology and themes in 5:17–29? What period of Johannine history and experience (*Sitz im Leben*) is reflected by this further redaction?

Form. We noted earlier that the evangelist repeats the same forensic form that structured 5:10–16, 30–47 in 5:17–18, 19–29 by extending it to new issues, which lead to a new charge and a new defense.

Content. Commentators regularly note a certain repetition of terms and themes in 5:19–29 and 30–47.[50] A closer examination of these two blocks of materials, however, indicates that the alleged repetition is quite ephemeral and that deep differences exist just where similarity is claimed:

1. *Sabbath.* It is true that 5:10–16/30–47 and 5:17–29 deal with what Jesus did on the Sabbath. But how different is the perception that Jesus broke a Sabbath law (5:10–16) from the assertion that his Sabbath actions constitute a claim of creative power that makes him equal with God!

2. *Judgment.* In 5:30 Jesus says, "As I hear, I judge." This judgment, however, does not mean forensic judgment, but rather Jesus' evaluation of his Sabbath action and his knowledge of his authorization by God. As he says later, he does *not* exercise forensic judgment against his critics: "Do not think that I shall accuse you to the Father; it is Moses who accuses you" (5:45). Yet in 5:22 and 27 Jesus will actively execute forensic judgment as an official judge of all people.

3. *Works.* Jesus' works, which include healing on the Sabbath, are an important witness on his behalf. They "bear testimony that the Father has sent me" (5:36). Yet Jesus' works in 5:19–20 are the works that "he sees the Father doing"; for "*whatever* he does, the Son does likewise." Jesus' "works" are not limited in scope, for "the Father shows him *all* that he himself is doing." And "greater than these will he show you . . . "—the works of raising the dead (chap. 11) and even of raising himself (10:17–18). Prophetic credentials (5:36) are simply not the same works as "all that God himself is doing" (5:20).

4. *Authority.* Jesus says, "I can do nothing on my own authority" (5:30a) because his whole identity rests on being authorized as God's agent. While Jesus admits in 5:19 that "the Son can do nothing of his own accord," he goes on to explain that, in fact, he can do *all* because God has given him all power and authority, which surpasses that of a mere agent.

5. *Eschatology.* Whereas it rests on the believer to hear God's word, believe, and so have eternal life (5:39–40), in the second redaction, it is Jesus who makes alive (5:21) and who raises the dead to a resurrection of life or judgment (5:29). Self-judgment characterizes 5:39–40, but Jesus' eschatological judgment dominates 5:21–29.

6. *Honor/Glory.* In 5:41 Jesus boasts that "I do not receive glory from men," as does his audience, "who receive glory from one another" (5:44).[51] In 5:30–47 Jesus' glory and honor are solely from God, for only God's evaluation really counts. Yet 5:23 states that honor from men should be given Jesus, not just honor

as God's agent and emissary, but honor equal to God's. This reflects a shift from accepting Jesus as a prophet with a word of God to confessing him as a heavenly being who is "equal to God." Because of his special status, "all may honor the Son even as they honor the Father."

This list indicates that while Jesus' healing on the Sabbath precipitates both forensic processes, and while the same terms ("works," "authority," "judgment," "honor") occur in both versions of the controversy, they are used in quite different senses. The passage in 5:17–29 can hardly be a doublet of 5:10–16, 30–47, for it argues a completely different case. The hands may be the hands of Esau, but the voice is that of Jacob. The similarities exist because the second redaction was a substantive reworking of the earlier material, from which the evangelist borrowed existing, useful materials. Just as Renaissance Rome quarried the ancient ruins of the imperial city for stones and pillars with which to construct new palaces, so the evangelist used the existing form and terminology as the stone of his new building, the defense of Jesus' equality with God.

Collection. In understanding the composition of 5:17–29, one needs to recognize, for example, how the eschatological materials in 5:21–29 are in fact a *collection* of differing traditions and perspectives.[52] We can discern that 5:21–29, although a new redaction, was not cut of totally new cloth. On the contrary, the verses contain a variety of old and new, Johannine and traditional eschatological statements.

The presence of 5:24 in this passage constitutes the best evidence for the claim that 5:21–29 is a collection of old and new eschatological statements. Readers of the Fourth Gospel hear in it echoes of other typical Johannine remarks about realized eschatology and self-judgment. The synopsis at the top of page 32 indicates a remarkable degree of similarity between Jesus' remarks to Nicodemus and the eschatological perspective of 5:24.

It is also possible to hear in 5:21 echoes of earlier Johannine eschatological traditions; for that ambiguous remark about making alive could just as handily reflect what is stated in 10:10, "I have come that they may have life and have it abundantly," or in 20:31, "These things have been written that you may have life in his name."

Even 5:25 might be said to reflect an older tradition in the Fourth Gospel, related to an earlier version of the raising of Lazarus. As I

31

3:16–18	*5:24*
16. For God so loved the world that he gave his only Son that whoever believes in him should not perish but have eternal life.	24. He who hears my word and believes him who sent me has eternal life,
17. For God sent the Son . . . not to judge the world, but that the world might be saved through him.	he does not come to judgment, but has passed from death to life.
18. Who believes in him is not judged; who does not believe is already judged because he did not believe in the name of the only Son of God.	

---

will show in a later chapter, the raising of Lazarus is indeed an old tradition that was subsequently redacted by the evangelist.[53] John 5:25 need not refer to a future eschatological raising of the dead (as in 5:28–29), but is satisfied by the story of the raising of Lazarus. John 5:21, 24, and 25, then, reflect characteristic Johannine eschatological materials that had been part of the Fourth Gospel for quite some time. But they were collected and put alongside traditions of another stripe. In the text as it comes to us, the characteristic Johannine materials stand in considerable tension with 5:22, 27, and 28–29.

For example, the present possession of "eternal life" (5:24) stands in some tension with Jesus' future calling of the dead from their tombs to a resurrection of "life" or "judgment" (5:28–29). Again, while 5:24 states that "the believer does not come to judgment," the argument in 5:22 and 27 insists that God has given all judgment to the Son, who will judge all the dead (5:28–29). It can be shown, moreover, that these newer eschatological materials are old materials that belong to the established body of New Testament traditions.[54]

Since Bultmann, it has become a commonplace of Johannine criticism[55] to note that in 5:21–29 two types of eschatological statement are juxtaposed, that is, realized or present eschatology and futuristic eschatology. The issue is, Who put them side by side, and why? Bultmann's classic explanation for the juxtaposition depended on his view of the history of the Johannine Gospel: Originally the evangelist proclaimed only a present or realized eschatology, but a second-century redactor added the futurist statements for the purpose of taming the Johannine remarks and making the Fourth Gospel more orthodox for general consumption among the apostolic churches. But I have shown that there is a special christological argument operative in 5:17–29 in support of the distinctive *Johannine* high Christology that Jesus is equal to God. In proof of Jesus' genuine equality with God, the evangelist himself argued that Jesus has God's full eschatological power. The evangelist himself, not a second-century redactor, added the futurist statements in support of the high Christology, not to tone down any position. In explaining Jesus' equality with God, the evangelist collected older Johannine materials and traditional materials as well, to which he added special, new materials:

1. Older Johannine materials
   - 5:21   "to make alive"
   - 5:24   "self-judgment"
   - 5:25   "calling the dead to life"
2. Traditional futuristic materials
   - 5:22, 27   "Jesus as judge"
   - 5:28–29   "Jesus as eschatological judge"
3. Distinctive eschatological materials
   - 5:23   "to be honored equally with God"
   - 5:26   "to have life in himself"

In collecting these materials together, the evangelist gave a certain primacy to the new perspective, in which Jesus exercises active power. This means that in a certain sense the older traditions are modified. Yet the purpose of this collection was not to domesticate Johannine eschatology, but precisely to promote the Johannine high christological confession that Jesus is "equal with God."[56]

Topic Statement. A significant piece of evidence in regard to the composition and content of 5:17–29 lies in the next three chapters of our study. For as figure 1 (p. 34) indicates, 5:21–29 functions as a characteristic Johannine topic sentence, which serves as the agenda for the development of new eschatological predications made of Jesus in John 8, 10, and 11. This offers convincing proof that 5:17–29 reflects a later redaction of 5:10–16, 30–47, a redaction that focuses on the Johannine high Christology, indeed, Jesus' full eschatological power.

Occasion. What, then, of the occasion of this later redaction? What period of Johannine history is reflected in it? If I am correct in

FIGURE 1

ESCHATOLOGICAL POWER IN JOHN 8, 10, 11

Eschatological Power	John 8	John 10	John 11
1. *equal to God*			
He makes himself *equal to God* (5:18)	—	10:30, 33	—
2. the Son *gives life*			
As the Father raises the dead and *gives them life*, so also the Son *gives life* to whom he wills (5:21)	8:51	10:28	11:25a
3. *judgment*			
The Father . . . has given *all judgment* to the Son . . . and has given him *authority to execute judgment* because he is the Son of man (5:22, 27)	8:21–30	10:26	—
4. *equal honor*			
Honor the Son even as they *honor* the Father (5:23)	the name "I AM"	(10:31; 10:39)	11:4
5. *the dead hear and live*			
The *dead will hear* the voice of the Son of God, and those who *hear* will *live* (5:25)	—	(10:3–4)	11:43–44
6. *life in himself*			
As the Father has *life in himself*, so he has granted the Son also to *have life in himself* (5:26)	8:24, 28, 58	10:17–18 10:34–36	11:25a
7. *resurrection and life*			
All who are in the tombs will hear his voice and come forth, those who have done good to the *resurrection of life*, and those who have done evil, to the *resurrection of judgment* (5:28–29)	—	—	11:25a

discerning in 5:19-29 that the evangelist confesses Jesus to be "equal with God" in both creative and eschatological power, then the redaction of John 5 would belong to the same period of Johannine history in which the Prologue (1:1-18) and the confession of Thomas (20:28) were added to the Fourth Gospel. As I hope to show, this pattern of redaction can be discerned also in the eschatological claims of Jesus in John 8, 10, and 11. This second redaction of John 5, then, belongs to a later period of Johannine history and is reflected in the larger pattern of redaction of the Johannine Gospel which articulated the high Christology.

This literary development would seem to be occurring around the occasion of the community's excommunication from the synagogue. As the christological confession of Jesus rose to special heights, it was perceived by some as blasphemy, as a claim of ditheism.[57] This leads not only to persecution and excommunication, but also to a perceived death threat (5:18; 8:59; 10:31-33; 16:1-2). In this context, the articulation of Jesus' eschatological power served an important social function.[58] That Jesus should be honored equally with God (5:23) is affirmed as a God-given command, which is what the Johannine Christians are obeying in their high confession of Jesus. Their honoring of Jesus, of course, is costly for Jesus' followers. But since Jesus has all judgment, he will judge the faithful ones who so confess him and give them life, even as he will judge and condemn those who refuse him this honor (see 8:24). A guarantee of future resurrection unto life for the faithful and resurrection unto judgment for unbelievers and persecutors becomes important in the context of persecution and death threats against Jesus and his followers from the synagogue. The proclamation that Jesus has both creative and eschatological powers serves apologetically to support the persecuted group. As Jesus acted providentially to maintain creation on the Sabbath (5:17), so he has power to guard, protect, and defend his covenant followers. And as he will have the final word in history, he will vindicate himself and his followers who name him as Lord and God, even as he rebukes those who refuse him this honor. Although the evangelist credits Jesus with the active exercise of eschatological power as proof of his "equality with God," this new and different doctrine comes to serve an important social function in the Johannine community, thus assuring its place in the high christological confession of the group. What may have started out as a profound confession survives because of its utility.

SUMMARY AND CONCLUSIONS

In summary, this chapter has argued for the following points. (1) The tradition history of John 5 consists of a traditional healing story (5:2–9), which was redacted into a Sabbath controversy with a forensic defense (5:10–16/30–47), and which was later again redacted into a claim and defense of the Johannine high Christology (5:17–18/19–29). (2) The dominant form in John 5 was and remained that of a forensic process in which Jesus did or said something (claim), which led to a formal charge, and a defense. (3) Form-critical analysis indicated how different were the two charges of Sabbath violation (5:16) and blasphemy (5:18) and how these distinct charges led to different but appropriate defenses. (4) Different also were the confessions about Jesus either embedded in the controversy or formally expressed. Jesus' sinlessness and his authorization by God represent what I am describing as "low" Christology, confessions of him as an earthly, human figure. Confession of him as "equal with God," however, is of a higher order and represents the Gospel's "high" Christology, which acclaimed him as having God's two powers. As a result of the argument that Jesus fully has God's two powers, he may be correctly named God because of his creative power and Lord because of his eschatological power. (5) John 5:21–29, moreover, can be recognized as a collection of divergent eschatological statements. The evangelist himself collected old and new statements, although not because the older doctrine was too liberal and needed toning down. On the contrary, the ascription to Jesus of active eschatological powers and the addition of such novel ideas as equal honor (5:23) and life in himself (5:26) indicate that the evangelist himself was making even bolder claims on Jesus' behalf, claims that are distinctively Johannine, namely, equality with God. (6) The claims made on Jesus' behalf in 5:21–29 function as a typical Johannine topic statement, which contains the agenda of the redaction of John 8, 10, and 11, as the next three chapters will show.

2

JESUS'
ESCHATOLOGICAL POWER:
JOHN 8

We noted in chapter 1 that John 5 attributes God's two basic powers to Jesus: creative power (5:19–20) and eschatological power (5:21–29). The Johannine Gospel frequently presents a thematic statement or paragraph, which in subsequent dialogue the author unpacks word by word and theme by theme.[1] It is the hypothesis of this chapter that the remarks on Jesus' eschatological power in 5:21–29 function as just such a topic statement. That statement is subsequently explained, argued, and demonstrated in John 8, 10, and 11.

As this chapter hopes to show, John 8 explains in considerable detail Jesus' eschatological power, especially his power to judge (5:22, 27; 8:21–59). Other aspects of Jesus' eschatological power discussed in John 8 include (1) life in himself (5:26; 8:24, 28, 58), (2) honor (5:23; 8:49–50), and (3) gift of postmortem life (5:21; 8:51–53). John 8, then, carefully advances and articulates earlier claims that Jesus is equal to God by virtue of his eschatological power.

In regard to Jesus' judgmental power, however, John 8 contains a typical Johannine *aporia* or inconsistency, whereby Jesus initially insists that he does *not* judge (8:12–20), yet subsequently states that he has much to judge (8:26).[2] As we shall see, forensic process is the dominant formal structure of the narrative in John 8, as Jesus conducts a trial in which some people are formally charged, tried, convicted, and sentenced. This *aporia*, moreover, suggests that the narrative of chapter 8 has gone through a complex growth and development in the history of the Johannine community, a growth in which the high Christology was only later distinctively articulated and included.

JESUS THE JUDGE: 8:21–59

If we would argue that Jesus functions as judge in 8:21–59, we must be clear about his status and role in the earlier version of John 8, where he avows that he is *not* a judge. We begin, therefore, with a discussion of the precise forensic procedure described there as a point of contrast with 8:21–59.

Jesus, the Plaintiff: 8:12–20

Regarding 8:12–20, scholars agree that it is of a piece with the controversy narrated in John 7.[3] The occasion is still the Feast of Tabernacles (7:2), and Jesus claims to offer Christian replacements for the prayed-for water (7:37–39) and light (8:12). The forensic process against Jesus begun in John 7 continues in 8:12–20, as the following synopsis indicates.

1. TESTIMONY

8:12	*7:37*
I am the light of the world.	If any one thirsts, let him come to me and drink.

	7:38
He who follows me will not walk in darkness, but will have the light of life.	He who believes in me, as the Scripture says, "Out of his heart shall flow rivers of living water."

2. BASIS FOR TESTIMONY: FIRSTHAND KNOWLEDGE

8:14	*7:27*
Even if I bear witness to myself, my testimony is true; for I know whence I have come and whither I am going.	We know whence this man comes; when the Christ appears, no one will know whence he comes.

	7:17
	If any man's will is to do his will, he will know whether the teaching is from God or whether I am speaking on my own authority.

3. CRITERION FOR JUDGMENT

8:15	*7:24*
You judge according to the flesh; I judge no one.	Do not judge according to appearances, but judge with right judgment. (See debate over whether the Christ or a prophet can come from Galilee, 7:27, 40–44, 52)

4. ACCEPTABLE TESTIMONY:
TWO WITNESSES

8:16–18	*7:16–17*
Yet even if I do judge, my judgment is true, for it is not I alone that judge, but I and he who sent me. In your law it is written that the testimony of two people is true. I bear witness to myself and the Father who sent me bears witness to me.	My teaching is not mine but his who sent me; if any man's will is to do his will, he will know whether the teaching is from God or whether I am speaking on my own authority.

5. AUTHORIZED TESTIMONY:
AGENT SENT FROM GOD

8:19	*7:18*
"Where is your Father?" Jesus answered: "You know neither me nor my Father; if you knew me, you would know my Father also."	Who speaks on his own authority seeks his own glory; who seeks the glory of him who sent him is true and in him there is no falsehood.

6. SETTING OF THE FORENSIC DISPUTE

8:20a	*7:14*
These words he spoke in the treasury, as he taught in the temple.	Jesus went up into the temple and taught.

8:20b	*7:30a*
But no one arrested him	They sought to arrest him, but no one laid hands on him,

8:20c	*7:30b*
for his hour had not yet come.	for his hour had not yet come.

John 8:12–20 is linked with John 7 not only in terms of Jesus' claims to be the replacement of the Feast of Tabernacles. It is also formally shaped like chapter 7 according to an elaborate forensic procedure against Jesus.[4] In both texts, (1) a claim is made before the assembly of Israel in its most sacred location, the temple: Jesus is Israel's water (7:37–39) and light (8:12). (2) The basis for this testimony is examined: a witness should have firsthand information (8:14)[5] or be informed on the topic to which he witnesses (7:15). What makes Jesus an apt witness in this instance is that he is truly in the know: he knows whence he comes and whither he goes (8:14),

and they do not know (7:27). They might be in the know, if they were devoted to God (7:17). Because of his superior knowledge, Jesus' testimony ought to be acceptable at court. (3) Instructions are given to the judging public to judge justly and fairly; they should not judge with partiality,[6] according to the flesh or appearances (8:15; 7:24). (4) The testimony of a single witness is not acceptable in Israel's court (Deut. 19:15); yet two witnesses testify to Jesus' claims: Jesus and the one who sent him (8:16–18; 7:26–28). (5) Jesus claims to be a valid witness, deputized by the most honorable person as his personal agent,[7] and so an acceptable witness (8:19; 7:18, 28). In form, then, 8:12–20 resembles the kind of forensic procedure found in 5:30–46 and 7:13–52. The christological claims are still modest by the standard of this Gospel, and belong to earlier stages of the Johannine group's development.

Jesus, the Judge: 8:21–30

In a number of important ways 8:21–30 stands in considerable discontinuity with 8:12–20 and its themes, patterns, and argument. Characteristic of this Gospel, 8:21 serves as a fresh topic statement consisting of three items that will subsequently be developed: (1) "I go away and you will seek me," (2) "You will die in your sins," and (3) "Where I am going you cannot come."

Topic	A.	I go away and you will seek me (8:21a)
	B.	and you will die in your sins (8:21b)
	C.	where I am going you cannot come (8:21c).
Development	C'.	Then the Jews said: "Will he kill himself, since he says, 'Where I am going you cannot come'?" (8:22).
	B'.	You will die in your sins, for you will die in your sins unless you believe that I AM (8:24).
	A'.	When you have lifted up the Son of man then you will know that I AM (8:28).

The development of these topic items proceeds chiastically,[8] starting with the third, and so will our discussion of them.

(C) While the statement, "Where I am going you cannot come," sounds similar to 7:34, the narrator interprets it in 8:23 as a statement of fact that Jesus and his hearers belong to two different worlds: "You are from below, I am from above; you are of this world, I am not of this world." This is a damning statement in the Johannine idiom, a formal forensic charge. Jesus and his listeners belong to two irreconcilable, hostile worlds. He belongs to God's world, which they cannot enter, for they are truly outsiders to God and God's covenant.

(B) Jesus pronounces a sentence on the hearers, that they will die in their sins and never come into God's presence. This is explained in 8:24 to mean that "unless they believe that I AM" they will be sinners and die fixed in that sin, thus truly *not* of the world above which is God's world. As we shall see, this is a patent demand for acceptance of the Johannine high Christology. It is, moreover, the latest and most exalted of the absolute demands issued in the Fourth Gospel:

> Unless one is born anew, he cannot see the kingdom of God. (3:3)

> Unless one is born of water and the spirit, he cannot enter the kingdom of God. (3:5)

> Unless you eat the flesh of the Son of man and drink his blood, you have no life in you. (6:53)

> As the branch can bear no fruit of itself, unless it abides in the vine, neither can you, unless you abide in me (15:4).

Whereas these functioned at one time as formal criteria according to which one is reckoned either an insider or not, 8:24 becomes the new and transcendent forensic norm of judgment according to which Jesus' listeners will be judged. The ultimate and fatal sin becomes noncompliance with the demand to acknowledge Jesus according to the special formula, "I AM."

(A) The original remark of Jesus, "I go away and you seek me," again sounds similar to a remark in 7:33.

8:21	*7:33*
—	I shall be with you a little longer
I go away	and then I go to him who sent me.
and you will seek me	You will seek me
and die in your sins,	and not find me;
for where I am going	where I am
you cannot come.	you cannot come.

But in Johannine logic, 8:21a contains a statement of double meaning.[9] Its cryptic significance is lost on Jesus' listeners, but the narrator finally explains it in terms of his death. Jesus' going away and their seeking him refer to their attempts to kill Jesus: "When you have lifted up the Son of man . . ." (8:28). Verse 8:21, then, serves

41

as a topic sentence of three items containing the Johannine double-meaning words that are subsequently explained in 8:23–30. The issue of Jesus' being the light of the world and his apologetic defense of that claim (8:12–20) has vanished in favor of dramatic new matters.

The form of 8:21–30, moreover, differs from the forensic procedure described in 8:12–20, for it exemplifies the typical Johannine pattern[10] of statement/misunderstanding/explanation. Jesus makes an initial statement in 8:21 containing a double-meaning remark which the hearers misunderstand because they are outsiders and do not grasp the inner, spiritual meaning of his words (8:22). Jesus then issues an explanation, a further word (8:23–30), which exposes the extra meaning encoded in his original statement. This pattern can be found throughout the Fourth Gospel:[11]

FORM

Statement	3:3	4:10	4:32	6:41	8:21	11:11
Misunderstanding	3:4	4:11	4:33	6:42	8:22	11:12
Explanation	3:5	4:12	4:34–38	6:43–48	8:23–30	11:13–15

In shape and form, then, 8:21–30 differs significantly from 8:12–20.

The content of 8:21–30 is likewise distinctive. Whereas Jesus claimed to be "light" (8:12), he presents himself as "I AM" in 8:24 and 28, which should be interpreted as statements of the Johannine high Christology. Second, on the level of forensic procedure, 8:21–30 presents a quite different picture than does 8:12–20, where Jesus acted primarily as a witness testifying to a message he was authorized to speak. He is but a witness there, for as he says, "I judge no one" (8:15); the Jews assembled in the temple are the judges who are advised not to "judge according to the flesh" (8:16). But in 8:21–30, Jesus assumes the role of judge: "I have much to say about you and much to judge" (8:26). This shift in roles from witness to judge can be verified in the content and tone of the two passages. In 8:12–20, Jesus speaks an apology in defense of his claims, whereas in 8:21–30 Jesus as judge charges his hearers with a terrible punishment ("You will die in your sins") for noncompliance with a serious norm (" . . . unless you believe that I AM"). His tone is strongly aggressive as he charges his listeners with being totally different from himself: "You are from below, I am from above; you are of this world, I am not of this world" (8:23). Third, the reactions of Jesus' audience become significant. Whereas in 8:13 the listeners object to his words on legal grounds, in the subsequent narrative they totally misunderstand him (8:25, 27) and so prove Jesus' charge true: They are of a different realm from Jesus, they are outsiders, sinners, from below and of this world. From a forensic point of view, the Jews are formally charged with being outsiders to God's world (8:23). John 8:21–30, then, moves from defensive apology to aggressive judgment, from low to high Christology, and from testing Jesus' own claims to proof of the listeners' unbelief and sin.

The Trial of Pseudobelievers: 8:31–59

John 8:31–59, which necessarily continues the dialogue of 8:21–30, states that Jesus speaks to the Jews "who had believed in him," which links the audience in 8:31–59 with "the many who believed in him" (8:30). Scholars[12] have argued whether the audience in 8:30 and 31 is the same, for considerable ambiguity clouds whether those whom Jesus accuses of being slaves and sons of the devil in 8:31–47 could possibly have been believers. But this is precisely the point; the evangelist knows the ambiguity created in 8:30–31. Because there are pseudobelievers among Jesus' disciples, some attempt must be made to find out the truth according to accepted procedure, namely, a forensic process.[13] The critical issue in 8:31–59, then, is not whether some hearers historically did believe in Jesus on the occasion noted or whether Jesus could speak with such hostility. Rather, the Gospel portrays Jesus conducting a forensic inquiry to resolve the very ambiguity surrounding their claims in 8:30 to be believers—their testimony must be tested.

Many formal features in 8:31–59 unify the diverse elements in the narrative and present the reader with a strikingly coherent story. On a strictly formal level, 8:31–58 is structured in the typical Johannine pattern of statement/misunderstanding/explanation:

FORM	JOHN 8				
Statement	31–32	38	41a	51	56
Misunderstanding	33	39a	41b	52–53	57
Explanation	34–37	39b–40	42–47	54–55	58

Furthermore, the allusions to Abraham, his two sons, and his deeds also unify the discourse.[14] The subtext of this dialogue, however, carries the main argument, for it presents a lengthy forensic process in which Jesus functions as a judge. First, in 8:31–43 Jesus submits the testimony of the ambiguous disciples to careful scrutiny, pointing out that it is deceitful, false testimony. Second, in 8:44–47 Jesus formally charges these disciples with crimes of murder and lying. Finally, in 8:48–59, Jesus leads the accused in such a way as to prove his earlier charge, that they are of this world and from below, for they refuse to confess him as "I AM," and so will die in their sins. The tone, moreover, remains aggressive throughout, as Jesus judges them and relentlessly proves that they are in fact pseudobelievers. Three features, then, unify the dialogue in 8:31–59, the most significant one being the forensic trial that Jesus conducts. Let us move through 8:31–59, taking note of the forensic elements as they occur in the narrative.

1. As the trial begins, Jesus the judge[15] conducts a typical *cognitio*[16] of the testimony of the defendants to see whether it is true or false. *Cognitio* is the technical legal term for a judge's personal examination of the testimony of witnesses and plaintiffs. Are "the many who believed him" (8:30) truly his disciples? Jesus states his perception of this central issue clearly in his opening remark: "You are truly my disciples, if you continue in my word" (8:31). But how to get at the truth? In his *cognitio* of the case, the judge will make a series of formal statements to which the defendants must reply; and depending on their reply, the judge will know if they are telling the truth or not, which explains the conditional nature of his remark in 8:31.

In terms of the Johannine narrative, the form of the dialogue, statement/misunderstanding/explanation, serves the forensic process described above. Jesus' *cognitio* as judge consists in his statement to his so-called followers ("You are my disciples"). Their very misunderstanding of his words illustrates the falseness of their testimony that they are his disciples, for they do not "remain in his word." The judge repeats this pattern five times, which gives him ample evidence of the falseness of their testimony in 8:30 that they are his disciples. For example, Jesus asserts that true disciples continue in his word and know the truth, which makes them free. The negative reaction by the audience to Jesus' remark proves that they are not "free" descendants of Abraham through Isaac but slave descendants through Ishmael (8:32–37) because, as he shows, they do not remain in his word (8:32a) and his word finds no place in them (8:37b). Second, Jesus makes a remark about his Father and "their father" (8:38). It elicits more false testimony from the defendants as he proves that Abraham is not "their father" as they claim, because they do not do what Abraham did, namely, show hospitality to a divine visitor

44

(8:38–40).[17] A third time Jesus makes a leading remark about the defendants doing "what 'your father' did." It prompts them to make further false testimony, as they claim that "We have one Father, even God" (8:41). Jesus can then prove that they are wrong, for "If God were 'your Father,' you would love me, for I proceeded and came forth from God" (8:42). And so the judge has proved that the so-called disciples have from the start spoken only false testimony and are not his disciples at all. The *cognitio,* then, reveals that the audience always misunderstands the judge's statements, thus proving that they cannot be his disciples, because his "word does not remain" in them (8:31).

2. The judge's *cognitio,* moreover, leads to specific formal charges against those being examined. As the trial continues, Jesus formally accuses them of being enemies of God, offspring of Cain, and spawn of the Devil (8:44).[18] "You do what your father did" (8:41a), a general accusation that includes the specific charges of murder and lying. Concerning murder, Jesus states, "You are of your father the devil . . . he was a murderer from the beginning" (8:44b). This explains the cryptic double meaning in the remark that they were "seeking" Jesus, for while on the surface it might mean that they were seeking the truth, Jesus proves that their "seeking" (8:21, 28, 40) was rather a "seeking to kill" him (8:37). At first Jesus ambiguously remarks, "You will seek me" (8:21), whose sinister meaning is hinted at in the remark, "When you have lifted up the Son of man . . ." (8:28), but which is finally exposed for what it really is when Jesus states plainly: "You seek to kill me" (8:37) and ". . . but now you seek to kill me" (8:40). Inasmuch as they actually take up stones to throw at him (8:59), they prove the truth of Jesus' charge of murder. Like their father, moreover, they were murderers from the beginning.

Regarding lying, Jesus conducts a more complicated proof. Of their lying father it was said: "He has nothing to do with the truth, because there is no truth in him. When he lies, he speaks according to his nature, for he was a liar and the father of lies" (8:44). Lying, then, has two aspects: (1) having nothing to do with the truth yet (2) dissembling that one knows and says the truth. Of the listeners it is argued in fact that they have nothing to do with the truth, for if they were truly Jesus' disciples, "they would know the truth and the truth would make them free" (8:31). They dissemble, moreover, when they claim to be (legitimate) "descendants of Abraham" (8:32) but are not,[19] and boast that they are "sons of God" (8:41) but are not.

Finally, in 8:55, Jesus finishes his argument proving them liars. Speaking of God, Jesus claims to be the complete opposite of his audience: "You do not know him; I know him." This judgment of fact serves as the basis for Jesus' next remark: "If I said, 'I do not know him,' I should be a liar like you; but I do know him." Implied in this comparison/contrast is an accusation that they are liars. Were Jesus to dissemble, he would reverse his statement and say, "I do not know him." But Jesus speaks the truth when he claims ". . . but I do know him." The liars, on the contrary, dissemble when they say "I know him [God]," for their judge has persuasively shown that they *do not know God* or understand God's words, their dissembling to the contrary.

Besides the remarks above, John 8 contains elaborate forensic proof that the hearers "do not know God":

A. They say to him: "Where is your father?" Jesus answered: "You know neither me nor my father; if you knew me, you would know my father" (8:19–20)

B. They did not understand that he spoke to him of his father (8:27)

C. "I proceeded and came forth from God; I came not on my own accord, but he sent me. Why do you not understand what I say?" (8:43)

Constantly claiming to know God, the audience has never known God's agent or God's intentions. Besides being hopelessly ignorant (8:23), they are liars of the first order, for they dissemble concerning an object of the greatest importance, knowing God.

In proving them liars, Jesus demonstrates the forensic purpose of the dialogue in 8:31–58. Recall that Jesus already judged his listeners to be "from below" and "of this world" (8:23). To paraphrase, "they speak according to their nature" (8:44), that is, they naturally dissemble and lie when they say that they believe Jesus (8:30). It belongs to Jesus the judge to ferret out the truth, which in this case is to demonstrate that like their father, they are "liars *from the beginning.*" They always were and will be outsiders to God's word and God's covenant.

3. Thus far Jesus' trial of these pseudobelievers has proved their testimony to be false. Jesus has also formally accused them of murder and lying, serious charges indeed. The trial, however, is not over yet, as the accused proceed to convict themselves out of their own mouths. Mutual name calling takes over in the trial, as Jesus accuses

them of demonic allegiance, a charge they turn back on him. It is typical of accusations and slurs that they be returned in kind (It takes one to know one!). After Jesus proved that his listeners were neither children of Abraham nor children of God but of the devil, they attack Jesus with the same charges, accusing him of being: (1) a covenant outsider ("You are a Samaritan") and (2) son of the devil ("You have a demon"). The very fact of these charges against Jesus demonstrates that his accusers deny his message and reject its source, and so goes to prove that they are in fact "liars" and not his disciples. Those who malign Jesus as a Samaritan or demon-possessed could never in 8:30 have confessed him as "I AM."

4. After these opening slurs, the familiar pattern of statement/misunderstanding/explanation resumes in 8:49b–50. In the first instance, Jesus issues a complex statement:

> I honor my father, and you dishonor me.
> Yet I do not seek my own glory;
> there is One who seeks it and he will be the judge.
> Truly, truly, I say to you: if any one keeps my word,
> he will never see death. (8:49b–50)

The listeners pick up but a fraction of this statement and misunderstand even that. They clearly do not understand what is meant by "not seeing death forever." In fact, they do not even cite Jesus' words accurately, ironically demonstrating their perverse ignorance. Their misunderstanding, moreover, takes Jesus' more spiritual remark in a literal, physical sense, once more proving that they are "from below."

Jesus' word (8:51)	Their version (8:52)
. . . not see death forever (au. trans.)	. . . never taste death

Because of their misunderstanding, the listeners are put in the position of asking questions, a mode of syntax showing that they lack knowledge:[20] "Are you greater than our father Abraham, who died? Whom do you make yourself?" (8:53). In the irony of the moment, the people who were so sure that Jesus was a heretical son of the devil are now questioning whether he is greater than the archetypal patriarch.

Jesus' explanatory clarification (8:54–55) goes back to the substance of his remarks in 8:49b–50:

Statement (8:49–50)	*Explanation (8:54–55)*
I honor my father and you dishonor me.	
Yet I do not seek my own glory	If I glorify myself, my glory is nothing;
there is one who seeks it	it is my father who glorifies me,
and he will be your judge.	of whom you say he is your God. But you have not known him; I know him. If I said, I do not know him, I should be a liar like you; but I know him;
If anyone keeps my word he will not see death forever.	and I keep his word.

Since he is from above, Jesus speaks of heavenly things, especially of God. The listeners, however, are from below, and pick up only fragments of his discourse, fragments they understand in a literal fashion and in a fleshly mode. Although Jesus knows God and can speak of God, they have not known him, and so they misunderstand all of Jesus' remarks about God.

5. John 8:58 serves one more important function in the flow of the dialogue. Earlier in the text Jesus had made his listeners liable to a terrible punishment for noncompliance of a formal norm: "You will die in your sins unless you believe that I AM" (8:24). They seemed to have no clue at that point what he meant by "I AM," asking him, "Who are you?" (8:25).[21] Already in 8:28 he had instructed them concerning the meaning of "I AM" (8:28). When, moreover, he proclaims himself explicitly as "I AM" in 8:58, they know at least that he is claiming to be "greater than Abraham, who died" (8:53), and that he claims power over death (8:51). They reject this claim, as "they took up stones to throw at him" (8:59), and so demonstrate definitively that they do not believe him to be "I AM." The audience, then, would draw the correct conclusion that the pseudodisciples are justly condemned to die in their sins, as Jesus had charged. John 8:58 has served to dramatize the formal rejection of Jesus precisely as "I AM."

Forensic Process: A Resume

The evangelist apparently redacted John 8 to present the whole episode as an extended forensic proceeding, complete with all of the elements of a normal forensic process: a judge, a norm of judgment, testimony from witnesses, a judge's *cognitio*, formal charges, and proof. *Judge:* Although 8:12–20 records the testimony of Jesus as a knowledgeable, deputized witness to his Jewish judges, 8:21–30 portrays a shift in forensic roles, whereby Jesus becomes the judge and his listeners the plaintiffs.[22] *Norm of Judgment:* As judge, Jesus establishes a most solemn law, complete with punishment for noncompliance:

Law: Unless you believe that I AM

Punishment: you will die in your sins (8:24)

Along with this, Jesus the judge goes so far as to accuse his hearers of being totally sinful, that is, of not belonging to Jesus' world, which is the world of God: "You are from below, I am from above; you are of this world, I am not of this world" (8:23). His audience alleges belief in him (8:30), thus pleading not guilty, which would mean that they do not come under his judgmental statement in 8:23. But how true is their testimony of belief? *Judge's cognitio:* In 8:31–58, Jesus the judge conducts an elaborate *cognitio* of his plaintiffs to see whether they are in fact telling the truth that they are authentic believers (8:31). *Testimony of witnesses:* As the judge speaks to them, they bear testimony against themselves, proving that they are liars and so pseudobelievers. In forensic proceedings this is considered to be the best testimony at a trial, to have unwilling witnesses testify against themselves.[23] As a result of his *cognitio*, Jesus has discovered that they are really slaves of sin, bastards of Abraham, murderers, liars, and sons of the devil. *Formal charges:* Jesus' *cognitio* issues in formal charges of murder and lying. *Proof:* The proof that they are not truly Jesus' disciples comes from their repeated misunderstanding of his words. They are duly charged, tried, convicted, and sentenced.

More devastating, however, is the forensic demonstration of the truth of Jesus' charge in 8:23 that these alleged believers and Jesus belong to two different and irreconcilable worlds. This was no statement of tolerant pluralism, "We agree to disagree." Rather, it is an accusation by Jesus the judge that his listeners are neither genuine covenant members nor obedient children of God. This charge, if sustained, warrants the most severe punishment. And so a plethora of contrasts is produced that distinguishes true disciples from false, true sons of Abraham from bastard, and true sons of God from sons of the devil.[24] These all serve the judge's inquiry into his listeners' state of soul, a most serious forensic investigation.

A. *True Covenant Members*

  1. free

  2. sons, who remain

  3. descendants of Abraham, through Isaac

  4. they do what their father did: hospitality

B. *Father is God*

  1. my father, who is God

  2. I told you the truth from my father

C. *True Disciples*

  1. remain in my word

  2. who is of God hears God's words

  3. I honor my Father

  4. I know him

A. *Pseudo–Covenant Members*

  1. slaves

  2. slave sons, who do not remain

  3. descendants of Abraham, through Ishmael

  4. they do what "their father" did: murder

B. *Father is the Devil*

  1. your father is the devil

  2. there is no truth in your father

C. *Pseudo-Disciples*

  1. my words find no place in you

  2. the reason you do not hear them is that you are not of God

  3. and you dishonor me

  4. You have never known him

Every time the text records that the listeners misunderstand Jesus' remarks on a fleshly or literal level, they are shown to be from below and of this world. Likewise, every objection they make to Jesus' words only confirms their distance from what is from above and not of this world. The conclusive proof of Jesus' charge in 8:23–24 occurs in 8:59 when they take up stones to throw at him for his revelation that he is "I AM." The plaintiffs, then, have demonstrated beyond a shadow of doubt that they do not in fact believe in Jesus as "I AM," and so they stand condemned to "die in their sins." Jesus' initial judgment that they are "from below . . . of this world" has been proved true. Equally demonstrated is their refusal to confess him as "I AM." Both parts of 8:23–24, then, have been argued and demonstrated. The law, which was stated in 8:24, is shown by 8:58–59 to apply to them with devastating effect.

What, in fact, goes into judgment?[25] On one level, a judge hears charges and claims, which he tests for validity. Yet in the Gospel tradition, judgment has to do with separating the good and the bad. For example, Matthew records at least five parables in which judgment is described as an act of separation:

13:36–43	separation of wheat from tares
13:47–50	separation of good from bad fish
22:11–14	separation of those with from those without wedding garments
25:1–13	separation of wise from foolish maidens
25:31–46	separation of sheep from goats

It belongs to a judge to sift witnesses' testimony so as to know what kind of characters they are. The wicked have no place with the just and must be winnowed out, as chaff is separated from wheat (see Matt. 3:12). As noted above, Jesus' dialogue with the pseudobelievers in John 8:31–58 generates an elaborate series of contrasts which force a separation of (1) true, free sons of Abraham from false, slave sons; (2) sons of God from sons of the devil; and (3) true disciples from false ones. Jesus' discourse, then, is a forensic judgment in which he separates what is from above from what is from below and what is not of this world from what is of this world.

John 8 and Jesus' Eschatological Power to Judge

Although there should now be little doubt about the forensic character of 8:21–59, how should we construe this motif? I suggest once more that the presentation of Jesus as judge should be seen as his exercise of God's eschatological power granted him in 5:22, 27, and so as a demonstration of his equality with God. The essential relationship of Jesus' judgment and the high Christology of John may be seen from the following arguments. First, the criterion of Jesus' judgment is precisely the confession of high Christology, for people will be judged on whether they confess him as "I AM" (8:24). As we shall shortly see, "I AM" should be understood as a coded phrase for many of the tenets of the high Christology: (1) as a synonym for Jesus' eschatological power to "have life in himself" and (2) as the name of the appearing deity of the Scriptures. Second, 8:23 declares that Jesus is totally a heavenly figure. As I will show in chapter 5, 8:23, just like 6:62–63, encodes a statement about Jesus' radical heavenliness, his equality with God.

According to the argument that Jesus is equal to God, moreover, eschatological power is given to Jesus: "The Father judges no one, but he has given all judgment to the Son" (5:22); and "The Father has given him authority to sit in judgment, because he is the Son of man" (5:27). This grant of eschatological power has long presented a problem for interpreters of the Fourth Gospel. Although Jesus does not judge according to 3:17 and 12:47, according to 5:22, 27 and 9:39 he does judge. The solution I propose to this seeming contradiction is the one I am employing throughout this study, namely, that John's community went through many stages of development, which are reflected in the successive redactions of the document. The transformation of Jesus the witness into Jesus the judge belongs to a stage of development when Jesus was credited with being equal to God because of God's gift to him of eschatological power, especially power to judge.

JESUS HAS LIFE IN HIMSELF:
8:24, 28, 58

John 8:24, 28, and 58 all contain Jesus' special name "I AM." But what does that name mean? And what relationship does it have to the argument that Jesus has God's eschatological power? As we attempt in this second part of the chapter to specify the content of "I AM," one important clue to its meaning comes from the perspective that John 8 has an explicit connection with the powers credited to Jesus in 5:19–29. It is my hypothesis that the "I AM" statements in 8:24, 28, and 58 are explicitly related to the special aspect of eschatological power credited to Jesus in 5:26: "As the Father has life in himself, so he has granted the Son to have life in himself" (5:26). As we begin our investigation of the "I AM" statements, then, we must briefly pause to be clear about the content of 5:26 which, I suggest, has a connection with 8:24, 28, and 58.

If commentators attempt to treat 5:26 at all, they explain it as life-giving power such as was expressed in creation. John's text, however, discusses this verse as an element of Jesus' *eschatological* power (5:21–29), not his creative power (5:19–20), and so we should ask what 5:26 means in that vein.[26]

It is claimed in the Prologue that Jesus is an ancient figure who was "in the beginning" (1:1–2). This suggests an eternal figure, that is, one who is ungenerated, a conclusion strengthened by the absolute claim that "in him was life" (1:4).[27] Jesus was, was alive, and was "in the beginning." When 5:26 claims that Jesus "has life in himself," in one sense that statement looks backward to the remarks about Jesus in 1:1–4 as an eternal, living figure who was from of old. But in 10:17–18, something else is claimed for Jesus. He has power to lay down his life and he has power to take it again (10:18). No one takes his life from him, as in the case of mortals, who are victims; Jesus lays it down of his own accord (10:17). His taking back his life after death, moreover, implies that Jesus raises himself to life after his death on the cross. And so "having life in himself" looks forward as well, explaining how God gave this command to Jesus (10:18b) and how he can be imperishable, despite the hiatus of his death. Only one who has life in himself can do this, a power that belongs to no mortal. Thus, 5:26 says two things: (1) Jesus is an eternal figure in the past, who already "is" in the beginning and (2) Jesus is an imperishable figure in the future, who can lay down his life, take it back, and be alive forever. This, I suggest, is the content of the "I AM" statements in John 8.

The Temporal Content of "I AM"

Verses 8:28 and 58 together deal with the past and future aspects of his "having life in himself." When Jesus states that "before Abraham came to be I AM" (8:58), he makes a distinction between is *(eimi)* and becoming *(genesthai)*, that is, a distinction between existence that is eternal and hence divine, and existence that has a beginning and so is mortal.[28]

Jesus	*Abraham*
I AM *(eimi)*	came to be *(genesthai)*
	died *(apothanen)*

Eimi here denotes existence that is eternal (ungenerated, without beginning) and imperishable, which existence belongs to God alone. *Genesthai* denotes existence that not only came into being at a fixed time, but that also ends in death, the existence of a mortal. John 8:58, moreover, argues that Jesus already "is" prior to Abraham's "coming to be," and so it denotes a mode of being for Jesus like that described in 1:1–4.[29] This statement looks in the same temporal direction as 1:1–4, attesting that Jesus is an eternal, ancient figure who "is" from of old because he had life in himself even "from the beginning."

When, however, Jesus states that "when you have lifted up the Son of man, you will know that I AM" (8:28), he is likewise drawing a distinction between a mortal's death and God's imperishability. Jesus, of course, died; but because he "has life in himself," his death is not typical mortal corruption, but is best interpreted according to 10:17–18 as his laying down his life so as to take it back again. The same quality of life that was in the beginning ("I AM," 8:58) is predicated of the risen Jesus who is still "I AM" after being lifted up. John 8:28, then, looks forward in time and attests to Jesus' radical possession of imperishability in the future.

The "I AM" statement in 8:24 sums up both the past and future aspect of Jesus' eternity.[30] True believers must acknowledge Jesus absolutely as "I AM," that is, confess his eternity in the past (8:58) and his imperishability beyond death (8:28). For, as the Gospel has argued, "to have life in himself" (5:26) embraces both ends of this spectrum of Jesus' life and being. In confessing this, one acknowledges that Jesus is equal to God in that he, too, is both eternal in the past and imperishable in the future.

Eternity and Imperishability
in the Fourth Gospel

The argument that the name "I AM" contains a dual reference to past eternity and future imperishability can be supported from a background study of Exod. 3:14 and other references to God's eternal duration, which is found in Appendix 1 at the end of this study. But for the present, we may ask what this dual notion of past eternity and future imperishability has to do with the understanding of the high Christology in the Fourth Gospel. In summary form, the Gospel states concerning Jesus:
1. He is a heavenly, rather than terrestrial figure:
   he is bread "come down from heaven" (6:41, 50);
   he is the one who came from God and returns to God (13:3);
   he is the one who had glory with God before the world was made (17:5);
   although no one has ever ascended into heaven, the Son of man has because he descended from heaven (3:13).
2. He is eternal, ancient, and existing from of old:
   he already "was" *in the beginning* (1:1–2);
   he already "was" before Abraham (8:58) and before John the Baptizer (1:15, 30).
3. He is imperishable, a being not limited by future death.
It is here that the Johannine confession becomes subtle and sophisticated. Jesus died, however apologetically his death is explained as lifting up and glorification. Yet in the face of this fact, it is nevertheless maintained that he "has life in himself," just as God has (5:26). I suggest that *imperishability* belongs exclusively to God, and it is an adequate way to express what "having life in himself" means.

54

Although he died, he has power such as no mortal has; he is able to lay down his life and take it back again (10:18). Indeed, it is argued, no one takes his life; he is no passive victim, no helpless mortal. Rather he lays down his life—a thing unheard of for a god. And he takes it back again—a thing unheard of for a mortal. Unlike the immortal heroes who are made deathless by another after their death, the eternal Jesus makes himself alive after death, and so he is imperishable in a genuine but analogous way. Jesus is "greater than Abraham, who died" because he existed before Abraham and because he lives eternally after dying.

This investigation of the relationship of John 5:26 and John 8 has taken us somewhat afield, so let us pull together what we have learned. I contend that the gift of eschatological power, given to Jesus in 5:26, is alluded to and developed in the "I AM" statements in 8:24, 28, and 58 regarding Jesus' eternity in the past and imperishability in the future. Having life in one's self makes Jesus truly equal to God. One simply cannot talk about the Deity in postbiblical Judaism or in Greco-Roman culture without speaking of uncreated eternity and imperishable endurance. John 8:58, moreover, refers to Jesus' past, eternal existence, and 8:28 speaks of his future and everlasting endurance beyond death. The "I AM" statements, then, treat both aspects of God's being which both Jews and Greeks considered the unique, distinguishing characteristic of authentic deity.

JESUS' HONOR: 8:49–50

Continuing our investigation of John 8, we focus now on a third aspect of Jesus' eschatological power, God's will that "All honor the Son, even as they honor the Father. Who does not honor the Son does not honor the Father who sent him" (5:23). Most commentators understand this verse according to the rules of agency,[31] whereby in receiving and honoring an agent, one receives and honors the agent's sender.[32] According to Johannine logic, "honoring" Jesus equally to God is functionally equivalent to believing in him.

In the development of John's high Christology, however, Jesus' honor and glory are more than that of an agent. Twice we are told that Jesus enjoyed glory with God before being sent as an agent. For example, Jesus prays to God to reaffirm his glory ("And now, Father, glorify me"), a glory which was his as a permanent quality even before creation (". . . which I had with you before the world was made," 17:5, 24). C.K. Barrett rightly tried to describe this as "the glory of Christ within the Godhead, his glory as God."[33] To honor

Jesus even as one honors God means to consider Jesus "equal to God," that is, a divine, eternal figure who was with God before creation and who resumes that position.

These remarks have an obvious bearing on John 8. First, Jesus demanded of his listeners under pain of eternal death that they believe in him as "I AM" (8:24), that is, they must honor him as a heavenly figure equal to God in eternity and imperishability. Yet at the end of John 8, Jesus' hearers dishonor him: "You are a Samaritan and have a demon" (8:48). Refuting these dishonoring slurs, Jesus continues:

> I have not a demon, but I *honor* my Father
> and you *dishonor* me. Yet I do not seek my
> own *glory* [i.e., *honor*]; there is One
> who seeks it, and he will be your judge. (8:50)

This remark echoes 5:23, where it was stated that God seeks Jesus' honor and will hold the Johannine world to account for it. That is, God will "judge" in this regard, even though all judgment has been put in Jesus' hand.

Again in response to the listeners' ridicule (8:52–53), Jesus alludes once more to his divine grant of honor: "If I glorify [i.e., honor] myself, my glory is nothing; it is my Father who glorifies me, of whom you say that he is your God" (8:54). John 8, then, demands the honoring of Jesus as a figure who is equal to God, a demand based on God's express will.

In conclusion, John 8 equates honor with belief and dishonor with unbelief, such that failure to honor Jesus (8:49b) indicates radical nonbelief. Dishonoring Jesus, the listeners are certainly not Jesus' disciples, but neither are they obedient worshipers of God. In denying Jesus honor as "I AM," his listeners more importantly reject the Johannine high Christology (8:23–24). Failure to honor Jesus, therefore, proves that the audience has no part in God's world above and so they will die in their sins. Yet as 5:23 stated, an essential element of Jesus' eschatological power was his right to honor equal to God's.

JESUS GIVES LIFE: 8:51–53

The evangelist discusses in 8:51–53 one final aspect of Jesus' eschatological power, to make alive. A claim is made in 5:21, "As the Father raises the dead and makes them alive, so the Son 'makes alive' those whom he wills." Since it belongs uniquely to God "to kill and make alive, to bring down to Sheol and to raise up" (1 Sam. 2:6),[34] Jesus is credited with a unique divine power. Yet "giving life" has many meanings in John: (1) resurrection on the last day (5:28–29); (2) life through faith (10:10; 3:16; 5:24); and (3) raising Lazarus back to life (chap. 11).[35]

The statement in 5:21, moreover, appears at one point to have been interpreted in the Johannine community in a rather literal sense to mean that true believers will not or should not die because Jesus has given them a gift of divine life. We find in the Fourth Gospel statements attributed to Jesus suggesting this interpretation: (1) "Your fathers ate manna and died. This is the bread which comes down from heaven, that a man may eat and not die" (6:49–50). "If any one eats of this bread, he will live forever" (6:51). "The fathers ate [manna] and died; he who eats this bread will live for ever" (6:58). (2) In John 11 there is great consternation over the fact that a "beloved disciple," Lazarus, becomes sick and dies (11:21), a thing that should not happen since true believers have "passed from death to life" (5:24). (3) John 21:20–23 rephrases Jesus' remark about another beloved disciple of whom it was popularly assumed that he would never die.

Jesus' Statement	*Interpretation of the Statement*
If it is my will that he remain until I come, what is that to you? (21:22)	The saying spread abroad that this disciple was not to die; yet Jesus did not say that he was not to die, but "If it is my will that he remain until I come, what is that to you?" (21:23)

However 5:21 might have been interpreted in the history of the Johannine group, it was carefully nuanced in 8:51 to exclude any literal misunderstanding of it, such as is made in 8:52. Jesus never said that his followers would "not taste death," but that they would "not see death for ever." Just as the qualification was added to the bread of life discourse that Jesus will "raise up on the last day" even those who ate the bread of life (6:39, 44, 54), so the remark in 8:51 indicates that Jesus is claiming to give postmortem life to believers. The fact that "Abraham died, as did the prophets" (8:52) is no argument against Jesus' claim in 8:51, for he never claimed that patriarchs and prophets who received theophanies would never taste death. I suggest, then, that the gift of eschatological power given Jesus in 5:21 was finally understood as the power to raise the dead. And this is the power claimed by Jesus in 8:51, but misunderstood by his listeners in 8:52–53.

CONCLUSIONS AND FURTHER TASKS

From this analysis we may now gather certain conclusions. John 8 has evidently undergone a complex development. John 8:12–20 appears to reflect an earlier tradition, which depicted Jesus acting as the plaintiff who defends his actions on the Sabbath against hostile Jews. However, 8:21–30 portrays Jesus as judge, suggesting a later redaction of the narrative portraying Jesus conducting a scrutiny of pseudofollowers who do not genuinely accept the high christological confession of the Johannine group.

Regarding the high christological confession, John 8 was shown to take up the topic statement of Jesus' eschatological power from 5:21–29 and explain and demonstrate four aspects of that power credited to Jesus whereby he is truly equal to God: (1) a judge with judgment (8:21–50); (2) one who has life in himself (8:24, 28, 58); (3) one who deserves honor equal to that of God (8:49–50); (4) giver of postmortem life (8:51–53). Even Jesus' appearance to Abraham as the "I AM" figure supports this, for "I AM" was shown to be a condensed expression of God's eternity in the past and imperishability in the future, which were cross-cultural criteria of authentic deity in the ancient world. The importance of the "I AM" statements points in two directions. First, Jesus is "equal to God" in that he is given God's own unique name. Second, inasmuch as the contents of "I AM" point to Jesus' eternity and imperishability, they reinforce the claim that Jesus truly has "life in himself," just as God does. John 8, then, serves as the first demonstration of Jesus' eschatological powers, a demonstration that will continue in John 10 and 11, to which we now turn.

3

JESUS'
POWER OVER DEATH:
JOHN 10

John's exposition of Jesus' eschatological power, surveyed in John 8, continues in chapters 10 and 11 of the Gospel. Whereas John 8 stressed Jesus' power to judge, John 10 focuses on his power over death, both his own and that of his followers. It is a power that makes him equal to God.

John 10, however, is not readily accessible to the reader. Many scholars perceive a lack of coherence in the chapter, an observation that produces various suggestions about its displacement and rearrangement.[1] Although it is beyond the scope of this study to offer a complete analysis of the history of the materials in John 10, our concentration on Jesus' power over death offers a specific focus that may contribute to scholarly conversation on the chapter. It is our hypothesis that a redaction theory offers a better explanation of the logic and structure of John 10 than a displacement theory. Concentrating on the statements about Jesus' power over death and his equality with God, we will argue that 10:17–18 was added to 10:1–16, and that 10:28–38 was added to 10:22–27. The additions explicitly proclaim Jesus' power over death, both his own and that of his followers. In virtue of this claim, Jesus is "equal to God" (10:30), a claim defended in 10:34–38. These additions, moreover, are of a piece with the claim that God has given Jesus full creative and eschatological powers, a claim first made in the topic statement in 5:19–29.

Our focus, then, rests on two interrelated texts. In 10:17–18 and 28–30, Jesus claims absolute power over death, first his own and then that of his followers. Claims of this power lead to a confession of him as equal to God (10:30, 31–33), a confession that is vigorously defended (10:34–38). This chapter will examine these materials in their contexts, indicating their distinctive content and the narrative dynamic they produce.

JESUS' OWN POWER OVER DEATH:
10:17–18

Beginning with 10:17–18, we immediately ask about the relationship of these verses to the collection of parables in 10:1–16. Do they reflect the ideas in 10:1–16 and comment on them in any way? Or do they communicate totally different information about Jesus? Since any answer presupposes that we have a clear assessment of 10:1–16, let us briefly examine that material.

10:17–18 in Relation to 10:1–16

Odo Kiefer[2] argued persuasively that 10:1–18 is structured in terms of alternating statements of antithesis and benefit:

Antithesis	10:1–3a	Shepherd vs. Thief/Robber
Benefit	10:3b–5	Shepherd and Sheep
Antithesis	10:7–8	Door vs. Thief/Robber
Benefit	10:9–10	Door and Sheep
Antithesis	10:11–13	Shepherd vs. Hireling
Benefit	10:14–18	Shepherd and Sheep

Sometimes it is suggested that 10:11 and 15 form an *inclusio* around the parable of the good shepherd in virtue of the double mention of one characteristic of the shepherd: "I lay down my life for the sheep."[3] But Kiefer's suggestion about alternating statements of antithesis and benefit seems to make more sense of 10:1–16,[4] although we cannot help but notice the importance of the special hallmark of the Shepherd, who "lays down his life."

Kiefer, moreover, suggested a chiastic structure for 10:17–18.[5]

A. For this reason the Father loves me (17a)

B.   because I lay down my life
        that I may take it again (17b)

C.   No one takes it from me
            but I lay it down of myself (18a)

B'.   I have power to lay down my life
        and I have power to take it again (18b)

A'. This command I have received from my Father (18c)

The chiastic form clarifies the basic message here: (A) References to the Father and my Father frame it, expressing God's agreement with the content of 10:17–18. (B) Twice the point is made that Jesus both lays down his life and takes it again, thus underscoring its importance. (C) This "laying down of life" is emphatically in Jesus' sole control and his alone.

Concerning the relationship of 10:17–18 to 10:1–16, however, Kiefer's arguments lack persuasiveness. He suggested that 10:17–18 forms a parallel with 10:10 on the theme of "life,"[6]

10:10   the gift of life
10:17–18   the laying down of life.

This appears to be a false parallelism, because "life" in 10:10 is *zōē*, that is, life that belongs to the sheep, while "life" in 10:17–18 is *psychē*, that is, Jesus' own physical life. In 10:10, Jesus gives generic life to his sheep, whereas in 10:17 he lays down his own life without mention of them.

Differences abound, moreover, between 10:1–16 and 17–18. (1) On the basis of Kiefer's own pattern, 10:17–18 presents Jesus neither as the antithesis to thief, robber, or hireling nor as benefit for the sheep. The narrative focuses exclusively on Jesus, who has God's power and command to "lay down his life and to take it back again"; neither an alternate shepherd nor Jesus' flock is mentioned. (2) In 10:17–18, Jesus both "lays down his life" and "takes it again," which latter remark is not found at all in 10:11–15, where only "laying down life" is mentioned. (3) John 10:17–18 is devoid of soteriology attached to Jesus' death, which is hardly the case in 10:11–15, when the life laid down is a benefit "for the sheep." (4) In 10:17–18, Jesus is emphatically not a victim whose death results from the agency of another ("No one takes it from me!"), which is not the case for the good shepherd. (5) The Christology of 10:17–18 makes a point quite different from that of the messianic shepherd of 10:11–15. (6) Whereas Jesus' messianic claims in 10:11–15 need no justification, the remark in 10:17–18 to "lay down my life and take it again" comes with a forensic legitimation in Jesus' claim to have power to do this, a command received from God (10:18). (7) The antithesis in 10:11–15 lies between authentic and inauthentic shepherds; but if a contrast exists in 10:17–18, it is between those who lay down their lives so as to take them again and those whose lives are taken from them, lives which they themselves cannot recover. These differences may be summarized:

1. *Passive vs. active death:* "To lay down one's life" is passive in 10:11–15, but active in 10:17–18

2. *Soteriology vs. Christology:* "To lay down one's life" has a soteriological purpose in 10:11–15, but a uniquely christological one in 10:17–18
3. *Taking one's life again:* The good shepherd made no claims to raise himself after laying down his life for the sheep, claims that are the very heart of 10:17–18

Like others, Kiefer asserts that 10:17–18 speaks of Jesus' death and resurrection, which he would see in soteriological perspective.[7] While I agree that the topic is death and the undoing of death, "resurrection" is much too technical a term for labeling what is discussed in 10:17–18. For example, "resurrection" is the specific term that refers to Jesus' power to raise the dead (6:39, 40, 44, 54), which resurrection is also the threshold to judgment (5:29). According to 10:17–18, Jesus himself is not raised up by anyone, and certainly not for judgment. Jesus' resurrection, moreover, may have a certain soteriological significance in other New Testament texts; for example, in 1 Cor. 15:21, where Jesus' resurrection is cause of our rising; in Acts 2:33, where the Risen Jesus sends the Spirit; and in Rom. 4:25, where his resurrection is "for our justification." But this notion remains alien to the Fourth Gospel.

The text states that Jesus lays down his life not for the purpose of benefiting the sheep, but so as to take it again. While there is a stream of Johannine thought that speaks of the death of Jesus as ascending, returning to the Father, and being lifted up, that perspective simply is not expressed in 10:17–18. Jesus is not going anywhere! He is taking his life back again. It is true that Jesus has a "commission" to save the world (3:16–17), which usually has to do with speaking God's word or revealing a heavenly secret. The commission in 10:17–18 differs in that it refers not to revelation or salvation, but to Jesus' laying down his life and *taking it back.* Too facilely do commentators insert words like resurrection and soteriology into discussion of 10:17–18.

The language in 10:17–18 is exclusively christological, but not like the argument about the authentic shepherd in 10:1–16. In 10:17–18 we find a double reference to "laying down one's life" which, while similar to remarks in 10:11 and 15, serves a different purpose. According to 10:17, God loves Jesus because he lays down his life. But the reason God loves him is not because he lays down his life on behalf of the sheep, as was the case in 10:11 and 15. Rather, God loves him because "I lay down my life so that I take it again." The purpose of laying down one's life is now different:

10:11	*10:17*
The Good Shepherd lays down his life for the sheep.	For this reason the Father loves me, because I lay down my life so that I take it again.

Some scholars comment on the nonaltruistic character of the purpose clause in v. 17,[8] comparing it with the rich "life for others" comment in 10:11 and 15. Wishing Jesus to be the model of love, they explain the clause "so that I might take it again" to mean Jesus' resurrection which becomes the source of life for the sheep.[9] But this waters down the point of 10:17–18 and introduces a notion of resurrection alien to this Gospel. The purpose expressed in 10:17 has less to do with soteriology than with a new christological point of view, as 10:18 explains.

John 10:18 juxtaposes the new remark about Jesus' "laying down his life" with comparable remarks in the parable (10:11, 15). Formerly he was a victim whose life is taken from him by a wolf or some other agent of death (see 11:45–52). Here it is emphasized that Jesus is not a victim at all: "No one takes my life from me!" This is explained by a remarkable claim found nowhere else in the New Testament: "I have power to lay it down and I have power to take it again. This command I received from my Father" (10:18). While both 10:11–15 and 17–18 speak of Jesus' death, his laying down his life, they view that death from quite different perspectives. It will be helpful to see these two remarks against the background of the Johannine understandings of Jesus' death.

The Meaning of Jesus' Death in 10:17–18

At the outset, we recall a current axiom of Johannine scholarship that "notions of expiation, sacrifice and vicarious satisfaction for sin play a peripheral role in the thought of the evangelist or are completely non-existent."[10] What have we then? First, we can note in the Gospel an apologetic approach to Jesus' death as the fulfillment of Scripture:

2:17 (Ps. 69:9) "Zeal for your house has consumed me"

3:14 (Num. 21:9) "As Moses lifted up the serpent in the desert so must the Son of man be lifted up"

13:18 (Ps. 41:9) "The one who eats my bread has lifted up his heel against me"

15:25 (Ps. 35:19/69:4) "They have hated me without cause"

19:24 (Ps. 22:18) "They divided my garments among them"

19.28   (Ps. 22:15) "I thirst"

19:36   (Exod. 12:46) "Not one bone of it shall be broken"

19:37   (Zech. 12:10) "They shall look on the one whom they have pierced"

By happening according to God's providential plan, Jesus' death is no accident, not a lapse of God's providence nor a shameful thing.

Second, the Fourth Gospel more characteristically describes Jesus' death as a "glorification" and a "lifting up,"[11] terms that serve both apologetic and revelatory purposes. The Fourth Gospel apologetically interprets Jesus' death, which to human eyes was a shameful event and even a "curse,"[12] as a "glorification." His death, moreover, "was an integral part of Christ's saving mission of revealing the Father to men."[13] Third, there seems to be another view of Jesus' death. It speaks in terms of its benefit to humankind: it will draw all of God's dispersed sheep into one fold (12:32, 11:51–52) or result in rivers of living water flowing from his side (19:34; see 7:37–39 and 1 John 5:6–8). Jesus will also die "for the sheep," that is, in benefit to them and for their sake (10:11, 15, 18:8, 14).[14]

These perspectives on Jesus' death, of course, both draw upon early church tradition and reflect Johannine characteristics. They belong, moreover, to what J. Louis Martyn has called low Christology, for there is no sense here of Jesus being a divine figure or doing something beyond the range of what it belongs to humans to do.[15]

Yet other aspects of Jesus' death in this Gospel go beyond these apologetic and kerygmatic perspectives. Jesus' death is no mere heroic apotheosis[16] but actually constitutes his return to the glory he had with God before the creation of the world (17:5, 24). His death becomes the occasion when his parabolic career turns toward completion, when Jesus knew that he "had come from God and was going to God" (13:3). This is no mere turning of the tables or vindication of the rejected, motifs that stand behind the apologetic remarks that his death was ironically glory-in-shame and exaltation-in-humiliation. Death becomes the occasion to resume his true existence with God in glory. This perspective belongs to the high Christology of the Fourth Gospel.

Finally, Jesus' death in 10:17–18 emphasizes that he himself has the power to lay down his life and to take it back again. I suggest that this constitutes the formal explanation of what was claimed in 5:26, namely, that God's gift to Jesus to have life in himself is the grant of eschatological power whereby Jesus is equal to God. To have life in himself, however, cannot mean that Jesus escapes death (see such a misunderstanding in 8:52–53). By no means! He genuinely lays down his life, but he has power to take it back again. To have life in himself (5:26), I suggest, is identical with power "to lay down my life and power to take it again" (10:18). This suggestion might explain the troublesome *hina* in 10:17, where Jesus lays down his life for the purpose of taking it again. As a result of the claim made in 5:26, what is needed is a demonstration by Jesus of "having life in himself," a demonstration of eschatological power. What greater proof can there be than Jesus' own power to lay down his life so as to demonstrate that he has power to take it again? The issue is not soteriology, but Christology, and that of a very high order. This should be seen in conjunction with the assertion made in the previous chapter that "I AM" (8:28, 58) implies imperishability, a characteristic only of a true deity.

In summary, Jesus' death tells us something unique about him. Unlike any mortal, his death is not that of a victim whose life is taken from him; Jesus lays down his life of himself. Unlike any mortal, his death is neither final nor a prelude to vindication by another, for he himself will take it again. It is not enough that Jesus can raise the dead, that is, his followers who have died (5:25, 28–29; 11:43–44), although that is certainly a remarkable claim. He has power over his own death, a power that does not depend on "faith" or realized eschatology. He has power over his own death. He genuinely dies and he truly takes back his own life again. The content of 5:26, I suggest, is fully developed in the remarks in 10:17–18. It demonstrates the earlier claim of eschatological power whereby Jesus is equal to God.

JESUS' POWER OVER OTHERS' DEATHS:
10:28–38

Just as we identified 10:17–18 as a redactional addition to 10:1–16, so it is part of our hypothesis that 10:28–38 is a comparable redactional addition to 10:22–27. Scholars generally note that 10:22–38 is structured around two basic questions, whether Jesus is truly "Messiah" (10:24) and "God," "equal to God" (10:30, 33, 34).[17] According to the criterion of Christology developed in this book, these are hardly duplicate accounts,[18] but rather passages that make different christological claims. I suggest that 10:22–27 and 28–38, while formally similar as forensic processes, argue different christological issues and so come from different periods of the Gospel's history. But let us examine these two blocks of material more closely.

Literary Analysis of 10:22–27

We begin with an analysis of 10:22–27 because it is the narrative context to which 10:28–38 was later added. The passage 10:22–27 resembles other Johannine passages where a forensic process gives shape to the narrative:

Claim	Messianic shepherd (10:1–16)
Judgment	"Tell us plainly, if you are the Christ?" (10:24)
Apology	Defense of Jesus as shepherd (10:25–27)

The parables in 10:1–16 contain various aspects of the messianic claim,[19] especially claims that only the true shepherd enters the gate (10:2) and that Jesus is both "the gate" (10:7) and the "Good Shepherd" (10:11). A popular judgment about Jesus' claim is already occurring in the crowds, as some judge him to be demonic while others defend him (10:19–21). Verses 22–27 indicate that a more formal forensic setting is required where competent officials, not the uneducated *am ha-aretz*, can decide the issue (see 7:47–49). And so the claimant is queried before a legal assembly gathered in solemn assembly "in the temple, in the stoa of Solomon" (10:23). A formal question is put to Jesus, which addresses the substance of his claims: "Tell us plainly, if you are the Messiah?" Although it has often been noted that this setting, question, and answer resemble that of the Synoptic trial of Jesus before the sanhedrin,[20] more important is the observation that they parallel the forensic inquiry in John 7 about (1) Jesus' doing things "plainly" (7:4, 26); (2) his identity as Messiah (7:26, 31, 41); (3) popular judgments about him (7:25–27, 31, 40–44); and (4) a demand for a formal hearing before the legal authorities of Judaism (7:45–52). Schematically John 7 and 10 run parallel as follows:

JESUS SPEAKS PLAINLY

1. No man works in secret if he seeks to be known "plainly" (7:4)	1. How long will you keep us in suspense? If you are the Christ, tell us plainly (10:24)

JESUS IS THE CHRIST

2. Can it be that the authorities really know that this is the Christ? (7:26) This is the Christ (7:41)	2. If you are the Christ . . . (10:24a)

POPULAR JUDGMENT

3. When they heard these words some said, "This is really the prophet." Others said: "This is the Christ." But some said, "Is not the Christ to come from Galilee?" . . . So there was a division among the people over him (7:40–43)

3. There was again a division among the Jews because of these words. Many of them said, "He has a demon, and he is mad; why listen to him?" Others said, "These are not the sayings of one who has a demon. Can a demon open the eyes of a man born blind?" (10:19–20)

NEED FOR A FORMAL HEARING

4. The Pharisees heard the crowds thus muttering about him, and the chief priests and Pharisees sent officers to arrest him (7:32). The officers went back to the chief priests and Pharisees . . . (7:45–49)

4. Jesus was walking in the temple in the portico of Solomon. The Jews gathered around him and said to him, "How long will you keep us in suspense?" (10:22–24)

While Jesus did not appear in John 7 for the investigation, in 10:22–28 he finally resolves the controversy around him in what can only be described as a formal trial, a forensic proceeding.[21] The messianic claims in 10:7 and 11 bring the issue to a head (see 7:31). Now a formal question can be put to Jesus, which also challenges him and demands forensic testimony: Tell us plainly, if you are the Messiah?

The apology rests on testimony, not that of Jesus (see 8:12–20), but the testimony of Jesus' works: "The works that I work in my Father's name, these witness to me" (10:25; see 5:36). In the eyes of some, these works are precisely the legal problem, for Jesus does them on the Sabbath (5:16; 9:16, 24), and so some construe his works as those of a sinner (9:24) or of a man possessed of a demon (10:20). What would constitute Jesus' works as valid evidence to this court? Nothing less than acceptance of him as God's agent and shepherd, or, as the text puts it, being one of his sheep.

As is often the case with trials in John, the tables are turned: the judges are judged and the one being judged becomes the judge. The very judgment that the judges make about Jesus constitutes a judgment about the judges themselves.[22] Jesus turns on his judges and charges them with being unbelievers and outsiders, that is, not being sheep in God's flock: "You do not believe because you are not of my sheep!" (10:26; see 8:23). The rest of Jesus' remarks in 10:26–27 serve to prove this charge against them. The parables in 10:1–16 not only define the authentic messianic shepherd, they also contain remarks about the sheep which the true shepherd tends, remarks that can be construed as three criteria for identification as authentic sheep in the flock of Israel.[23]

10:1–16	*10:27–28*
1. The (true) sheep hear his voice (10:3b)	1. My sheep hear my voice (10:27a)
2. He calls his own sheep by name (10:3c) I know my own and my own know me (10:14)	2. I know them (10:27b)
3. The sheep follow him, for they know his voice (10:4)	3. And they follow me (10:27c)

Authentic sheep hear the shepherd's voice and follow him, but these "Jews" clearly do not accept Jesus' testimony nor do they become his disciples (see 9:28). In judging Jesus' claim, the judges judge that he is *not* Israel's shepherd, and in so judging they judge that they are *not* his sheep. This trial, its claims, and charges are of the utmost seriousness, for the sentence in this trial will be death, either for the judges or for Jesus. Jesus has claimed that authentic sheep will through the shepherd find pasture, life, and protection from the evil ones. But if these Jews are not his flock, they will not find "life in abundance" (10:10). They will instead be subject to the powers of this world and die in their sins. These self-confessed nonsheep, then, will lose their place in God's flock and perish forever. And if the judges judge against Jesus , they will seek his death (see 10:39).

Verses 22–27, then, constitute the natural conclusion of the process begun earlier in which claims are made (10:1–16), which in turn result in popular judgments about Jesus (10:19–21), and conclude in a forensic proceeding (10:22–27). The issue is Jesus' identity as authentic messianic shepherd, a significant christological point, but one that belongs to the low Christology of the Fourth Gospel.

Jesus' Unique Claims in 10:28–33

Continuing with 10:28–38, we find a second forensic process focusing on a new claim by Jesus. Verses 31–33 tell of a violent reaction to a statement by Jesus that sounds to the Jews like "blasphemy": "You, being a man, make yourself god" (10:33). The response of Jesus in

10:34–38 constitutes his apologetic defense of this. But where is the claim that is challenged? What is the cause of this new forensic proceeding? The reaction in 10:31–33 points back to Jesus' remark in 10:30 that "I and the Father are *hen,*" which is Jesus' new claim. The shape of 10:30–38, then, is another forensic process, similar in form to that in 10:22–27.

	Early Trial John 10:22–27	Later Trial John 10:28–38
Claim	Good Shepherd (10:1–16)	I and the Father are *hen* (10:30)
Judgment	Tell us plainly, if you are the Christ? (10:24)	Blasphemy: Being a man, you make yourself God (10:33)
Apology	Defense of Jesus as Good Shepherd (10:25–28)	Defense of Jesus as God (10:34–38)

The issue is no longer Jesus' claim to be the messianic shepherd, but to be equal to God. The shift in perspective between 10:22–27 and 28–30, then, is truly enormous and reflects a shift in the development of the Johannine narrative.

Returning to the claims made in 10:30, how are we to interpret Jesus' word that he and God are *hen?* Are they one or equal or what?[24] First, since the audience correctly understands it as a claim to parity with God ("You being a man make yourself god"), *hen* in 10:30 does not mean moral unity with God. Jesus' obedience to God is the shared ideal of every covenant member, the apex of Jewish piety and something for which each and every person strives. In this, Israelites are not striving for divinity! No, moral unity[25] with God is not enough.

It has been suggested, however, that *hen* be translated not as "one" but "equal": "I and the Father are equal." The argument is based on a similar use of this language in 1 Cor. 3:8, in which the status of Paul and of Apollos are compared.[26] In a conciliatory move, Paul insists that he and Apollos, while quite different in Paul's eyes, are on a par when contrasted with God: "Neither he who plants nor he who waters is anything, but only God who gives the increase" (3:7). And he continues, "He who plants and he who waters are *hen*" (3:8), which must be translated in this context as "equal" or "on a par." In the conflict at Corinth, Paul senses that in many ways Apollos is perceived as superior to him, for Paul lacks eloquence, wisdom, and "power" (1:17; 2:1, 4; 4:9–12). Yet Paul can claim the superior place at Corinth as its "skilled master builder" (3:10). But for the purpose of quelling the factions and strife, he will agree that he and Apollos are "equal" in regard to their mission to the church. *Hen* in 3:8 does not refer to moral unity or metaphysical identity, but to equality of power, role, and status.

In 10:30, the Fourth Gospel does not claim that Jesus is the Father or that he replaces Yahweh, but rather proclaims him "God" alongside God (1:1–2) and "equal to God" (5:18). As we saw, according to John 5, claims of Jesus' equality with God were precipitated by a Sabbath healing which was interpreted in 5:17 as an act of creative power (5:19–20). Nothing in John 10 speaks of creative power, but as we saw in regard to 10:17–18, there are ready to hand references to Jesus' eschatological power. In regard to what aspect of eschatological power are Jesus and God equal? Verses 28–29 put them on a par in regard to "snatching out of the hand":

Jesus (10:28)	*The Father (10:29)*
I give them eternal life	My father
and they shall not perish forever,	who has given me
and no one shall snatch them out of my hand	and no one is able to snatch them out of the Father's hand

About the text of 10:29 there is considerable scholarly discussion, the results of which may further clarify the meaning of 10:30. C. K. Barrett[27] and those who took up the discussion of this text[28] all agree that *meizōn*, not *meizon*, is the correct reading, so that the text says, "My Father . . . is greater than all." The statement that God is "greater than all" has considerable relevance for the argument in 10:28–30, where it minimally means that God is more powerful than the "snatchers." But J. Whittaker suggested that "greater than all" is a formulaic way of referring to the supreme deity,[29] noting that this greatness is based not only on God's creative power, but especially his ruling and executive powers as *pantocrator, despotēs,* and *basileus.*[30] Regarding John 10, Jesus claims a power in v. 28 that, according to v. 29, is a power of God who is "greater than all"—the executive of the cosmos. But in 10:30, having just said that God is "greater than all," Jesus claims that "I and the Father are equal." Regarding the substance of the claims made in 10:28–30, if God is rightly called "greater than all" and if "greatness" consists of executive and eschatological power, then when Jesus claims equality with this God he claims these very powers as *despotēs* and *basileus.*

70

The juxtaposition of "greater than all" and "equal" was bound to cause an explosion.

If God is "greater than all," God has, nevertheless, given "all" to Jesus:

> The Father loves the son and has given all into his hands. (3:35)

> The Father loves the son and shows him all that he himself is doing. (5:20)

> The Father has given all judgment to the Son. (5:27)

> Jesus, knowing that the Father had given all into his hands . . . (13:3)

This "all" might be "the words of God" (3:33), that is, heavenly revelation, creative power (5:19–20), but also God's eschatological power (5:21–29; 10:17–18). The context of John 10 suggests that we examine Jesus' equality with God in the light of eschatological power; in particular, power over death.

John 10:28 says three things about Jesus' eschatological power: (1) I give them eternal life, (2) and they do not perish forever; (3) no one snatches them out of my hand. As we saw in the case of 8:51–53, we cannot take this literally to mean that followers of Jesus do not taste death. Jesus is not promising to prevent death, for in John 11 a "beloved disciple" will die to the great chagrin of his sisters (11:21, 32). Jesus even predicts death for Peter (21:18–19) and for other loyal followers (16:1–2). Rather, we should construe 10:28 in the light of the eschatological power given Jesus according to 5:21, 25, and 28–29, namely, power over the dead: to give life to the dead and to keep them from perishing. We are beyond the proclamation of 3:16 where, according to a self-judgment principle, believers do not perish but presently have eternal life. Here Jesus himself holds the keys of death and the underworld; he has power over death.

If Jesus' power over the death of his followers means that he raises them *from* death, in regard to his own death Jesus exercises complete control. He prevents his own death as a victim at the hands of others: (1) there is no question of others "handing him over" (*paradidonai*)[31]; (2) he is never "in their hands" (7:30, 44; 10:39); (3) he controls "the hour" (7:30; 8:20); (4) in fact, "no one takes my life from me, but I lay it down of myself" (10:18); and (5) his power over death extends to his "taking it back again" (10:17–18). Jesus' power over his own death, then, is absolute: he controls the if, when, and how of his death, and he controls death itself, for he can undo it.

Yet in regard to his sheep, Jesus will not prevent death, so that "no snatching them" cannot mean that he acts to forestall their death. Rather, he claims power that his sheep "not perish forever," that is, be lost, corrupted, destroyed.[32] He can rescue them from death so that they do not perish in death. When seen in this perspective, Jesus' equality with God (10:30, 33) is constituted by his total power over death. New claims, then, are made in 10:28–30, claims that lead to a new forensic charge of blasphemy in 10:31–33. We turn now to the apologetic response to this new charge.

Apology for the New Claims (10:34–36)

The brunt of the apologetic response to the new charge of blasphemy rests with the citation of Ps. 82:6. What is the understanding of the psalm, and how does that relate to the argument in 10:34–36? In appendix 2 of this volume, I have briefly shown that Ps. 82:6 was interpreted in postbiblical Judaism in a historicized manner to refer to Israel on Mt. Sinai, when God made them deathless once more, because they became holy once more in virtue of hearing God's word. A man, then, may be called god because of deathlessness. Psalm 82:7, moreover, was said to refer to the death Israel subsequently died because of the sin of the golden calf. Psalm 82:6 and 7, then, refer to deathlessness because of sinlessness (v. 6) and to death because of sin (v. 7).

Although the dating of a midrash is always a difficult task, John 10:34–36 might well be the earliest witness to this traditional interpretation of Ps. 82:6 discussed in appendix 2, for it too understands the historical setting of Ps. 82:6 as the giving of the Torah on Sinai and likewise presupposes the psalm's equation of godliness with power over death. (1) Both John and the midrash deal with a common issue: how can mortals be called gods? Verse 33 explicitly focuses on this issue: "You, being a man, make yourself god," whereas Ps. 82:6–7 contrasts "You are gods" with "You will die like men." (2) John 10:34–36 cites the psalm precisely as it is embedded in its midrashic explanation, that is, in the context of the giving of Torah at Sinai:

Psalm 82 in Legend	Psalm 82 in John 10:35
1. Proclamation: "I say 'You are gods'"	1. Proclamation: Is it not written in your law: "I say 'You are gods'"
2. Occasion: on Sinai, when God gave Israel the Law	2. Occasion: "If he called them gods, to whom the word of God came . . . "

72

The most economical reading of 10:35 ("to whom the word of God came . . . ") is the historicized context of Psalm 82, the giving of God's word of Torah at Sinai. (3) When Ps. 82:6 is linked with Sinai, Israel's godlikeness is first and foremost its deathlessness. In John 10, Jesus' predication as god rests on his claim to have God's power over death (10:17–18, 28–29, 37–38). (4) Finally, Israel's deathlessness is linked to the holiness that resulted from its gift of Torah (Exod. 24:8). Perhaps it is merely part of the apology, but in this passage Jesus emphatically defends his holiness, his radical sinlessness.

Unlike Israel, to whom holiness was restored after sin, there is no restoration of holiness for Jesus! The evangelist makes the issue quite explicit in Jesus' response to the charge of blasphemy: "Do you say of him whom the Father consecrated and sent into the world, 'You are blaspheming,' because I said, 'I am (the) Son of God'?" (10:36). Examining this complicated argument, let us not think that Jesus is watering down [33] his claim to be "god" or "equal to God" by identifying himself as "son of God." On the contrary, Ps. 82:6 still applies to 10:36, for the psalm makes no difference between "god" and "son of God": "I say, 'You are gods, sons of the Most High, all of you.'" The psalm is still being quoted.

Second, Jesus' holiness or sinfulness becomes the formal issue as the text juxtaposes "You are blaspheming" with "whom the Father consecrated. . . . " The Gospel has repeatedly taken up the explicit issue of Jesus' alleged sinfulness, recording a mounting popular judgment of him as a sinner (9:16, 24), based on his two healings on the Sabbath (5:1–17; 9:1–7). His enemies charge him with being thoroughly evil, that is, possessed of a demon (7:20; 8:48; 10:20). Here in 10:33 and 36 he is charged with a new sin, blasphemy, for claiming to be equal to God. And it belongs to sinners to die, for "there is no death without sin" (b. Shab. 55a). If in fact Jesus dies, does this not imply sin?

In the face of these accusations the Fourth Gospel affirms Jesus' holiness and obedience. Jesus himself laid down the challenge: "Which of you convicts me of sin?" (8:46). John 10:36 represents but the most recent evidence of this defense, as it proclaims that God consecrated Jesus. We have, moreover, heard God's evaluation of Jesus elsewhere, that "the Father loves the Son" (3:35; 5:30). Sinners, of course, find no place in God's presence, yet Jesus was face to face with God (1:1–2) and in God's bosom (1:18). And Jesus will return to God's presence at the completion of his mission (13:3; 17:5, 24). Nor could anyone convict Jesus of sin (8:46). His working on the Sabbath constituted no breach of God's law, but must be perceived precisely as obedience to God's will (7:21–23). In fact, Jesus' very ability to open the eyes of the blind testifies to his closeness to God (9:31–33). Jesus' holiness (6:69) and his consecration (10:36) attest to his sinlessness. And where there is sinlessness, there should be deathlessness. Jesus, then, is god because he is deathless because he is sinless.

In summary, like the midrashim, John employs Ps. 82:6 as it was contextualized and historicized. And like the midrashim, John's version implies and alludes to a rather complex argument, although only key pieces of that argument are explicitly mentioned. The Sinai context is alluded to as the historical occasion of the psalm.

Psalm 82 in the Midrashim	*Psalm 82 Applied to Jesus in John*
1. Israel called god	1. Jesus called god and equal to God (10:30, 33),
2. because sinless	2. consecrated by God (10:36),
3. and made deathless once more	3. and given power over death (10:17–18, 28–29);
4. on the occasion of the giving of God's word at Sinai	4. he is God's word to Israel (1:1–2, 18);
5. yet Israel sinned and died	5. he dies, but *not* because of sin (10:17–18)

Jesus, however, is not just another example of Psalm 82, although that might suffice in the apology in 10:34–36. In its use of Ps. 82:6, the Fourth Gospel heightens the midrashic interpretation of the psalm in three ways when applying it to Jesus by stating that: (1) he has never sinned, (2) his death has nothing to do with sin and punishment, (3) his power over death is radically different from Adam's or Israel's deathlessness. In essence, the Fourth Gospel proclaims of Jesus a radical power over death, a power quite different from the deathlessness given Israel. With the argument from Scripture, the first part (10:34–36) of Jesus' apology comes to an end.

Further Apology in 10:37–38

The second part of the apology (10:37–38) justifies the special predication of god to a man by explaining its basis. In 10:37–38 three key terms are linked to form an argument, *works, know,* and *in.*

Works. The topic becomes Jesus' *erga,* his "works." But the reader should not simply look back to Jesus' good works, which in

10:32–33 were formally excluded from the current judicial inquiry. Rudolf Bultmann[34] gave three reasons why in 10:37–38 the defense could hardly be speaking of Jesus' miracles as such: (1) such a discussion would be more in place following a miracle itself; (2) the miracles in John 5 and 9 caused offense, so it is hard to see why they would be appealed to here; and (3) the parallel with 14:10–11 indicates that words and works, that is, the whole of Jesus' special revelation, is meant in 10:37–38. A fourth point can be added to Bultmann's argument: the context is *not* a discussion of miracles or credentials, but of Jesus' equality with God (10:30, 33), equality based on a specific work, which is power over death.

Jewish lore occasionally notes that God gave Elijah, Elisha, and Ezekiel the key to three things that are exclusively in God's power, namely, the key to rain, the womb, and the grave.[35] The issue here, however, is neither prophets nor miracles but "the works of my Father." Works in John, moreover, are not simply synonymous with miracles or *semeia*.[36] In fact, the Fourth Gospel speaks often of "the works of so-and-so," a usage we should carefully examine. In 8:39, Jesus alluded to "the works of Abraham," which means Abraham's hospitality; Jesus' hearers, however, are doing "the works of their father," the devil (8:41), referring to murder and lying. On one occasion, people queried Jesus about doing "the works of God" (6:28), to which Jesus replied that there is but one work of God: "This is the 'work of God,' that you believe in him whom He has sent" (6:29). I am persuaded that the discussion of Jesus' works in 10:37–38 not only refers to Jesus' eschatological works, but is related to a remark made earlier in 5:20. In that place, Jesus admits that God shows him all that God does, so that the Son does what the Father does (5:19), that is, creative works. But in 5:20, Jesus boasts that God will show him greater works than his creative acts, which are then immediately itemized as works of eschatological power.[37] This remark occurs in the apology for Jesus' equality with God (5:18), which was shown to be Jesus' exercise of God's two basic powers, the creative power (5:19–20) and the eschatological power (5:21–29). "The works of so-and-so," then, is a phrase that refers to deeds characteristic of or proper to a patriarch or God.

Most commentators suggest that 10:38, the conclusion to be drawn from Jesus' works, alludes back to 10:30.[38] C. H. Dodd was more precise when he urged that 10:38 refers back not only to 10:30 but to 10:28 as well. The works that argue for Jesus' unity with the God are *zōopoiēsis:* "It is in this unity with the Father in

75

exercising the divine prerogatives of vivifying and judging that the unique Sonship of Christ is manifested."[39] The issue in 10:28–38 is not miracles, but special powers claimed by Jesus which make him "equal to God," even eschatological power over death.

Even the way the miracles/*semeia* are presented in a formal argument in the Fourth Gospel differs from the way these "works" function in 10:37–38 on Jesus' behalf. Miraculous works are twice explained as having probative value: (1) "The works I do witness about me that the Father sent me" (5:36); and (2) "I have said this on account of the crowd standing by, that they may believe *that you sent me*" (11:42). As with prophetic credentials, Jesus' miracles and signs refer to his authorization by God, ("that the Father sent me"), and so the object of belief is expressly God, who sent Jesus. The christological identity the miracles suggest is that of prophet (6:14) or king/messiah (6:15), important titles, but still titles of low Christology. They argue, moreover, that Jesus is no sinner, but a "man from God" (9:31–33).

The works in 10:37–38, however, have a different function and argue for a different Christology. Completely absent from 10:37–38 is any mention of works as demonstration "that the Father sent me." Rather, the works function precisely in the formal argument that "the Father is in me and I am in the Father," not agency from God but parity with God. When miracles or signs function in an argument, moreover, the logic is linear, as Jesus' signs point beyond him to God:

5:36 . . . that the Father sent me
9:33 . . . if he were not from God
11:42 . . . that you sent me

The works of Jesus in 10:37–38, however, have a different logic, for the trajectory is not linear or unidirectional (Jesus—sign—God), but circular (God-in-Jesus and Jesus-in-God), where circularity implies parity, "equality with God" (10:33).

Miracles	*Works in 10:37–38*
. . . in order that	. . . in order that
they believe	they come to acknowledge
that you sent me	that the Father is in me
	and I am in the Father

The Christology implied in 10:38 is hardly that of prophet or messiah, but, as the context indicates, "equality with God" (10:30, 33) and "God" (10:33). Authorization from God is not the issue here, but rather parity with God. Miracles, even the special ones granted to Elijah, Elisha, and Ezekiel, do not prove their heavenly status which, however, is precisely the issue in 10:28–38.

Know. Analogously, it is argued that "to know" Jesus leads one to know God—again a linear chain of evidence whose goal is God:

8:19 If you knew me, you would know my Father also.

14:7 If you had known me, you would have known my Father also.

In 10:38, however, knowledge is not linear but circular once more: " . . . that you may come to know that the Father is in me and I am in the Father." The works here have as their object both God-in-Jesus and Jesus-in-God, which at least puts Jesus on a par with God, the very claim made in 10:30.

In. Commentators argue two things about 10:38: it refers to mutual indwelling, and back to 10:30, the cause of the debate in 10:30–38. The first comment remains mysteriously vague, especially if the basic parallels for comparison are 14:10–11 and 17:21. One might understand that God's Spirit or power can be said to be "in" Jesus or a Christian; Christians can be said to be "in" Christ. But in these two instances a radical distinction is maintained (1) between the superior figure, God, and an inferior figure, humankind, who is the recipient of a gift. Or, (2) a distinction is made between a dominant figure, Jesus or God, and a subordinate figure (a Christian disciple) whose whole identity derives from association with the dominant figure. Verse 10:38 seems not to be making any distinctions, certainly not in terms of superior/inferior or dominant/subordinate relationships. The Fourth Gospel asserts here a formal balance or equality between God and Jesus: "The Father is in me and I am in the Father."

This equality must be remembered as we survey how John tends to use "in God" and "in Christ" statements. I am persuaded that most of the Johannine "in so-and-so" statements are variant forms of "remain in so-and-so" and may be classified as follows:

1. Disciples remain "in" Jesus (15:4–7)
2. God remains "in" them (1 John 3:24; 4:15)
3. God and Jesus are "in" them (14:20)
   or they are "in" God and Jesus (17:21)

Of paramount importance in the Fourth Gospel is the question of where one is. Being in God's covenant and being God's children or Abraham's descendants are contrasted with being an outsider, a child of the devil, apart from the vine. It does not seem to matter whether

God is in the true disciple or the disciple is in Christ, so long as a genuine relationship exists, for in virtue of this, they are insiders. Outsider vs. insider—the issue never drops, as criteria are developed to determine genuine membership (3:3, 5; 6:53; 8:24) and to identify authentic disciples (8:31; 10:4–5). After all, there can only be one flock and one shepherd (10:16). Being in God or in Christ basically means that one is an insider and a member of the covenant.

In this line of thought we find clearly expressed the role of superior/inferior and master/follower, for only God and Jesus are leaders or shepherds and we are all their sheep, their followers. Any note of equality or balance is out of the question here, since the issue is obedience and loyalty to God and God's Christ. Yet as the argument develops in 10:28–38, exact balance and equality between God and Jesus become the formal issues. As commentators have noted, 10:38 harks back to 10:30 and so to 10:33.

10:30   I and the Father are equal (*hen*).

10:33   A man is God?

10:38   The Father is in me and I am in the Father.

Yes, a man (*anthrōpos*) is god (*theos*)! Yes, Jesus and God are on a par! Yes, God is in Jesus and Jesus is in God. There are no superiors or inferiors in this relationship. Furthermore, as we have seen in regard to 10:17–18 and 28–30, what makes Jesus and God equal is the exercise of the same power (works of the Father), that is, God's eschatological power over death.

In conclusion, the new forensic proceeding redacted onto 10:22–27 argues for the following points. Jesus makes a claim beyond that of being Messiah. He claims that he is "equal to God" (10:30, 33). God, who is "greater than all," has made Jesus "equal to God." His equality, moreover, consists in eschatological power over death. Jesus defends this equality with God and the acclamation of himself as god first from Ps. 82:6, which equates godliness with deathlessness. Although not strictly deathless, Jesus nevertheless is imperishable and has power over death, both that of his followers (10:28) and especially his own death (10:17–18). Further defense in 10:37–38 of Jesus' equality with God rests on Jesus' claim to do certain works, which we saw were the works of eschatological power, that is, to raise the dead, both his followers and himself. In 10:28–38, therefore, Jesus' equality with God rests on his eschatological power over death.

SUMMARY AND CONCLUSIONS

Regarding the history of some of the materials in John 10, I have argued that 10:17–18 was added to 10:1–16, and 10:28–38 to 10:22–27. This rests on the observation that 10:17–18 and 28–38 both assert that Jesus has God's eschatological power over death, both to raise himself and to raise his followers. The substance of this claim points to a very high christological confession of Jesus as "equal to God" (10:30, 33). For that reason it is judged to belong to a redaction of the Fourth Gospel which contains especially the claim that Jesus is god and lord because he has God's two powers to the full.

Regarding the specific content of the high christological confession in John 10, the substance behind the claims that Jesus is God and equal to God rests on God's gift to Jesus of power over death. Jesus claims power over his own death (10:17–18, 34–36), as well as power over the death of his sheep (10:28–30, 37–38), in virtue of which he and the Father are equal.

This power over death, moreover, needs to be seen in light of the claims made in 5:21–29 that Jesus is indeed equal to God because God gave him specific eschatological powers. "To have life in himself" (5:26) stands behind Jesus' claim in 10:17–18 to "lay down my life and take it again." "To raise the dead" (5:21, 25, 28–29) surely finds its echo in the claim in 10:28 that Jesus "gives eternal life," that no one "perish," and that no one can permanently "snatch" Jesus' sheep from him. "Equality with God," first raised in 5:18, is explicitly the focus of 10:30–33 and the claims that precede and the apology that follows that claim. The discussion of power over death in John 10 purposely takes the reader back to the claims made in 5:21–29 that Jesus has God's eschatological power to the full.

Although defense of the confession of Jesus as "equal to God" tends to be made in terms of further intensified claims, John 10:34–35 cites the Hebrew Scriptures (Ps. 82:6) as justification for calling Jesus god. As we saw, the substance of the citation embodied a midrashic understanding of the psalm in reference to deathlessness. As Israel was rightfully called god because it was made deathless by virtue of hearing God's word on Sinai, so Jesus is rightfully equal to God precisely because he is deathless, that is, he has power over death.

As Figure 1 (p.34) indicated, therefore, John 10 continues the bold confession of Jesus as god and equal to God precisely because of his parity with God in terms of eschatological power. If judgmental power was stressed in John 8, power over death, both his own and that of his followers, constitutes the substance of the claims in John 10. Discussion of this aspect of Jesus' equality with God will not end with John 10, but develops more dramatically in the subsequent narrative of Jesus' raising of Lazarus in John 11, to which we now turn as we complete the exposition of Jesus' eschatological power begun in 5:21–29.

4

JESUS'
RESURRECTION:
JOHN 11

No discussion of Jesus' eschatological power over death would be complete without some consideration of the raising of Lazarus in John 11. Our hypothesis is that John 11 continues the demonstration of the eschatological power credited to Jesus in 5:21–29, whereby he is "equal to God." This suggestion is not entirely new, inasmuch as scholars regularly suggest some connection between John 11 and 5:21–29, although there is little agreement on the precise parallels:

Dodd[1]	John 11//5:25
Hoskyns[2]	John 11//5:26
Lindars[3]	John 11//5:24
Schnackenburg[4]	John 11//5:21, 26, 28–29.

Commentators note these parallels randomly, but do not indicate how John 11 might be demonstrating the claims made in 5:21–29 or how older traditions in John 11 might be reinterpreted in light of these claims. Nor do scholars suggest that this new demonstration of Jesus' power over death confirms the christological claim that Jesus is equal to God. Yet the perception that John 11 has some thematic relationship to 5:21–29 is a major datum of lasting interpretive significance.

We are focusing on the relationship of 5:21–29 and John 11, with particular attention to 11:25, where Jesus reveals himself as "the resurrection and the life." It is also part of our hypothesis that the discussion of Jesus' eschatological power over death and its formal demonstration in John 11 constitute a later redaction of a more traditional story. And so we begin our investigation of John 11 with an examination of the history of the story of the raising of Lazarus.

CRISIS IN ESCHATOLOGICAL
DOCTRINE

Discussion of John 11 has stayed at a fairly low level of exposition, because the dominant exegetical inquiry has been into the source of John 11 and its place among the Johannine signs.[5] Yet this discussion has advanced the understanding of John 11 and can serve as a point of departure. A strong degree of consensus exists about the basic shape of the source of this story and of its earliest Johannine redaction:[6]

Source: 1–3, 17–18, 33–34, 38–39, 43–45
Redaction: 4–16, 19–32, 35–38, 40–42

The Johannine redaction of the original tradition includes: (1) the catechesis of the disciples in the Johannine pattern of statement/misunderstanding/explanation (vv. 5–16, esp. 11–16); (2) the centrality of Martha[7] (vv. 5, 19, 20–27, 28) and especially Jesus' catechesis of her (vv. 23–27); (3) the schism over Jesus in vv. 35–37; (4) the prayer of Jesus in vv. 41–42; and (5) the special function of the incident "for the glory of God" (11:40), as proof that God sent Jesus (11:42). Yet when the question is asked, What is the occasion and function of the Johannine redaction? commentators become reticent. W. Stenger[8] pointed to 11:24–27 and suggested that John's interest lies in Jesus' eschatological revelation and the corresponding demand for faith. More interesting is James Martin's suggestion of a crisis in the Johannine community over eschatological doctrine; Martin himself pointed to the problem of the delay of the Parousia as the immediate historical background of the Johannine redaction.[9] Although there is scant evidence in the Fourth Gospel about a crisis over the delay of the Parousia (see Matt. 24:48–51; 25:1–13), Martin's question deserves attention, for it urges us to consider John 11 in the light of contemporary scholarship: What event or crisis in the community might be addressed in the redaction of this passage?

Two aspects of the story suggest the appropriateness of such a question. First, a sense of crisis exists in the narrative: Jesus delays (v. 6); he is reproached for not being there on time (vv. 21, 32); crowds comment sarcastically on Jesus' seeming impotence (v. 37). Second, a new insight and a fresh confession of faith are demanded: the disciples will be led to a new faith through the episode (v. 15); Martha herself is led step by step to a new faith in Jesus (vv. 23–26), which crystallizes in a solemn confession (11:27). And so crisis, new insight, and fresh confession are the literary evidence that warrants further scrutiny of the narrative in the light of the experience of the Johannine group.

Why the crisis? What is it about? I suggest that the crisis arose over the group's eschatological doctrine which spoke of believers having life, even eternal life. Readers of the Fourth Gospel can readily recall numerous passages in the narrative that link belief with the promise of immediate life under the code label of "realized eschatology."

> Whoever believes in him should not perish, but have eternal life. (3:16)

> Whoever hears my word and believes him who sent me, has eternal life; he does not come into judgment, but has passed from death to life. (5:24)

> This is the bread come down from heaven, that a man may eat of it and not die. (6:50)

> If anyone eats of this bread, he will live forever. (6:51)

> Whoever lives and believes in me shall never die. (11:26b)

How was this eschatological doctrine understood? As we saw in the discussion of 8:51–53, some understood it literally as a promise of undying physical life, yet people in John 8 who think this way are outsiders who are "from below . . . of this world" (8:23). At one point, however, even true believers entertained such ideas, as is suggested in the case of the alleged imperishability of the beloved disciple in 21:21–23. On balance, it would seem that the depth of the crisis in John 11 indicates that some people at least took the early Johannine doctrine on "realized" eschatology quite literally.[10]

This issue as it is framed in John 11 does not focus on the faith and life of a marginal disciple, but on that of a genuine insider. It is hardly accidental that the family at Bethany is presented as intimates of Jesus. Mary (11:2; 12:3) showed singular marks of hospitality to Jesus, an action contrasting her with the pseudodisciple, Judas. Martha likewise demonstrated hospitality in her service of Jesus (12:2). Yet Lazarus was Jesus' intimate, even his "beloved" disciple:[11]

> He whom you love is ill . . . (11:3)

> Now Jesus loved Lazarus . . . (11:5)

> Our beloved Lazarus has fallen asleep. (11:11)

> See how he loved him . . . (11:36)

Lazarus, moreover, is later linked with Jesus' death, becoming the second object of the plot that will engulf Jesus. "So the chief priests planned to put Lazarus to death . . . " (12:10). The Gospel, then, portrayed him as not only intimately linked with Jesus on a personal basis but also sharing his fate. The sickness and death of a genuine beloved disciple, then, provoked a crisis of the first order for the Johannine group. His death ought not to have happened (11:21, 32)! Jesus ought to have been able to prevent it (11:36)! After all, Jesus' own teaching indicated that death would not occur!

The crisis necessarily provoked a fresh evaluation of the community's eschatological doctrine. Was it erroneous or merely inadequate? Was it misunderstood? The redaction of John 11 grappled with these issues in the way it structured how the disciples and Martha are led to fresh understanding of the group's eschatological teaching. The evangelist, moreover, formally presented this growth in understanding in the double instance of the pattern statement/misunderstanding/explanation.[12] First, in 11:6–16 the disciples are catechized to accept a new teaching and so grow in belief. Jesus states: "Lazarus has fallen asleep," which the disciples misunderstand: "They thought that he meant taking rest in sleep" (11:11–13). Jesus' explanation removed the ambiguity ("Lazarus is dead"), even as it summoned the disciples to special faith: "For your sake I am glad that I was not there, *so that you may believe*" (11:15). Jesus, however, gives no indication here in what the new belief consists, only strongly demands that the disciples "believe."

Second, in 11:21–27 Martha is catechized, but in a way that leads her to receive a specific revelation and to confess a specific confession of faith. Jesus states: "Your brother will rise again" (11:22). Martha misunderstands Jesus to speak of a future time of resurrection, similar to that proclaimed in 5:28–29. In contrast with Jesus' listeners in 8:31–58, Martha's misunderstanding does not brand her as hopelessly impervious to Jesus' word. She does not understand Jesus on an earthly, fleshly level as others do (3:4; 8:33, 39). Her insight represents a traditionally orthodox belief in a future resurrection, although one not entirely in accord with the Johannine promise that believers already have life, even eternal life. Too easily does Martha disregard Jesus' earlier statements and opt for a solution less specifically Johannine. Jesus explains in 11:25b that believers have everlasting life: "He who believes in me, though he die, shall live." This new statement in 11:25b, which contains the correction in eschatological perspective, is deliberately juxtaposed to an older formulation in 11:26.

11:25b	11:26
He who believes in me though he die will live	Whoever lives and believes in me shall never die.

Both statements address the issue of the life and death of believers. I take 11:26 as representative of the type of eschatological perspective that is challenged in John 11 by actual, physical death, for it implies that believers already live and will never taste death (8:52). Lazarus's death stands as proof that this simply cannot be true. And so it is qualified by the addition of 11:25b. This verse provides an adjusted perspective, which takes the new experience into account: believers die, but live.[13] The very sequence of terms in these two statements conveys the necessary adaptation of perspective:

11:25a	11:26
(*a*) believer	(*a*) believer
(*b*) dies	(*b*) lives
(*c*) but lives	(*c*) and does not die

This juxtaposition occurred also in John 6, where statements that those who eat the bread of life do not die stand side by side with remarks that Jesus will raise them on the last day.

6:39

And this is the will of him who sent me, that I should lose nothing of all that he has given me,	but raise it up at the last day.

6:40

This is the will of my Father that every one who sees the Son and believes in him should have eternal life;	and I will raise him at the last day.

6:44

No one can come to me unless the Father draws him;	and I will raise him at the last day.

6:54

He who eats my flesh and drinks my blood has eternal life;	and I will raise him at the last day.

The refrain, "and I will raise him at the last day," clashes with the bold claims that: (1) those who believe in Jesus "shall not hunger . . .

shall never thirst" (6:35) and "have eternal life" (6:47); and (2) those who eat the bread of life "do not die" (6:50), "live forever" (6:51, 58) and "have eternal life" (6:54). The refrain qualifies these claims by not allowing them to be taken too literally. For this reason it appears to be a secondary qualification of the earlier doctrine of realized eschatology which was being understood all too literally. The pattern of juxtaposing eschatological statements in John 6 resembles that in 11:25b–26.

According to this redaction of John 11, Jesus speaks a qualifying eschatological word that moderates earlier claims. How will death be understood, especially in the framework of Johannine ideology? What new element or correction is suggested? Death is a fact not to be denied—neither Jesus' death nor that of his followers. But perhaps Martha, and the whole Johannine group for whom she speaks, took Jesus' words too literally, equating "life" with physical deathlessness. Literal, earthly interpretation of Jesus' eschatological words did occur. Jesus then urges her to understand them in a more spiritual, heavenly mode, much like the way the Samaritan woman was moved from buckets of water to waters of revelation (4:10–26). Jesus really meant that belief truly leads to eternal life, but this claim does not exclude physical death.[14]

Yet how to overcome death? What proof is there that belief really does lead to life, life *beyond death*? What is called for is a demonstration of power over death, a sample event proving that: (1) belief does lead to life, (2) Jesus' very word is the power to effect life after death. The original sign miracle, which served to validate Jesus' credentials as one sent from God, is now interpreted as a demonstration of the new eschatological doctrine. At this point, the notes in the text that Lazarus is genuinely dead, four days in the tomb and already subject to corruption, become the unimpeachable evidence of death that constitutes the acid bath for the demonstration of Jesus' new doctrine. If Jesus can overcome these conditions, then death in all its forms and duration is subject to his control. The raising of Lazarus, then, is no mere sign of Jesus' credentials, no humanitarian action, no act of prophetic power, but a demonstration of power in support of a specific doctrine: *He who believes in me, though he die, will live.*

What level of Christology is expressed by this? Jesus leads Martha to a confession that is supposed to embody this new doctrine. Yet she acclaims Jesus by titles that are still expressions of low Christology: "I believe that you are the Christ, the Son of God, he who is coming into the world" (11:27). Her confession formally contains titles also found in Nathanael's confession and in the original conclusion of the sign source.[15]

1:41–48	*11:27*	*20:31*
the Christ	the Christ	the Christ
the Son of God	the Son of God	the Son of God
the King of Israel		

As Martyn has shown, these titles basically acclaim Jesus as a human figure. Nothing in Jesus' claims or Martha's confession demands that Jesus be acclaimed equal to God.

In summary, then, we can see how an early Johannine redaction of the Lazarus story was precipitated by a crisis in the community over its eschatological doctrine. The naked fact of death demanded a review of Jesus' promise that believers would not die, for some of his followers understood him too literally. True insiders came to see that when Jesus said that a believer would not die, he meant not die forever. A believer would be raised to life after death. Proof of this lies in the immediate grant of life to a dead believer. Yet this is not the only redaction of John 11, as the following investigation indicates.

HIGH CHRISTOLOGY IN JOHN 11

John 11 would seem to have undergone still another redaction.[16] The fact that so many scholars see parallels between 5:21–29 and John 11 indicates that it is capable of being read from another perspective, the perspective of the Johannine high Christology and the claim that Jesus has God's eschatological power. This redaction may not rest so much on the infusion of new materials into the text, which was the case with the first redaction, as in the reassessment of its remarks from a higher perspective. The redaction of John 10, which we studied in the previous chapter, indicates that at this point in the Gospel's history, special new claims were made on Jesus' behalf: (1) claims by Jesus to rescue his followers out of death, after death (8:51; 10:28), and (2) claims by Jesus to be able to take back his own life after death (8:28; 10:17–18). As we saw, these claims belong to the confession of Jesus as a figure "equal to God" (10:30, 33). They are, moreover, claims that hark back to the assertion in 5:21–29 that Jesus fully enjoys God's eschatological power. This level of discourse constitutes a new horizon from which to view the materials in John 11. What issues is a fresh reading of John 11. Filtered through the high christological confession of Jesus as equal to God, it labels his power to raise the dead as God's eschatological power.

I Am the Resurrection

Our focus moves in particular to two verses, 11:4 and 25a. Let us first examine the great revelatory statement: "I am the resurrection [and the life]." Although in form 11:25a resembles other "I AM" plus predicate statements in John, it functions on a level proclaiming Jesus as the replacement of Jewish cult and experience. Not manna, but Jesus is the true bread. Not the sun or Torah, but Jesus is the light. Not Israel's rulers, but Jesus is the model shepherd. Not the way of the synagogue, but Jesus is the true way to life. Not the covenant with Moses, but Jesus is the true vine. In 11:25, however, Jesus does not replace any obsolete or false Jewish cult object or expectation, for he does not merely revive Lazarus, replacing prophets of old who could do the same act of power. He claims to have an eschatological power that belongs to God alone. Martha's confession of Jesus as Christ and Son of God may be adequate to Jesus' former eschatological word, but the christological confession implied in the revelation "I am the resurrection" is nothing less than Jesus' claim to be equal to God and Lord.

Just what is claimed in 11:25? On the level of eschatological doctrine in John's Gospel, 11:25 stands apart from other claims to give life. Raymond Brown summarized the other "I AM" plus predicate statements as descriptions of Jesus as the source of life for his followers:

> In his mission Jesus is the source of eternal life for men ("vine," "life"); he is the means through which men find life ("way," "gate"); he leads men to life ("shepherd"); he reveals to men the truth ("truth") which nourishes their life ("bread").[17]

Yet a prophet like Moses might likewise give bread, shepherd God's covenant flock, and plant it as a vine in the promised land. The separate functions described in these "I AM" statements are all functions of a human figure.

I suggest that the contents of "I am the resurrection" are identical with the claims made in 5:25; 10:17–18, and 28. Jesus claimed power *over death:* not that his disciples would not taste physical death, but that they would not "perish" or die eternally. And so his sheep "hear his voice," and he gives them "eternal life and they shall never perish" (10:27–28). Jesus' power over death likewise extends to his power to raise himself to life after death (10:17–18). This, of course, is what he claimed in 8:28, that after being "lifted up," he would still be "I AM," that is, imperishable.

Equal Glory with God

Jesus' raising of Lazarus will result in equal glory for God and the Son of God: "It is for the glory of God, so that the Son of God may be glorified by means of it" (11:4)."Glory" in John's Gospel has several distinct meanings. In the early stages of the Fourth Gospel, Jesus does not seek his own glory (5:40, 44; 8:50, 54), for he is but a sign of God's word, revelation, and presence. His miracles may "manifest his glory" (2:11), but they function as signs of his credentials, namely, that God sent him. But at a higher level, the one who is equal to God did manifest his glory (1:14), even as Isaiah saw his glory in the christophany in Isaiah 6 (see John 12:41). These last statements relate to 5:23, where it is claimed that God wills us to "honor the Son, even as we honor the Father." The reader is reminded of the discussion of 8:49–50 and 54, where it was argued that "honor" and "glory" there were demonstrations of the equal honor demanded of Jesus in 5:23. In this vein 11:4 indicates that the argument in John 11 will be equally for the glory of God and the Son of God: "For the glory of God, so that the Son of God may be glorified by means of it" (11:4).

In John 11, there are two references to "glory," which cannot simply be equated:

11:4	*11:40*
It is for the glory of God, so that the Son of God may be glorified by means of it	Did I not tell you that if you would believe you would see the glory of God?

The remark in 11:40 corresponds to the use of "glory" in the early Johannine traditions, where Jesus' signs serve as credentials that God sent him (11:42), and so they are for God's glory. In the remark in 11:4, however, Jesus is not pointing to God through a sign as in 11:40–42, but is claiming something that belongs to God alone,[18] eschatological power as the resurrection.

This is confirmed when we note that Jesus is "glorified" especially in the context of his death and victory over death.[19] In a prayer quite different from Jesus' prayer in 11:41–42, Jesus prays on the eve of his death to be "glorified with the glory I had with you before the world was made" (17:5, 24). Glory, then, has to do with Jesus' status as the eternal and imperishable one, who is "equal to

God." As the eternal one, he had glory with God before the world was made, "Father, glorify thou me in thy own presence with the glory which I had with thee before the world was made" (17:5). And as the imperishable one he will resume that glory[20] in overcoming death: "Father, I desire that they . . . behold my glory which thou hast given me in thy love for me before the foundation of the world" (17:24). And so the mutual glory of God and the Son of God in 11:4 has to do with their equality, both as eternal, but especially as imperishable figures who have absolute power over death. One is reminded of a similar argument in 10:30 and 38.

Verses 11:4 and 25a, therefore, should be seen as expositions of the eschatological power granted Jesus in 5:21-29. God demanded that Jesus be given equal honor with God (5:23), which relates to the new function of the raising of Lazarus according to 11:4—equal glory. And the claims to have life in himself (5:26), to be able to raise the dead (5:21), and to call them from their tombs (5:25) are summarized in the assertion in 11:25a that Jesus is the resurrection and the life. It would seem, then, that John 11 underwent still another redaction that interpreted and manipulated the earlier materials which deal with the Johannine eschatology to demonstrate the claims of divine eschatological power given Jesus in 5:21-29.

John 11 and Jesus' Eschatological Powers

The suggestion that John 11 underwent a second redaction which highlighted his eschatological powers whereby he is equal to God can be demonstrated by sharpening the differences between the two redactions of the basic story of the raising of Lazarus. (1) Occasion: The first redaction was occasioned by a crisis over eschatological doctrine caused by death; the second redaction occurs in the context of the proclamation of the high Christology. (2) Function: The first redaction serves as an apologetic correction to an inadequate eschatological doctrine, the second as part of the demonstration of the new christological claim that Jesus has God's eschatological power. (3) Symbolism: The raising of Lazarus symbolizes Jesus' power and is an earnest of his claim that "Who believes in me shall live, even though he dies." But in the last redaction, the raising of Lazarus becomes a demonstration of Jesus' absolute power over death, that Jesus himself is the resurrection. (4) Level of eschatological doctrine: In the first redaction the eschatological doctrine primarily treated the validity of faith in Jesus to produce genuine life, despite death. But the second redaction argues that Jesus has God's eschatological power over death because he is equal to God. (5) Christology: Martha sums up the Christology reflected in the first redaction in confessing Jesus by titles of low Christology, namely, Christ and Son of God. In the second redaction, Jesus is acclaimed as equal to God, even Lord, because of his heavenly power. (6) God's glory: In the first redaction, God is glorified in Lazarus's raising when people "believe that you sent me" (11:42). But in the second redaction, the incident will be for the equal glory of God and God's Son, glory related to their "imperishability," or power over death. (7) Relation to Jesus' death: In the first redaction, Jesus' death is treated on the same level as Lazarus's death; as Lazarus was the object of a death plot (12:9–11), so Jesus is likewise a victim of plots (11:8, 16).[21] In the second redaction, however, Jesus is heralded as one who has power over death. If he is "the resurrection," his power is equally over the death of his followers as well as over his own death. The second redaction, then, picks up four specific elements of the eschatological powers credited to Jesus in 5:21–29, as the following table shows.

5:21	give life	11:25, 43
5:23	equal honor	11:4
5:25, 28	call dead from their tombs	11:43–44
5:26	have life in himself	11:25a

Most obviously 11:43–44 fulfills in detail the claim that the dead in the tombs will hear the voice of the Son of God and come forth and live (5:25, 28):

John 5:25, 28	*John 11*
1. "The hour is coming . . . "	"Are there not twelve hours in the day?" (11:9)
2. "when the dead . . . "	"Lord, by this time there will be an odor, for he has been dead four days already" (11:39)
3. "will hear the voice"	"He cried out with a loud voice: 'Lazarus, come out!'" (11:43)
4. " . . . of the Son of God"	"It is not unto death; it is for the glory of God, so that the Son of God may be glorified by means of it" (11:4). "I believe that you are the Christ, the Son of God, he who is coming into the world" (11:27)
5. "and hearing, they will live"	"The dead man came forth . . . " (11:44)

91

Jesus' raising of Lazarus, we saw, will result in glory for him equal to God's glory (11:4), echoing the demand in 5:23 that Jesus be given "equal honor" with God. Furthermore, Jesus' claim to "have life in himself" (5:26) would seem to be expressed also in his claim that "I am the resurrection" (11:25a). And the generic claim to "make alive" (5:21) would also seem to be illustrated both in Jesus' claims in 11:25b–26 and in the actual raising of Lazarus in 11:44. The close relationship of John 11 and 5:21–29 only confirms our assertion that John 11 enjoyed a second redaction and came to be read in the light of the claims in 5:21–29, that is, in terms of the Johannine high Christology.

SUMMARY AND CONCLUSIONS

In our quest for the high christological confession in John 10 and 11, the investigation inevitably led us to consider the growth and development of the materials in those chapters. The basic parables of 10:1–16, the popular judgment in 10:19–21, and the forensic defense of Jesus' claims in 10:22–27 would appear to belong to an early stage of development, the replacement stage, where the Gospel acclaims Jesus as the authentic shepherd and the true gate. The new claims of Jesus to have life in himself (10:17–18) and to be equal to God (10:28–30), as well as the ensuing forensic trial defending these claims (10:31–38), represent the Johannine high christological claim that Jesus is equal to God, which we have judged to stem from a later stage of development.

In regard to John 11, it would appear that the account of the raising of Lazarus enjoyed a prominent place among Jesus' signs. That early story was later redacted to treat a crisis in eschatological doctrine occasioned by the death of Jesus' beloved disciple. And, I suggest, the basic story underwent still another redaction in which Jesus' eschatological power over death was demonstrated (11:4, 25).

The elements of high Christology in John 10 and 11 were shown to be demonstrations of Jesus' eschatological power: (1) Jesus' power to lay down his life and take it back (10:17–18; 11:25a); (2) his power over death, whereby he is equal to God (10:30); (3) his defense for being called "god" because of his gift of deathlessness (10:34–36); (4) his grant from God to do "the works of God," that is, the exercise of eschatological powers (10:37–38); (5) his claims of power over death (11:25) and power to call the dead from their tombs (11:43–44); and (6) his demand for "glory" equal to God's (11:4).

The first four chapters in this book, moreover, have shown that the Fourth Gospel dramatized the contents of the summary of eschatological powers credited to Jesus in 5:21–29 in John 8, 10, and 11. The earlier grant of power functioned as a topic statement subsequently unpacked idea by idea and phrase by phrase in the narratives that followed, as figure 1 indicates. Each and every item of the summary of eschatological power credited to Jesus in 5:21–29 has been fully demonstrated by the end of John 11. And so Jesus may rightfully be called equal to God because he has the fullness of God's power.

The previous chapters operated according to traditional methods of exegesis, explaining in detail the content of the high christological confession in the Fourth Gospel. There can be no doubt that this Gospel proclaims that Jesus is fully and completely equal to God, that is, a heavenly, divine figure. Whatever can be said of Israel's God or any other deity in the ancient world can be said unequivocally also of Jesus. The traditional exegetical methods, then, have served us well up to this point in our investigation. But a full evaluation of the high Christology is far from over, for it remains for us to examine how it functions as ideology for a social group, how the person who is equal to God is emphatically not of this world. This is the task of the second part of this book.

5

EQUAL
TO GOD, BUT
NOT OF THIS WORLD

RESUME

As we gather together the threads of the previous discussion, we can finally appreciate how Jesus' equality with God means that God has fully bestowed on him his two comprehensive powers, creative and eschatological. Having both powers to the full, Jesus may correctly be called by the names corresponding to these two powers. In virtue of his creative power, Jesus may be acclaimed God (*Theos*, 1:1–2); and because he has eschatological power, he is confessed as Lord (*Kyrios*, 20:28).

An essential component of eschatological power, moreover, is Jesus' "having life in himself," just as God has life in himself (5:26). When examined, this was seen as the content of the "I AM" statements in 8:24, 28, and 58, whereby Jesus is acclaimed to be eternal in the past and imperishable in the future.

This conception of Jesus' past eternity and future imperishability interfaces necessarily with the two powers given to him. Himself uncreated, he is the eternal figure in the past who created the world "in the beginning." Imperishable, he is the future figure who triumphs over death (8:28) and raises the dead at the end of time (5:28–29).

Jesus' equality with God, therefore, is fully explained in the Fourth Gospel. Whatever could be said of Israel's Deity can be said fully of Jesus, regarding his eternity, powers, names, and functions:

1. God's creative power	1. God's eschatological power
2. God's name: *Theos*	2. God's name: *Kyrios*
3. God's ungenerated eternity in the past	3. God's imperishability in the future

94

The high christological confession of the Fourth Gospel unequivocally proclaimed that Jesus is equal to God, which should be seen
as the proper content of the confessions in 1:1-2, where Jesus
is "God," and in 20:28, where he is "Lord and God." We find
the substance communicated by those two names primarily in the
confession of him as equal to God, made first in 5:18-29 and
subsequently developed in the Gospel. This investigation, then,
would summarize most or all of the elements of the Johannine
high Christology under the inclusive concept of Jesus' equality
with God.

In regard to the high Christology, the Fourth Gospel exhibits
remarkable clarity of conception and narrative presentation. According to 5:18-29, the author is conceptually clear that God has
given Jesus two specific spheres of activity, which are themselves
compendiums of various aspects of unique divine actions summarized under the rubric of God's two powers. Clarity is shown also
in the exposition of the eschatological power in 5:21-29, which
includes four different elements correctly summarized under the
rubric of eschatological power. Remarkable clarity is also evident
in the way 5:18-29 summarizes not only Jesus' divine powers, but
necessarily suggests the names God and Lord corresponding to the
powers, and leads to the further perception of Jesus' eternity in
the past and imperishability in the future. Conceptually, then, the
high christological confession that Jesus is equal to God is clear,
succinct, and comprehensive.

Not only is the Gospel conceptually clear about Jesus' equality,
this clarity is embodied in the manner in which the high Christology
is presented in the narrative of the Gospel. As we saw, 5:18-29
functions as a topic sentence enunciating a theme, equality with
God, containing two elements or powers, which are the subject matter subsequently developed point by point in John 8, 10, and 11, an
observation illustrated in figure 1 (p. 34). Equality with God, then,
which appears to be the inclusive formula for the high Christology
of the Fourth Gospel, is a clear concept for the author and presented with exceptional narrative clarity.

It would be seriously misleading, however, to claim that the preceding discussion exhausts the content of the high christological
confession in the Fourth Gospel itself or in Christian and scholarly
imagination. For certain traditional ways of expressing the Johannine
confession that Jesus is "God" have tended to emphasize his (1) preexistence and descent into the world, (2) his incarnation as the Word

made flesh (1:14), and (3) the association of the Logos of the Prologue with the hypostasis of Wisdom. We are not ignoring this material, for much of it has been dealt with in the previous exposition,
although under a different rubric. For example, rather than speak
of Jesus' preexistence, a term not found in John, it seems better to
speak of his eternity in the past (1:1; 8:56–58; 17:5, 24). Rather
than speak of the Logos as hypostasized Wisdom who creates, the
Fourth Gospel would prefer to talk of Jesus' creative power,
whereby he is *Theos.* Wayne Meeks called attention to the motif of
Jesus' descent-ascent,[1] which I will discuss shortly as a specific perspective about the high Christology. It emphasizes Jesus' radical
status as an alien in this world. Jesus' descent from heaven necessarily involves his prior status as a figure who is eternal in the past,
and so some aspects of that theme are covered in the previous analysis. One aspect of the Johannine high Christology that has not
been treated is the claim that Jesus has functioned all along in Israel's history as its appearing deity who gave theophanies to Abraham (8:39, 56), Isaiah (12:41), and Jacob (1:51).[2] If the name of the
appearing deity is "I AM," then this is rightly included in our discussion of Jesus who is eternal in the past and who bears God's
name (17:6, 11–12, 26). Equality with God, then, can be said to be
an accurate summary of the Johannine high Christology. It does
not, however, automatically convey all of the nuances of that confession, such as Jesus' descent as an alien into an alien world, which is
precisely the task of the rest of this study.

THE PROBLEM OF PERSPECTIVE

An important critical question must arise at some point in the investigation of the high Christology. How was the confession understood
and how did it function? This is not a question about the genesis
of the confession, how monotheistic Jews might begin to talk about
another power in heaven,[3] or a Lesser Yahweh, and so forth.[4] The
precise origin of the Johannine high Christology continues to remain
inaccessible to us. Was it the influx of Samaritans who already acclaimed Moses as a divine figure that led to the conditions in which
Jesus could likewise be so acclaimed?[5] Was it wisdom speculation?[6]
The text remains mute here, although scholars continue to put this
question to the Fourth Gospel. At issue now, however, is not the confession's genesis, but rather its meaning and function for those confessing it. The distinction is important. For example, a fossil found by

an anthropologist may be properly identified as belonging to such-and-such an animal—its original meaning and genesis; but this same fossil might later be interpreted as an important piece of evidence about the evolution of apes and humans, and even function as a key argument for the priority of one theory of evolution over another. Original content, then, is not the same as subsequent meaning and function. In another example closer to home, Paul in Rom. 3:29–30 proclaims that "God is one," a monotheistic statement which normally implies a strong sectarian stance against the gods of other nations.[7] But Paul understands this theologoumenon differently, for it functions for him in an antisectarian argument for God's impartiality and inclusiveness vis-à-vis the Gentiles.

The genesis of the high christological confession, therefore, is neither accessible to us nor is it the focus of this inquiry. Rather, the dominant questions are, What meaning did Jesus' equality with God come to have for Johannine Christians? and, How did it function for them? These questions raise the critical issue of the perspective[8] from which the Fourth Gospel views the high Christology.

Perspective is constitutive of meaning. It matters whether the document studied is aristocratic in origin and perspective or whether it reflects peasant viewpoints. It makes a difference in our understanding if we can determine whether an author speaks with irony and satire, or whether the views advanced are to be taken at face value (e.g., the columns of Art Buchwald and Russell Baker on the editorial pages of newspapers). The perspective of statements written by university theologians in the United States must necessarily be assessed differently than that of documents issued by the official magisterium of a church, such as the Vatican. Perspective, then, is an essential component of a document's historical and cultural *Sitz im Leben*.

The perspective of the high christological confession in the Fourth Gospel comprises two elements, (1) the aspect of Jesus' nature that was deemed important or primary, and (2) his relationship to the world as implied in that first statement. Since the author of the Fourth Gospel does not doubt Jesus' equality with God, the perspective of the high Christology may indicate whether Jesus is primarily a heavenly figure, whose true place is with God in heaven, or a heavenly figure, who is pleased to tent on earth. And concerning the relationship of this divine Word to the world, the perspective of the high Christology may value Jesus' heavenliness over his becoming flesh, implying Jesus' ambiguous reception on earth, or it may value his pleasure to be flesh

97

and to tent on earth, implying just the opposite. The high christological confession, therefore, could mean two different things about Jesus and imply two different value systems. What, then, is the perspective of Jesus' equality with God?

Determining a document's perspective can be an extremely difficult task, an understatement when it comes to discovering the perspective of the Fourth Gospel. How to find it in a document that apparently underwent several redactions? Might not the Fourth Gospel have different, even conflicting perspectives in it?[9] Might the perspective have even changed because of specific historical experiences in the Johannine circle?

The Traditional Perspective

As a matter of fact, the Fourth Gospel provides in its introduction and conclusion two texts that have traditionally helped the reader discern the perspective of its high Christology. Jesus is acclaimed God in 1:1–2 and Lord and God in 20:28. The Prologue and the conclusion, the normal rhetorical places for controlling the proper perspective from which to view a document, are evidently addressed to insiders in the Johannine circle. Jesus-God creates the world and descends to tabernacle in it (1:14), thus in some way affirming the value of the physical, material world; and Jesus-Lord appears to Thomas to whom he shows his risen body, again indicating that what is death-conquering is also at home in what is mortal. Verses 1:14 and 20:28, therefore, have traditionally functioned as specific texts that serve to establish a perspective for the high Christology of this Gospel. Taken together, 1:14 and 20:28 might suggest the following points: they give equal importance to Jesus' divinity and humanity, and they imply a marriage of Jesus' heavenliness with earth, a compatibility of imperishability with mortality, and an intermingling of the divine in matter. But is this the perspective of equal to God? And is it even an adequate reading of 1:14 and 20:28?

The danger of reading the Fourth Gospel from this perspective lies in anachronistically interjecting the viewpoint of the councils of the fourth and fifth centuries back into the Johannine text. Surely in the creeds that emerged from the councils a certain harmony was seen to exist in the cosmos, a structure and unity whereby Jesus' absolute sovereignty as a divine person was mirrored in the structural authority given to both emperor and bishop in the world below as Jesus' lawful representatives.[10] But was this the perspective of equal to God in the Fourth Gospel? There are strong indications that it was not. It would be surprising if the ecclesiastical perspective of the creeds were identical with the actual historical perspective of the Fourth Gospel. We are urged, then, to examine once more the Fourth Gospel and its cognate documents for clues to the actual perspective of Jesus who is equal to God and to his relationship to the world.

Other Perspectives

As we pursue this task, we do not do it in a vacuum. Both ancient writers and contemporary scholars have offered us significant clues. We turn first to the Johannine epistles for their indication of a certain perspective in which the Johannine Christology appears to have been cast and understood, yet one judged by the author of 1 John to be false and demonic. Then we are advised to recall Meeks's argument about the alien character of Jesus in an alien world as a significant contribution to our understanding of the radical perspective of the high Christology of the Fourth Gospel.

1 John 4:3; 2 John 7. In literature connected with the Fourth Gospel and apparently written after the Gospel's many redactions, we find evidence of a christological perspective reprehensible to the author of the Johannine epistles. In substance, when 1 John 4:3 and 2 John 7 report the confession of some Christians that "Christ did not come in the flesh," that christological position is perceived as emphasizing only Jesus' heavenliness and placing no value in Jesus' flesh,[11] a radical value statement that would imply a relationship to the world that devalues his physical miracles, his earthly rites of water and bread, and his fleshly death on the cross. This devaluing of fleshly things would also extend to other traditions based on the fleshly Jesus, including the importance of eyewitness experience of Jesus and the legitimacy of apostolic leaders deputized by the earthly Jesus.[12]

This material will be examined in detail in chapter 7 of this book, but suffice it to remind us here that 1 John 4:3 and 2 John 7 indicate that the christological perspective of some Johannine group members placed no value in Jesus' flesh, his earthly history, and death. If no value can be predicated of Jesus in the flesh, then all value would seem to reside in Jesus' nonfleshly nature, a perspective that would seemingly clash with 1:14 and 20:28, or at least with the way these texts have been traditionally interpreted. Our two

passages from the Johannine letters indicate that the high christological confession did not necessarily celebrate the descent of the
Deity into flesh and did not value the deeds of the incarnate Word.
At the very least, we are made aware that the high christological
confession of certain Johannine followers of Jesus might be very
problematic. Being equal to God might not automatically signal an
agreeable marriage of heaven and earth, but might indicate a belief
that he is not of this world.

Sectarian Man from Heaven. As we try to grasp the perspective
of the Johannine high christological confession, we must recall
Meeks's important contribution to this project. In his celebrated article on Johannine Christology,[13] Meeks showed how the high christological confession of Jesus as a figure descending from heaven
came to imply that Jesus was perceived as an alien in an alien world
to which he descended. Meeks showed, moreover, that this particular slant on the Johannine high Christology reflected the social perspective of those who confessed it. They considered themselves as
aliens in the world below, just as Jesus was an alien here. Jesus is
surely a heavenly being, even one who descends to earth, but his
visit here was hardly congenial, which might indicate that the Word
was not at home in the world, not of this world.

. . . BUT NOT OF THIS WORLD

We must turn back to the Fourth Gospel and look more closely at
the context and function of passages where Jesus' equality with
God is expressed; and we must look as well at other passages that
embody that content. This must be done if we are to understand
more accurately the specific perspective of the high christological
confession.

A Transient Sojourner—1:14 Revisited

A careful reader would note that even in the Prologue we find
indications that Jesus' existence here in the world and on earth is at
best an uneasy presence, even a transient visit. Thrice it is noted that
the Word which came into the world met with rejection and hostility.

The darkness has not overcome it [the Light]. (1:5)

The world knew him not. (1:10)

His own received him not. (1:11)

The only home where the Word was pleased to dwell consisted of the small circle of believers "who believed in his name" (1:12) and who were "born of God" (1:13), certainly not the majority of the world or his own. And 1:18 subsequently locates Jesus back in God's bosom, his true home from which he descended (see 1:1–2). Several important contemporary studies of the chiastic form of the Johannine Prologue indicate that 1:14 is not the climactic pivot of the Prologue.[14] This shifts the passage's emphasis back to 1:1–2 and 18, Jesus' true home and status as "god" who is face to face with God, but away from the incarnational perspective of 1:14.

Although 1:14 might be thought to celebrate the delight of the Word to enter and dwell in flesh, thus giving value to flesh, other statements in the Prologue emphatically comment on the bankruptcy of material and fleshly criteria for birth into God's family: " . . . not of blood, nor of the will of the flesh, nor of the will of man" (1:13a). Association with the Word made flesh, therefore, does not depend on anything fleshly or material. This suggests that the Word may be in the world, but that his relationship to it is certainly strained.

At the very least, the Prologue describes the ambiguity, if not the hostility, the Word met when entering this world of matter and flesh. This world, then, can hardly be called a congenial dwelling place for the Word, nor do worldly criteria for membership have value in constituting anyone a child of God. John 1:14 may indicate to some a certain marriage of heavenliness with earthliness; but in the context of the Prologue as a whole, it suggests at best a narrow coexistence of imperishability with mortality and a tentative sojourning of the divine in matter. Whatever marriage exists is for the elite, few believers, not for the majority, as 1:5, 10, and 11 indicate. In its complete context, therefore, 1:14 is hardly an unambiguous celebration of the presence of the Word in the world. Even if Jesus is acclaimed "God" (1:1–2) who became flesh (1:14), it remains to be seen what this means in the rest of the Gospel narrative and how it functions for the Johannine community. For even in the Gospel Prologue, the divinity of Jesus, while affirmed, is not entirely at home in the world that he created.

As problematic as it is, moreover, 1:14 is not the only text in the Fourth Gospel that might help us understand the perspective and function of the high christological confession. When we look more carefully at the specific places in the narrative where Jesus is acclaimed equal to God, the traditional but ambiguous tranquillity of 1:14 is totally lost, as is the sense of a compatible marriage of opposites. Attention must be paid to the narrative contexts in which the confessions of Jesus as equal to God occur, for they indicate that another perspective is operative vis-à-vis the meaning and function of the high Christology.

Equal to God (5:18; 10:33)

In our continuing search for the perspective of the high christological confession, we turn back to the confession of Jesus as equal to God to examine it more precisely in its narrative context and to see how it functions there.

Three initial points need to be made concerning 5:18–29. According to the narrative, the opponents of Jesus first articulate the specific phrase "equal to God," precisely as a forensic accusation against him. Vigorously defended, it does not originate on the lips of believers as a formal confession. Although there is not doubt that equal to God constitutes the essence of the high christological confession, it is indeed curious that it never appears formally either on the lips of Jesus[15] or his disciples, but only as an accusation against him by his enemies.

Second, unlike the typical Johannine pattern whereby Jesus' statements tend to be misunderstood, the audience in 5:18 accurately interprets Jesus' remark in 5:17 about the parity of God's and Jesus' Sabbath working to imply Jesus' equality with God. Correct understanding of Jesus, however, does not indicate that they have become insiders who believe in Jesus, for the narrative states that this correct knowledge ironically divides them from Jesus and his group. They seek to kill him precisely because they perceive the correct implications of one of his sayings.

Finally, the narrative context of the remark "equal to God" is a formal forensic proceeding. Jesus makes a claim (5:17), which leads to a formal charge (5:18) and a forensic proceeding against him that might issue in his death. If we may safely distinguish the conceptual origin of "equal to God" from its narrative context in the flow of the Gospel story, the narrative context is conflict and forensic process. These three observations initially suggest that equal to God must be seen as embedded in a context of controversy, as a forensic accusation originating in conflict. A correct observation is ironically made by unbelievers, which produces not faith but hatred.

Probing further, we note the obvious fact that equal to God is offensive to Jesus' audience, causing them to stand critically over against Jesus. In short, it causes a division, a divorce. The apology for it (5:19–29) hardly seeks to ameliorate the offensiveness of the charge, but rather accentuates it, intensifying the division between the followers of Jesus and the synagogue. Defense of Jesus' equality with God in virtue of his miraculous healing power (i.e., his creative power) would easily satisfy the forensic issue raised in the narrative; but the apology emphatically capitalizes on the equality charge by insisting that this equality extends as well to eschatological power, about which there was no discussion or controversy in John 5. In fact, the apology spends most of its effort in affirming Jesus' eschatological power (5:21–29), effectively adding fuel to the fire.

In summary, the acclamation of Jesus' equality with God originates on the lips of his enemies for whom it is a forensic charge deserving of death. The narrative origin and context of the confession, then, are conflict-laden, a formal forensic process against Jesus which is only accentuated, not moderated, by the apology in 5:19–29. One might say that the defense of Jesus' equality serves a divisive function that only separates Jesus further from the synagogue. Its clear articulation in 5:19–29 makes no attempt to heal that division, but accentuates it.

In the other place in the Fourth Gospel where Jesus' equality with God occurs, it is again Jesus' opponents who object to certain of his remarks (10:28–30) and accuse him of "blasphemy" for "making himself equal to God" (10:33). Once more, the narrative context is a formal forensic proceeding against Jesus, a situation of extreme hostility and conflict. On the level of the narrative, just as he did in 5:17, Jesus himself gives adequate ground for the claim of equality (10:28–30). His remarks are correctly, if ironically, understood and are so highly offensive that they provoke hostility and the charge of blasphemy. Once the charge of blasphemy is made, Jesus neither denies nor moderates his equality with God, but boldly defends it. In 10:34–39, as in 5:19–29, Jesus defends his equality with God in such a way as to emphasize how radical it is and so to make unbridgeable the chasm between him and his accusers.[16] The remarks about Jesus' equality with God, then, serve a divisive function, separating him from the synagogue, widening the gulf between them, and causing a permanent divorce.

In summary, conflict is the narrative context of Jesus' equality with God in both 5:18 and 10:33. The so-called confession of equality is actually a formal forensic charge against Jesus, affirmed by him in such a way as to accentuate its scandal to his accusers, especially in 5:21–29. By his defense, Jesus emphasizes his differences with his audience, even to the point of accusing them of sin for contesting his claims; for "whoever does not honor the Son does not honor the Father" (5:23). One might go so far as to say that the emphatic defense of Jesus' equality with God functions as a definitive factor permanently separating Jesus and his audience. The perspective of equal to God, then, involves aggressive elements such as a forensic charge and a defense accentuating the scandal of the charge; the perspective relishes the division it causes.

"I AM" (8:24, 28, 58)

In chapter 2 we inquired into the abstract meaning of the "I AM" statements in terms of the claim made in 5:26, concluding that "I AM" implies that Jesus is both eternal in the past (8:58) and imperishable in the future (8:28). Yet the perspective of the "I AM" statements can be clarified only by examining more closely the narrative context where they occur, in particular 8:23–24.

In 8:23–24, which is part of another forensic controversy, Jesus formally takes the offensive and accuses his audience of monstrous evils for which they will be punished severely. As Jesus formulates the issue, *unless* his hearers acclaim him as "I AM," they will die in their sins. The confession of the high Christology, then, functions formally as a law, noncompliance with which means eternal death. As John 8 unfolds, the audience does not accept Jesus as "I AM" (8:56, 58) and so is condemned to destruction.

The confession of Jesus as "I AM," moreover, is contextualized vis-à-vis 8:23 to indicate that Jesus and his audience belong to two different worlds, so radically contrasted that they preclude any intermingling or compromise: "You are from below and I am from above; you are of this world, I am not of this world." Yet like Jesus, this audience can only belong to one world, either above or below; no other option is offered or desirable at this point. John 8:23–24 functions, then, not to celebrate how the heavenly one, who is from above and not of this world, descends to this world below to dwell here (1:14), but to accentuate how irreconcilable these two worlds are and where value is placed or denied. Those from below and of this world are they who do not confess Jesus as "I AM," and so are sinners who will die in their sins.

The perspective of the "I AM" statement in 8:23–24, then, affirms only Jesus' heavenliness ("from above . . . *not* of this world"), and it implies that all value resides in the world above, definitely not below. For to be from below and of this world are such serious charges that they warrant a death sentence! According to the absolute demand made in 8:24, the high christological confession "I AM" functions to separate peoples and worlds, not to unite them.

Like equal to God, the "I AM" statements arise in forensic controversy, and from start to finish serve to accentuate the differences between Jesus and his audience. But in this case a difference arises which is also cosmological: from above against from below and *not* of this world against of this world.

Not of This World (17:5, 14, 16, 24)

The prayer of Jesus in John 17 offers another excellent window into the way the high christological confession of Jesus as a heavenly being perceived Jesus as a figure radically out of place here in this world. Scholars more and more suggest that, like most parts of the Fourth Gospel, John 17 contains materials added to the Gospel at a later time, either in a late redaction or as a type of gloss.[17] The context is Jesus' farewell address, his final remarks on his departure, his relationship to the world, and his future status. More specifically, the author of John 17 portrays Jesus as eager to leave the world of hatred, which is ruled by the Evil One, and to resume his true status as God's equal in heaven (17:5, 24), his true home. Our interest lies in the many statements in John 17 that echo elements of the high christological confession that we studied in the previous four chapters, elements that unmistakably affirm that the Jesus who is equal to God is emphatically *not* of this world and eager to quit it. These remarks, precisely because they are embedded in this context, suggest an alien perspective, indicating how the high Christology was no neutral confession, but a statement of Jesus' being out of place in the world.

The substance of the high christological confession is found first in the affirmation of Jesus' eternity in the past. Twice Jesus remarks about "the glory which I had with Thee before the creation of the world" (17:5, 24), statements reminiscent of what was affirmed about the heavenly Jesus in the Gospel's Prologue (1:1–2, 18).[18] Inasmuch as Jesus, who is about to face his passion, prays that God restore his former glory, it seems that the prayer implies belief in Jesus' imperishability in the future, a perspective contained also in 8:28 (see 6:62).

Four times in John 17 the departing Jesus remarks that God gave him a name, which he has manifested and in which he has kept his disciples (17:6, 11, 12, 26). Raymond Brown[19] rightly suggests that this name is neither God nor Lord, but "I AM," the name Jesus manifested in 8:24, 28, and 58. As we saw, this name refers to Jesus' eternity in the past and imperishability in the future. This name, moreover, functions here in the same way as it did in 8:23–24, as a criterion of authentic membership. It links those who confess it to the world above, but distinguishes them from those who reject it, who belong to the world below. One's confession of Jesus' true home implies that in some way one shares that spatial location with him.

Jesus' equality with God is probably reflected in 17:7. At first glance, this remark sounds redundant, but that becomes one more clue to its meaning. Jesus confidently remarks that "Now they know that everything that Thou hast given me is from Thee." One might read "everything Thou hast given me" as an echo of the donation of God's two powers in 5:19–29. The seeming redundancy, however, whereby everything "Thou hast given" is clearly "from Thee," seems intended to deal with the repeated charge against Jesus that he "makes himself" God or equal to God (5:18; 10:31–33, 19:7). On the contrary, whatever power or claim Jesus makes is "from Thee," that is, God gave him powers and even demands that the same honor be given Jesus as God (5:23). Hence, Jesus is not violating traditional monotheistic faith, but affirming God's uniqueness and sovereignty (17:3), which means that true Israelites must acknowledge what God is now doing and saying in Jesus, namely, his equality with God.

Yet the context of these remarks and the perspective they give on Jesus' relationship to the world qualify how we should read them. First, Jesus' prayer to return to his former glory appears as a welcome quitting of this world. Although there is some positive evaluation of "the world" here (17:13, 21, 23), a negative perspective toward it dominates the prayer. The world is perceived as a place that not only hates him and his disciples (17:14), but also is ruled by the Evil One (17:15). Although for the present Jesus will leave his disciples in "the world" (17:11), he prays that, inasmuch as they too are truly not of this world, they join him in his glory, which is not here in this world (17:24).[20] Second, given the fact of 8:23–24, we must pay close attention to Jesus' emphatic remarks in John 17 that he is not of the world. His true place is not below, but above, where God is. Unlike "the world," which does not know God (17:25), Jesus knows God and shares God's own glory (17:5, 24). Yet not only is Jesus not of the world, his disciples also are out of place here; and so Jesus prays that they, too, eventually leave here and join him, so as to see his divine glory (17:24). Twice Jesus emphasizes that "even as I am not of the world, they are not of the world" (17:14, 16), indicating an irreconcilable revolt against it. These remarks about "not of the world," moreover, go hand in hand with the confession of high Christology in the same text segment.

Although one may fault Ernst Käsemann's study of John 17 on many points,[21] he nevertheless called attention to the fact that the presentation of the high Christology in John 17 implies a strange relationship of Jesus to the world, a point that will engage us in the remainder of this book. It is sufficient for the present to note that statements about Jesus' "equality with God" are inseparable here from radical, negative remarks about "the world." They suggest a divorce not a marriage, and a revolt not an accommodation with it. Although the prayer is made in this world, Jesus is "no longer in the world" (17:11); he eagerly returns to his true home after sojourning in an alien land.

Spirit over Matter (6:62–63)

We finally turn to John 6:62–63, a text that embodies the substance of the high christological confession we are examining and offers perhaps the best clue to the perspective and function of that confession. The narrative context of 6:62–63 is again one of conflict or, more precisely, rejection of Jesus .

The narrative locates Jesus' remarks in the controversy after the bread of life discourse, where unbelievers (6:60–65) are contrasted with believers (6:66–69). Jesus, of course, knew from the beginning those who did not believe in him (6:64), those who followed him merely because they ate their fill of bread (6:26). So, as they proceed to object to his words (6:60) and drop out of his group (6:66), Jesus shrugs off their rejection with the remark,"What if you were to see the Son of man ascending to where he was before?" (6:62). His remark relativizes the earthly rejection of Jesus by a compensatory affirmation that his true home is not earth anyway, but heaven.

According to our exposition, 6:62 embodies the high Christology of the Fourth Gospel in that it affirms that Jesus is the eternal figure of the past who will return in the future to his original status and position after his ordeal on earth, thus affirming his imperishability. Eternity and imperishability, then, are not simply stated for their own sake, but function in a polemical manner as a riposte to serious challenges to Jesus and his doctrine.

Formally, 6:62 resembles the response of Jesus to the high priest in his Jewish trial in the synoptic tradition (Mark 14:62//Matt. 26:64//Luke 22:70). Jesus, who is on trial, is rejected on earth by mortals, but proclaims a vindication in heaven by God. John 6:62, however, bears the stamp of the Johannine perspective, since it specifically acclaims Jesus' past eternity, a heavenly state that he had with God before the creation of the world (see 17:5, 24) and to which he will return. In 6:62, moreover, Jesus declares that he will ascend to heaven, implying that he does this by his own power (13:1–3; 20:17–18), unlike his being raised and vindicated by God, which is the perspective of the Synoptic Gospels at this point. Whereas the acclamation of Jesus' previous eternal glory is made to the disciples in John 17 in a context of prayer (albeit on the eve of catastrophe, in the context of a farewell address), here it functions as a riposte to those who reject him. Whereas 13:1–3 describes Jesus' return to the Father in the context in which his love for the disciples is noted (13:1) as well as God's donation of "all things into his hands" (13:3), the return of Jesus in 6:62 is phrased as a hostile rhetorical argument dismissing criticism of his teaching. The context of 6:62, then, is fierce conflict in which Jesus' remark functions as a riposte dismissing criticism of him, a function intended to divide permanently Jesus and his audience.

The Gospel, moreover, contextualizes 6:62 by linking it with 6:63, wherein Jesus states: "The spirit alone gives life; the flesh is of no avail." By this juxtaposition, the author intends 6:63 to comment on 6:62, the high christological remark about Jesus' true home, and vice versa. Because it is an unqualified value statement, 6:63 states that spirit is juxtaposed to flesh, just as Jesus is at home in heaven, not on earth. Spirit, moreover, is irreconcilably juxtaposed to flesh, as heaven to earth, replicating the pattern noted in 8:23. But 6:63 functions as a value remark. It places value only on the side of spirit (or heaven) and completely devalues flesh (or earth). Whatever might have been signaled in 1:14 about a possible marriage of heaven and earth comes into serious question. The context of the high christolog-ical remark in 6:62, then, is conflict and rejection; the particular way that 6:62–63 expresses that confession understands it as a statement that heaven/spirit have nothing to do with earth/flesh. And the con-fession functions to separate Jesus from others and conversely to pro-claim his superiority to them, even as Jesus' true home is superior to this world below.

THE JOHANNINE PERSPECTIVE

After examining the narrative context and function of statements that embody the high christological confession that Jesus is equal to God, we possess sufficient information to hazard a judgment about the Johannine perspective on that Christology, its meaning, and func-tion. At this point we are concentrating only on the substance of the confession, which was summarized in the first part of this chapter. We conveniently label it equal to God, and it includes Jesus' two pow-ers, their corresponding names (God and Lord) and Jesus' eternity and imperishability.

The narrative origin of this material resides in every instance in fierce conflict, and in three cases (5:18; 8:23–24; 10:33) in formal forensic proceedings. At no time was the substance of the Christology ever moderated or presented in a more palatable manner to those who initially took offense at it. On the contrary, in each case explana-tory or apologetic remarks from Jesus functioned only to accentuate the offensive content of the christological claim, thus dividing Jesus as permanently as possible from his unbelieving audience. The defense in 5:19–29 added to the claim of Jesus' creative equality with God his possession of eschatological power, effectively raising the ante in the conflict. The "I AM" statements are presented as forensic laws to the audience, laws they cannot keep because they are hopelessly from below and of this world. And the remarks in 6:62–63 serve to dismiss criticism of Jesus, effectively emphasizing division between Jesus and his audience. We must recognize, then, as key elements of the per-spective of the high Christology its conflictive context and its function to divide, dismiss, and condemn.

Concerning the perspective of Jesus himself on whether the high Christology celebrates a marriage of divine and human or whether it values primarily Jesus' heavenly otherness, the emphasis in the texts we examined unmistakably points to the latter. "I AM" is linked with being from above and not of this world; Jesus' return

109

to God (6:62) is intended to cancel the rejection he experiences on earth. Even in regard to his equality with God, the emphasis of that material was primarily on his eschatological power, whereby he is unlike mortals. He himself triumphs over death, he raises and judges mortals who have died, and he deserves divine honor. What is of value is what makes him equal to God, not what belongs to the human condition.

If the thrust of the high Christology affirms Jesus' heavenliness and celebrates his cosmic otherliness, this emphasis of value affects also the perspective of his relationship to the world in all of its materiality and fleshliness. And here again, it was noted that all value was placed on the side of what is from above and not of this world. John 6:63 and 8:23 reinforce each other in placing all value in heaven and spirit, while denying any value to earth and flesh. Although 1:14 and 20:28 might suggest to some a marriage of heaven and earth, the materials surveyed in this chapter point in the opposite direction, namely, a divorce between heaven and earth, an irreconcilable division between spirit and flesh and between the world above and the world below. If indeed the Word was once pleased to pitch its tent here below, we have seen evidence that at a later time this was not the case: the Word was pleased to stand against the world and to leave it for his true home. The perspective of equal to God, then, not only involves conflict and functions as division. It also celebrates primarily Jesus' heavenliness and values only the world above, a perspective apparently recognized by the author of the Johannine epistles, who found it reprehensible and condemned it in 1 John 4:3 and 2 John 7.

In summary, there appear to be two perspectives in the Fourth Gospel through which the high christological confession might be understood. They are represented by texts such as 1:14/20:28 and 6:63/8:23. At the risk of belaboring this point, I would like to develop even further the implications of these two contrasting perspectives. Verse 1:14 might signal not just an event but a value and a perspective, for it is a cosmological as well as a christological statement. The Word, who is divine, might be said to enter and tent in the human world; spirit comes into matter; heaven is wedded to earth. One meaning of 1:14, then, might be the joining of opposites and the marriage of irreconcilables. And this joining is considered a value, even as it establishes a perspective that such a joining is both possible and desirable. On one level, 1:14 might be said to accentuate the descent of Jesus.

But 1:14 is not the only statement in the Fourth Gospel about high Christology and cosmology, that is, about Jesus' nature and the relationship of heaven to earth, the divine to the human, and spirit to flesh. As 6:63 and 8:23 indicate, there is a stream of material in the Fourth Gospel suggesting that the heavenly Jesus was quite ready and willing to leave this earth, which had become a place of unrelieved hostility. If indeed 1:14 heralds a peaceful descent into this world, 6:63 and 8:23 speak of a necessary and all-too-welcome ascent from this world. Whatever value the world held as a place initially worthy of Jesus and God's gospel (3:16–17), Jesus' prayer in 17:5 to receive back the glory he had with God before the creation of the world suggests a subsequent desire to quit the world, which has become the place ruled by the Evil One (17:14–16) and tried by the Spirit (16:7–11). If 1:14 represents a christological perspective that envisioned a desirable marriage of opposites, we have seen evidence that speaks of another christological perspective in which opposites are hopelessly irreconcilable and ought not to be joined, no more than the sacred belongs in profane space. If 1:14 celebrated the marriage of opposites, other texts rejoice in their divorce.

CONCLUSIONS AND FURTHER TASKS

Our investigation of the perspective of "equal to God" in the Fourth Gospel indicates that this confession valued Jesus' heavenliness over his humanity and implied as well his radical stand against the world below, a world of flesh and matter. It would appear that the confession of Jesus as equal to God functions as a statement that he is not of this world. In fact, to ignore the latter assertion that he is not of this world would be to misunderstand his equality with God. In asserting this, we should not conclude that this was the only perspective of the Johannine high Christology,[22] but that it is a genuine if disturbing perspective which needs to be examined further.

In the terms of the tentative conclusions reached so far, the perspective of equal to God studied here appears to be in harmony with many of the assertions made by Meeks in regard to Jesus' descent and ascent. Even as Meeks continued his investigation of the christological formula and inquired about the type of social situation in which it originated and which it came to reflect, we sensed the need to inquire of the confession of Jesus as equal to God what type of social world might be implied and replicated by it when it is seen from the perspective of one who is not of this world.

In short, equal to God is not simply an abstract confession but an ideological statement. It not only asserts something about Jesus but describes his own relationship to the world as well as that of his followers to the world around them. These are new questions, which are not the focus of traditional exegesis but belong to the disciplines of the social sciences. What is needed, then, is a model to help us examine the social implications of equal to God as it functioned in the Johannine community. Constructing such a model becomes the task of part 2 of this book. What are the implications of believing in a figure who is equal to God, but not of this world?

PART TWO

Not of This World

CHRISTOLOGY IN
SOCIAL-SCIENCE PERSPECTIVE

6

A BASIC MODEL:
CHRISTOLOGY
AND REVOLT

NEW QUESTIONS, NEW METHODS

In one sense, our investigation into the meaning of the confession that Jesus is equal to God is just beginning. The presentation of its contents in Part 1 of this volume proceeded in an ideational manner which, until chapter 5, paid little attention to its meaning and function in the context of the social and cultural location of the community. But after seeing how "equal to God" becomes equivalent to "*not of this world,*" we must inquire into the way this Christology is related to the world view of the Johannine community. The perspective of equal to God suggests that its meaning and function have to do with a divorce between heaven and earth or between spirit and flesh, that is, with social alienation. This in turn implies that the high Christology functions as an ideology for some Johannine Christians, encoding and replicating their world view, in particular their estranged position relative to the synagogue and other apostolic Christians. Christology implies cosmology and is incomplete without appreciating the latter. It should come as no surprise, then, that we might give more attention in the second half of our study to cosmological texts rather than to the christological material considered in the first half. If we would truly grasp what equal to God means and how it functions, we must attend more seriously to what "not of this world" implies.

Questions about the cultural location and social function of confessional statements have long been regarded as both legitimate and necessary. They require, however, new methods of interpretation. Whereas our investigation in chapters 1–4 employed classical exegetical methods, they are simply inadequate for the present task. Even chapter 5 only indicated in a descriptive way the peculiar relationship of equal to God and *not* of this world. A description

115

can give no further insight into the necessary correlation between Christology and cosmology. Since the question of ideological meaning and function belongs to the discipline of the social sciences, the method and procedure of investigating that question must come from them. The new question, then, is the ideological meaning and function of equal to God, precisely as a cosmological statement, . . . *not* of this world. What is needed is a new method and model for pursuing this question.

Concerning question and method, Johannine students are grateful for the ground-breaking essay of Wayne Meeks as a paradigm for dealing with just these issues, namely, the relationship of the high christological confession to the lived experience of those who confessed it. Meeks began with a question about the function of myths in society, in particular the myth of Jesus' descent/ascent.[1] Surveying John 3 and the description of Jesus as the descending Son of man (3:13), Meeks asked what kind of cultural and social position was expressed by confessing Jesus as a figure totally above and beyond this world. He notes that the evangelist presented the myth of Jesus' descent/ascent throughout the Gospel in ways that constantly juxtaposed heaven with earth and juxtaposed being from above with being from below. The christological myth, moreover, functions not only to identify Jesus as a unique revealer but to distinguish him from those who belong to this world.[2] And so the descent of Jesus serves as a judgment of the world (9:39) especially by provoking misunderstanding, which proves that the person who does not understand belongs to this world and not to Jesus' world.[3] According to contemporary Johannine studies, Jesus' etiology symbolizes that of the Johannine community, such that in telling a myth of Jesus' descent/ascent, the Johannine Christians learn that, like their alien leader, they too are aliens in this world. The myth, then, "provides a reinforcement for the community's social identity which appears to have been largely negative."[4]

Meeks's essay broke new ground in Johannine studies. (1) On a literary level, it showed the coherence and redundance of Johannine Christology with the community's world view, how Jesus' descent/ascent was linked with other attitudes to "this world," and how it explained the social location of Jesus' followers. (2) On the level of theory, Meeks employed insights from anthropology and the sociology of knowledge,[5] thus offering a plausible hermeneutic for his suggestions. (3) Meeks indicated a dialectical relationship between Christology and experience: a certain christological formulation leads to alienation from the synagogue; the alienation in turn is explained by further christological development of the alien status of Jesus; this in turn pushed the group into further isolation. "It is a case of continual, harmonic reinforcement between social experience and ideology."[6]

This chapter takes obvious inspiration from Meeks's essay, but proposes to go beyond it in two areas. First, the data for analysis are not simply the descent/ascent myth, but the previous investigation of the confession equal to God. Since it came to mean not of this world, it will entail consideration of the important dichotomous, cosmological remarks about heaven vs. earth, spirit vs. flesh, and from above vs. from below. Second, I propose to use an explicit social-science model from the works of anthropologist Mary Douglas as a coherent and extensive device for assessing the social location of John, a model that offers greater precision than the elusive definition of a "sect" employed in Meeks's essay.[7] My hypothesis, nevertheless, resembles that of Meeks in that I am investigating the relationship of the ideology of the Johannine high Christology with the historical experience and social location of the Johannine community. New questions of the Johannine Christology, then, require new methods of investigation.

SOCIAL-SCIENCE PERSPECTIVE

The aim of the second half of this study is to interpret the high Christology of the Johannine text in light of Mary Douglas's cross-cultural modeling. We will assess the meaning and function of the confession of Jesus as equal to God, but not of this world. The procedure for doing this is quite direct and yet complex. As we noted in chapters 1–4, the document under consideration seems to have been redacted several times, suggesting a complex history of its development. Although those chapters focused on a late stage of development that reflects the emergence and articulation of the high Christology, the literary and thematic analysis there presupposed some model of the stages of development of both Johannine history and the history of the document. The stages of development need to be described more explicitly,[8] with a view to clarifying the late stage. This is characterized by the emergence and articulation of the high Christology. I posit four stages in the development of the Fourth Gospel: (1) an early stage characterized by missionary propaganda; (2) a middle stage, which acclaimed Jesus' replacement of Jewish patriarchs, rites, cultus, and so forth; (3) a still later stage characterized by the emergence and articulation of the high Christology; and (4) a final stage

117

represented by John 21 and the moderation of earlier spiritualist tendencies (see 1 and 2 John as well).[9]

The aim is still an investigation of the high Christology from a social-science perspective, but in fairness to the document and to the model to be used, it would seem that some attempt should be made to apply Douglas's model to the earlier two stages of development. This tests the model as well as clarifies what is distinctive about the high Christology in terms of its ideology and function. A sense of completeness is necessary as well as a sense of the utility and accuracy of the anthropological modeling.

Why models? Why Douglas? It is beyond the scope of this book to rehearse the contemporary arguments for employing social-science modeling for New Testament interpretation.[10] Perhaps it is enough to be reminded that the contemporary use of explicit models from the social sciences updates and realizes a long-lasting, basic thrust of Scripture studies to understand the biblical writings in their social context. The enterprise is old, but new, and its novelty resides in the formal application of explicit models for interpreting the text. This new thrust in biblical studies appeared at first quite eclectic,[11] as scholars searched for help wherever it could be found. Inevitably some criticism of the very models being employed was needed, as scholars debated the accuracy or applicability of models such as theories of cognitive dissonance[12] or Weber's study of charismatic leadership.[13]

In the search for usable models, Douglas's writings have enjoyed special consideration by students of Judaism[14] and the New Testament.[15] Douglas's basic model was formally introduced to students of religion in the article of Isenberg and Owens,[16] and then to students of the New Testament by Bruce Malina.[17] The conventions of the American Academy of Religion, the Society of Biblical Literature, and the Catholic Biblical Association regularly feature papers that analyze theological or biblical texts and themes using Douglas's material. On occasion, Douglas herself has addressed these conventions and participated in their seminars. Douglas's works, then, have found a congenial place in contemporary biblical scholarship.

Her writings represent in many respects a consensus among anthropologists and related fields on topics such as witchcraft, social cognition, body symbolism, food and eating, and so on. Her work, then, is hardly an esoteric system, but rather a judicious synthesis of the major results of cultural anthropology. The precise value of using Douglas's writings for New Testament purposes lies in their adaptability for biblical research, their comprehensiveness, and their suggestions about the consistency and coherence of a given cultural viewpoint.

Douglas's interest has consistently focused on the issues of order, structure, and control in social groups, even as these vary in intensity and complexity from society to society. To assess this basic phenomenon, Douglas has suggested a procedure for locating social units in terms of two basic variables, which she calls *group* and *grid*.[18] *Group* refers to the degree of societal pressure at work in a given social unit to conform to the society's definitions, classifications, and evaluations. The degree of pressure may be strong (hence, strong group) or weak (weak group). And so on an axis from 0 to 100, a given social unit may be located in terms of its relative pressure for conformity to societal norms. *Grid* refers to the degree of socially constrained adherence normally given by members of a society to the prevailing symbol system, its classifications, patterns of perception and evaluations, and so on, through which the society enables its members to bring order and intelligibility to their experience. Like the group variable, grid may be high, where there is a close fit between an individual's experience and the myths and norms of his or her society, or low, where the match is tenuous or wobbly. Just as group can be plotted, so can grid.

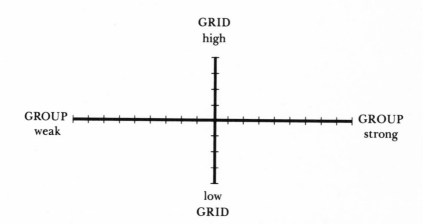

In her various writings, Douglas casts her anthropologist's eye on specific areas of interest, which collectively constitute the cosmology of a given group. The areas of interest include: (1) purity (or system), (2) ritual, (3) personal identity, (4) body, (5) sin, and (6) cosmology.[19]

Depending on where a social unit is located on the grid/group axes, the meaning and shape of these topics will vary correspondingly, as the pressure to conform varies and the degree of assent fluctuates. (See figure 2). Since this model of social ideology

FIGURE 2

BASIC GROUP AND GRID OUTLINE

Weak Group, High Grid   HIGH

Purity: pragmatic attitude toward purity; pollution is not automatic; bodily exuviae are not threatening and may be recycled

Rite: used for private as well as public ends when present; the individual remains superior to the rite process; condensed symbols do not delimit reality

Personal Identity: individualism, pragmatic and adaptable

Body: viewed instrumentally, as means to some end; self-controlled; treated pragmatically

Sin: basically caused by ignorance or failure; hence viewed as stupidity or embarrassment with loss of face; the individual is responsible

Cosmology: the universe is geared to individual success and initiative; the cosmos is benignly amoral; God is a junior partner; adequate causality

Suffering and Misfortune: an intelligent person ought to be able to avoid them; totally eradicable

Purity: anti the purity postures of the quadrant from which it emerged

Rite: anti the rites of the quadrant from which it emerged; effervescent; spontaneity valued

Personal Identity: no antagonism between society and the self; but the old society of the quadrant from which it derived is seen as oppressive; roles of previous quadrant are rejected; self-control and/or social control are low, highly individualistic

Body: irrelevant, life is spiritual; purity concerns are absent, but they may be rejected, body may be used freely or renunciation may prevail

Sin: a matter of personal ethics and interiority

Cosmology: the cosmos is likely to be impersonal; there is individual and direct access to the divinity, usually without mediation; cosmos is benign

Suffering and Misfortune: love conquers all; love can eliminate

Weak Group, Low Grid   LOW

WEAK GROUP

and social location can serve as a useful heuristic device for identifying and describing a given social unit, I propose to use it to describe and locate the various stages of development of the Johannine community.

FIGURE 2

Basic Group and Grid Outline

GRID   Strong Group, High Grid

Purity: strong concern for purity; well-defined purification rites; purity rules define and maintain social structures

Rite: a society of fixed rites; rites express the internal classification system of the group; rite symbols perdure in all contexts of life; permanent sacred places

Personal Identity: a matter of internalizing clearly articulated social roles; individual is subservient to, but not in conflict with, society; dyadic personality

Body: tightly controlled but a symbol of life

Sin: the violation of formal rules; focus is upon behavior rather than on internal states of being; rites are efficacious in counteracting sin; individual is responsible for deviance

Cosmology: anthropomorphic; non-dualistic; the universe is just and reasonable; personal causality; limited good

Suffering and Misfortune: the result of automatic punishment for the violation of formal rules; part of a "divine" economy; can be alleviated but not eliminated

Purity: strong concern for purity but the inside of the social and physical body is under attack; pollution present but purification rites are ineffective

Rite: a society of fixed rites; rite is focused upon group boundaries, with great concern to expel pollutants (deviants) from the social body; fluid sacred places

Personal Identity: located in group membership, not in the internalization of roles, which are confused; distinction between appearance and internal states; dyadic personality

Body: social and physical bodies are tightly controlled but under attack; invaders break through bodily boundaries; not a symbol of life

Sin: a matter of pollution; evil is lodged within the individual and society; sin is much like a disease deriving from social structure; internal states of being are more important than adherence to formal rules; but the latter are still valued

Cosmology: anthropomorphic; dualistic; warring forces of good and evil; the universe is not just and may be whimsical; personal causality; limited good

Suffering and Misfortune: unjust; not automatic punishment; attributed to malevolent forces; may be alleviated but not eliminated

GRID   Strong Group, Low Grid

STRONG GROUP

(from Bruce Malina, *Christian Origins and Cultural Anthropology* [Atlanta: John Knox Press, 1986], 14–15)

STAGE ONE:
MISSIONARY PROPAGANDA

Before we undertake a group/grid analysis, the data for it must be identified. The Gospel as we have it was not composed at one sitting, nor is it innocent of *aporiae* and contradictions. Matthew, for example, represents a text that incorporated the Q source, then Mark's Gospel, and, last, the perspective of the final redactor. What belongs to the first stage of development of the Fourth Gospel? The initial part of this analysis will be descriptive, assessing how the "signs" material coheres with a preaching form and titles of low Christology. The material thus gathered and described can serve as a clear basis for further analysis from an anthropological perspective.

Description of the Early Stage

Activity. The early history[20] of the Johannine group was characterized by missionary activity: preaching about Jesus, arguments on his behalf from the Scriptures, and the proclamation of his signs. This is clearly dramatized in the initial narrative of Jesus' ministry in John 1 in the activity of both the Baptizer and Jesus' first disciples. John the Baptizer heralded Jesus: "Behold, the Lamb of God, who takes away the sin of the world. I have seen and have borne witness that this is the Son of God" (1:29, 34). John then evangelized two of his disciples, who followed Jesus and became his disciples (1:37).

One of these first disciples, Andrew, then spoke a word about Jesus to his brother, Simon Peter: "'We have found the Messiah' (which means Christ)" (1:41). Another convert, Philip, evangelized Nathanael: "We have found him of whom Moses in the law and also the prophets wrote, Jesus of Nazareth, the son of Joseph" (1:45). Nathanael proved to be a difficult convert, but in the end confessed Jesus as "Son of God . . . King of Israel" (1:49). And so a pattern emerges that reflects not just the content of the early preaching but the normal process whereby a convert becomes a missionary to others: (1) a believer "finds" and evangelizes someone else, (2) using a christological title; (3) the evangelizer leads the person to Jesus: "Come and see!" (4) Jesus sees the newcomer, and speaks a confirming word; (5) the conversion is sealed.

The pattern can be confirmed in John 1:

122

A.	*1:35*	*1:40*	*1:43*	*1:45*
Believer evangelizes someone	John the Baptizer to two of his disciples	Andrew found Peter	X found Philip	Philip found Nathanael

B.	*1:36*	*1:41b*		*1:45b–46*
Christological title	Behold, the Lamb of God	Messiah	—	The One of whom Moses and the Prophets wrote

C.	*1:37*	*1:42*		*1:46b*
Evangelizer leads convert to Jesus	They listened and followed	He led him to Jesus	—	Come and see.

D.	*1:38–39*	*1:43*	*1:43b*	*1:47*
Jesus sees newcomer and confirms him	Jesus saw them: "Come and see"	Jesus saw him: "You are Cephas"	And said to him: "Follow me"	Jesus saw and said: "A true Israelite in whom there is no guile"

E.	*1:39*			*1:50*
Conversion sealed	They came, saw, and remained	—	—	"You will see greater things than these"

This episode serves a programmatic function in John for it describes a process whereby a believer evangelizes others about Jesus, a pattern that continues throughout the Gospel. For example, after being evangelized by Jesus, the Samaritan woman preaches to the people of Sychar: "Come and see a man who told me all that I have done" (4:29–30, 39). They came and saw, and became Jesus' ardent disciples (see also 12:21–23). This pattern also occurs in the Gospel's conclusion, where Jesus' disciples, after their own vision of the Risen Jesus, tell the absent Thomas of it, a word he refuses to accept without proof (20:25). After Jesus reproaches Thomas for his unbelief in the church's preaching, he then canonizes this basic missionary process: "Blessed are those who have not seen and yet believe" (20:29). The beginning and ending of the Gospel, then, indicate that the premier activity of stage one is the preaching of Jesus to relatives, friends, and even strangers.

Jesus' "signs" constitute the bulk of the early missionary propaganda. Their purpose is to lead people to accept Jesus as God's legitimate and authorized prophet or covenant leader, a purpose evident in the editorial comment after the first sign: "This, the first of his signs, Jesus did at Cana in Galilee, and manifested his glory; and his disciple believed in him" (2:11). Balancing this is a comment at the end of the Gospel about the missionary value of Jesus' signs: "Now Jesus did many other signs in the presence of his disciples, which are not written in this book; but these are written that you may believe that Jesus is the Christ, the Son of God" (20:30–31). Signs, like preaching, serve a missionary, propaganda purpose.

The preaching of the early Johannine missionaries was occasionally based on scriptural arguments, as the preachers tried within the synagogue to convince the crowds that Jesus is "the one of whom Moses in the Law and also the prophets wrote" (1:45). Yet this preaching meets with resistance. Nathanael, an astute student of the Scriptures, raises objections to this preaching when he points out that in the Scriptures Nazareth is not a fertile ground for prophets (1:46). Other synagogue Jews raise comparable objections to this line of argument. Jesus cannot be "the Christ": "Is the Christ to come from Galilee? Has not the Scripture said that the Christ is descended from David and comes from Bethlehem, the village where David was?" (7:41–42). Leaders of the synagogue dismiss the Christian preaching, "Search and you will see that no prophet is to rise from Galilee" (7:52). Nathanael, therefore, becomes a type of hero in this stage; for, although he too raised objections to the Christian preaching about Jesus from the Scriptures, he does come and see Jesus. Jesus then lavished praise on him, "an Israelite without guile" (1:47)—a commendation canonizing him as a Johannine saint. From this we gain some sense of the character of missionary preaching in the early Johannine group.

Membership. Although the majority of the members of this early group seem to be synagogue Jews, Christian preaching seems intended for a much wider audience. Samaritans, with whom the Jews have no truck (4:9, 27), are evangelized; and they confess Jesus, not just as a Jewish leader but as a universal figure of salvation, even as "Savior of the World" (4:42). The title over Jesus' cross is in three languages, "Hebrew, Latin, and Greek" (19:20), suggesting the universal significance of Jesus' mission. And his death is interpreted "not for the nation only, but to gather into one the children of God who are scattered abroad" (11:52; see 10:16; 12:32). In this early stage of its history, then, the Johannine group engaged in missionary preaching aimed at all peoples—Jews, Samaritans, and Gentiles.

Scriptures. These early Johannine Christians remained in the synagogue, committed to things Jewish. As they always had, they still acclaimed Israel's monotheistic belief in one God (see 8:41; 17:3). They accepted God's word in the Scriptures, which they interpreted as a valid and sacred document, but whose function they see as predicting the coming of Jesus, prophet and king. Apart from the preaching from the Scriptures noted above with regard to 1:45 and 7:42, 52, we often find Christians interpreting events in Jesus' life as "fulfilling the Scriptures." For example, when Jesus' seamless garment is made the object of a game of chance, the evangelist remarked, "This was to fulfil the Scripture, 'They parted my garments among them, and for my clothing they cast lots'" (19:24/Ps. 22:18). Again, in regard to the nonbreaking of Jesus' legs and his pierced side, the evangelist remarks: "These things took place that the Scripture might be fulfilled, 'Not one bone of him shall be broken' (Exod. 12:46), and again, another Scripture says, 'They shall look on him whom they have pierced'" (19:36–37/Zech. 12:10). The Scriptures remain the valid book of God's revelation for Christians, but they are basically understood as a prophetic document foretelling Jesus' identity and career (see 2:17; 5:39, 46).

Strategy. As they continued to pray in the synagogue and study the Scriptures alongside other pious Jews, Johannine Christians see all of Israel's history and literature pointing to Jesus and fulfilled in him. The idiom of preaching is taken completely from Jewish traditions. And so they implicitly claim to be "authentic Israelites" (1:47), urging a reformed reading of Scripture. This missionary group, moreover, is not aggressively seeking to overthrow the synagogue . and its structures, but to refocus them on a new prophet with a definitive word. We hear little from Jesus about how one lives from day to day as a true member of God's covenant people, which is presupposed in some sense in the Scriptures and the synagogue's traditions. Belief constitutes membership in God's kingdom and covenant group, and so there is a corresponding awareness of evangelization as the major experience of the Johannine Christians.

This strategy means reform of Israel's faith according to the word of Jesus, the new prophet who offers a reformed reading of the Scriptures and acts in a reforming way with his healings on the Sabbath. He is, of course, in competition for synagogue leadership with other reforming figures, and so legitimation of his status as a reforming prophet depends on the credentials of his sign. There is seemingly little by way of a formal program of reform other than the claims of this prophetic figure to be a legitimate reformer.

Christology. Regarding the Christology of this early group, we find traditional materials acclaiming Jesus as (1) the Messiah, the Christ (1:41; 4:25–26; 7:26), (2) the one predicted by Moses and the prophets (1:45; 5:39; 7:52), (3) Son of God (1:49), and (4) King of Israel (1:49; 12:13–15). These titles, which describe Jesus functionally as God's authorized and holy agent, sent to be the newest leader of God's covenant people, constitute what in Johannine studies is called "low Christology." This is the proclamation of Jesus as a special, even unique, agent of God, albeit only a human, earthly figure. Even Son of God refers here to Jesus as a leader like Israel's kings, who were also called sons of God (see Psalm 2).

These titles, which tell of Jesus' leadership of God's covenant people, are firmly attached to the signs of Jesus in the Fourth Gospel. In John, Jesus' miracles are distinctively labeled signs, that is, events that manifest Jesus' glory (2:11) and serve as his credentials (20:30; compare with Luke 24:19; Acts 2:22). Those who see these signs ought to conclude that the one who performed them is a special person sent from God: "If this man were not from God he could do nothing" (9:33); "When the Christ appears, will he do more signs than this man has done?" (7:31). Sinners can make no claim to be God's agent or to have access to God's power; Jesus' signs, therefore, argue that although Jesus did not keep the Sabbath in the traditional way, he *cannot* be a sinner (9:31–33; 10:21).

When people are open to God's revelation, they tend to interpret correctly the sign-miracles of Jesus as his credentials, and so acclaim Jesus as prophet or king. After Jesus multiplies the loaves (6:1–13), the crowd recognizes this as a sign and correctly concludes, "This is indeed the prophet who is to come into the world" (6:14). Signs, then, attest that Jesus is a holy figure sent to teach God's covenant people (i.e., prophet) and to shepherd them as their covenant leader (i.e., king). The crowd in John 6 who ate the multiplied loaves would make Jesus their leader: "They were about . . . to make him king" (6:15). Later, the crowd that greeted Jesus on his entrance into Jerusalem as "King of Israel" (12:13–15) did so because "they heard that he had done this sign" (12:18), namely, the raising of Lazarus from the dead.[21]

Social-Science Perspective: Strong Group / Low Grid

What does this data look like when examined in the light of Douglas's anthropological model? What is the cosmology or world view of a group engaging in this activity?

Purity.   Purity[22] is Douglas's abstract term for the overall system of ideology, values, structures, and classifications that give order to a given culture, which in this case is the system of Jewish religion. To be a good Jew, one minimally had to confess faith in Israel's one God[23] and accept God's word in the Scriptures. But in Jesus' time the normative expression of the system that is the faith of Israel was contained in the temple, in which God's creative ordering of the world was replicated and which served as a model for the rest of life.[24] Yet monotheistic faith in God and acceptance of God's scriptural word could result in quite different social configurations (priests, Pharisees, Qumran covenanteers, etc.).[25] In fact, the Judaism of Jesus' time was characterized by intense factionalism, as numerous challengers arose and argued for a structuring of Jewish life according to patterns quite different from those of Jerusalem's temple. The group factor was strong, as all claimed to adhere to the system of Judaism, even if under the program of reform,[26] but the grid was low or falling, as is evidenced by the emergence of numerous competing sects and parties.

In the Fourth Gospel, Jesus indeed presented himself as a member of the Jewish covenant community. He confessed faith in the one God of Israel (17:3) and accepted God's Scriptures (1:45; 5:39; 7:40–44, 52), but he challenged the way these were interpreted and used to structure life in Israel, as in the case of Sabbath controversies (7:21–24; see 5:16; 9:16). Construing the Scriptures as prophecy, not halakah, Jesus claims to stand in continuity with the overall thrust of Judaism (i.e., strong group), while contesting the current structures of Jewish life (i.e., low grid), many of which derived from a temple-oriented view of God and the Scriptures (see 2:13–21; 4:19–24). Jesus is heralded, then, as a reformer of the system, who accepts the basic order and orientation of his religious culture but contests many aspects of how that is structured in daily life.

Ritual. If a system exists, it must set lines and draw maps through time and space both to impose the order represented by its purity system and to maintain it. Rituals,[27] then, exist for two purposes: (1) to serve as boundary lines indicating who is in or out, and (2) to strengthen and maintain the structure or system of the group. Inasmuch as Jesus challenges the ideology and structure of the Jewish purity system (see temple: 2:13–22; Sabbath: 5:1–9; 7:22–23), he hardly appears interested in rituals that reinforce the system under his attack. Rather, the focus is on the articulation of boundary rituals, in particular the ways in which one joins Jesus' group and so passes from death to life. In stage one they consist primarily of accepting the missionary preaching about Jesus. The language of this ritual is spatial, suggesting movement across a boundary line. For example, whereas in Matthew one "inherits" life, in the Fourth Gospel the emphasis is on such boundary words as "crossing" (5:24) and "entering" (3:4–5; 4:38; 10:1–2). In 7:43 a *schism* takes place, which divides the crowd into two groups, a boundary drawn according to the confession made or lack thereof: "Some of the people said, 'This is really the prophet . . . the Christ.' Others said, 'Is the Christ to come from Galilee?'" (7:40–42; see 9:16; 10:19). Preaching and faith, then, are the primary rituals distinguishing insiders from outsiders.[28]

Personal Identity. One's basic identity in any strong group society is dyadic,[29] that is, one is embedded in a group and takes one's identity as a member of a given family, a particular group, or a specific locale. Dyad means two, in this case referring to a person and a dominant other, who gives a person his or her identity. For example, synagogue Jews describe themselves in a dyadic mode, as members of a group that follows Jewish Torah: "We are disciples of Moses" (9:28), and "We are descendants of Abraham" (8:33). When Jesus and the woman at the well converse, they initially understand each other in dyadic terms of ethnicity and locale: "How is it that you, a Jew, ask a drink of me, a woman of Samaria?" (4:9). Jesus is known according to his family stock as "son of Joseph" (6:42) or, according to his agency, on behalf of the one who sent him (4:34; 6:38; 7:16). A Christian's identity would be that of a "follower of Jesus," that is, one of the group that believes that he is God's Christ and agent.[30] This belief would distinguish Jesus' followers within the synagogue from those who are Moses' disciples.

Body. In general, as the social body builds and maintains boundaries to distinguish insiders from outsiders, this degree of social control is correspondingly exercised over the physical body and replicated in it.[31] When concern for social boundaries is strong, one anticipates comparable attention to the body's surface, its boundary, and to its orifices, the entrances into its interior.[32] Specifically this focuses on what is seen, heard, eaten, or spoken (see Mark 9:43–47).

By definition strong group/low grid is a conflictive situation, in which one finds a fundamental ambiguity, if not distrust of the externals of the body. According to the world view here, evil tends to masquerade as good. Replicated in terms of the physical body, this perception of ambiguity means that technically correct external bodily behavior may be "hypocrisy" and a disguise of righteousness, whereas technical violations of external bodily behavior may be irrelevant for knowing the heart or interior of a person. Thus Jesus, who works on the Sabbath, is not necessarily evil; but those who keep the Sabbath are not necessarily good. It is important, moreover, to "judge justly," and not according to the flesh or appearances (7:24; 8:15). While his enemies disparage Jesus for not having studied (7:15), one knows that schooling is no proof of wisdom or faith.

Sin. Given the distrust in externals yet the need for sharp, clear boundaries, sin for these Johannine Christians does not reside in the nonobservance of formal norms, such as traditional keeping of the Sabbath or temple rituals. Sin, however, consists of a wrong interior attitude, a false inner mind, a lack of correct faith.[33] If life and grace reside in "coming to the light" through belief in Jesus as the one whom God has sent, death and evil are correspondingly defined as an interior vice, an unbelief and refusal to come to that light. Sin in this context, moreover, is like a disease or pollution; one is either entirely clean or totally evil. It matters not at all that one keeps Torah perfectly if one refuses to accept God's agent, for this refusal makes one totally a sinner, an enemy of God (3:19–21; 6:28–29).

Cosmology. This world[34] is anthropomorphic, ruled by the God of Israel who rewards the good and punishes the wicked (see Exod.

129

34:6–7). In general it can be said that the world is just, so that one's fate follows one's actions (see 5:14). One's personal choices determine one's standing in God's sight, so accepting or rejecting God's prophets is a matter of life and death.

Seen from this perspective, stage one of the Fourth Gospel can be identified as strong group/low grid. Jesus stands within Judaism (strong group), accepting Israel's God and the Scriptures. Yet he stands outside of the mainstream of power and legitimation, claiming to be God's ascribed, reforming leader of the covenant people, its prophet and king. This implies a situation of challenge and reform (low grid), which issues in the formation of Jesus' faction or network among other such reform groups in Judaism. In this situation his signs serve to legitimate his challenge as the prophesied prophet or king. As a recent participant in the competition for disciples in the synagogue, Jesus' group is very missionary, which translates as an inclusive group with somewhat porous boundaries, yet whose membership criteria rest exclusively on acceptance of Jesus.

STAGE TWO:
REPLACEMENT

If stage one is characterized as a time of propaganda and mission, with attendant porous boundaries, stage two represents a period of intensification in claims and strategy, with much tighter boundaries. Now a specific, systematic program of reform is urged, as Jesus claims to replace the major elements of Judaism, its temple, feasts, and cult.[35] Now exclusive claims are made that only in Jesus can one find the true elements and structures of Judaism, with an attendant limiting of membership and tightening of group boundaries. Now is the time of bold and exclusive claims, confrontation, and fierce defense. The intensification characteristic of stage two is symbolized in the christological claims that Jesus is not just another prophet or king but the one greater than all previous prophets and leaders, greater than Jacob, greater than Abraham, and even Moses.

Description of Stage Two

Activity. Propaganda remains the chief activity, but there is a notable shift in the content and strength of the claims. The shift in the content of the group's proclamation can be observed in several formulas and topics: (1) the "I AM" plus predicate formulas, (2) boasts of truth and things true (vs. false), and (3) replacement claims. Jesus is not merely the fulfillment of the prophetic thrust of the Scriptures—he is the formal replacement of all that came before.

Johannine scholars are familiar with the formula, "I AM" plus predicate, in which Jesus claims to be the authentic version of an object or figure in Israel's cosmos:

I am the bread of life. (6:35, 51)

I am the light of the world. (8:12; 9:5)

I am the gate. (10:7, 9)

I am the good shepherd. (10:11, 14)

I am the resurrection and the life. (11:25)

I am the way, the truth, and the life. (14:6)

I am the vine. (15:1, 5)[36]

The formula argues exclusively that Jesus ("I AM") and no one else is the unique and essential giver of benefaction. This formula implies that former figures, who were shepherds of God's flock (David), givers of God's covenant (Moses), sources of life (Elijah), and revealers of God's truth (Jacob, Isaiah), are all replaced by Jesus, who insists that he alone performs all of these roles and gives all of these benefactions to God's people.

Similar to the "I AM" plus predicate formula is the Johannine use of the term "true," which implies that certain persons and objects are genuine and authentic in contradistinction to what is obsolete or false. Jesus himself is the *true* light (1:9), the *true* bread (6:32), and the *true* vine (15:1). Unlike Moses, who gave Israel the old and obsolete mode of relating to God, the law, Jesus gives "grace and truth" (1:14, 17), the authentic covenant. Jesus' followers must worship in a different but authentic manner: "True worshipers will worship the Father in spirit and truth" (4:23). Truth and true are also important claims in the growing forensic imagery of the Fourth Gospel, as Jesus' claims are tested in court and his testimony is subjected to close scrutiny. Being truthful (7:18), witnessing to the truth (5:33), and bearing true testimony (5:31–32; 8:13–14) reinforce the sense of exclusivity and authenticity claimed by Jesus, especially over against the synagogue.

Most notable in this stage is the repeated claim that Jesus replaces Israel's great personages and its sacred cultus. First, the Gospel formally asks whether Jesus is "greater than" either Jacob (4:12) or

Abraham (8:53). The initial question, whether Jesus is "greater than Jacob," is programmatic in the Gospel, for it builds on the pun in Jacob's name, "the Supplanter."[37] Jacob, whose name means "to grab by the heel" or "to supplant," demonstrated his name by supplanting Esau in birth (Gen. 25:26), birthright (25:34), and blessing (27:36). In this he exemplifies once more the traditional pattern in Israel of the younger son supplanting the elder,[38] a role for which he was popularly known in the first century.[39]

As the new Jacob/Supplanter, Jesus systematically replaces the central religious symbols of Israel. His risen body replaces the temple as the place where God's glory dwells and where Israel communes with its God (2:19–22). The evangelist located this episode, which in the Synoptics occurred at the end of Jesus' ministry, at the head of his Jerusalem ministry. The new location signals the programmatic theme of Jesus' replacement of Israel's cultic places, times, and objects. Place: Jesus, the new place, replaces Gerizim and Jerusalem as the authentic place of worship (4:20–24). Time: Jesus replaces old feasts: he is the new and authentic feast of Passover (6:4–14; 2:13), Tabernacles (7:2), and Dedication (10:22). Objects: Jesus replaces the cultic benefits desired by pilgrimage to the holy place at the holy time. Jesus is the authentic manna (6:32) of the authentic Passover, as well as the true light (8:12) and water (7:37–39) of the true Tabernacles. Purification: Jesus' water-made-wine is served last at the Cana feast, and it is served from jars reserved for rites of purification (2:6). This suggests that his fluids give true purification. The steward at that feast mouths the traditional wisdom that what is old is good but what is recent is uncertain or weak, only to correct it in Jesus' case: "You have kept the good wine till now" (2:10). Jesus, who is new, is superior to what went before him, especially in terms of purification.[40]

Replacement claims, which became the central theme of the preaching in stage two, admit no qualification and make no exception, for they are absolute and exclusive claims. The formula introducing two replacement rituals reflects this exclusivity: "Unless one is born anew, one cannot see the kingdom of God" (3:3, 5); and "Unless you eat the flesh of the Son of man and drink his blood, you have no life in you" (6:53). The claims of truth noted above imply that all else is false. The "I AM" plus predicate formula claims that in Jesus alone is God's benefaction. In a polemical vein, all privilege or value found in Israel's former prophets is denied, in particular, the position of Moses. The manna Moses gave is useless against death (6:49, 58); the covenant he established is obsolete by Jesus' standards (1:17); his Sinai revelations are challenged (3:13; 5:37). Jesus gives the true bread of life, establishes the authentic covenant, alone sees God and brings God's word.

In this regard, the preaching in stage two differs from that of stage one in content and exclusivity. Whereas Jesus was previously heralded as the latest and greatest king and prophet, he is now proclaimed as the superior figure who makes obsolete all previous personages. Whereas in stage one, other figures might take a rightful position alongside Jesus, now he is absolutely and exclusively Israel's leader in every aspect. The content and strength of the claims in stage two radically surpass that of the previous propaganda.

Scriptures. These claims imply a different interpretation of the Scriptures from the prophecy-fulfillment motif of the early preaching. Christian claims that Jesus replaces manna, circumcision, Passover, Tabernacles, and so forth, imply that one need not keep looking to the Scriptures for life and guidance, but to Jesus alone, his words, his rites, his cultus. They imply that the Scriptures are somehow becoming obsolete, as are the old rites. The synagogue naturally rejected these claims, but that only means the the Scriptures became a highly contested document, perhaps too controversial, ambiguous, and relative to be of use to the Johannine group any longer. The Scriptures, then, tended to lose value in the course of the development of the community of the Fourth Gospel. As revelation, they are replaced by Jesus' words (see 3:31–36).

Membership. A shift occurs also in the growing elitism and exclusiveness of the group in stage two, as membership no longer consists of hearers being convinced and freely accepting Jesus. Now membership becomes a matter of divine election. Jesus states that his only authentic followers are those *chosen by God:* "No one can come to me unless it is granted by the Father" (6:65; see v. 44). Jesus said this on the occasion of dropouts leaving the group, indicating by it that the dropouts never were true members, for they were not chosen by God. This harks back to other remarks of Jesus in the bread of life Discourse, that membership is a matter of

133

divine election, and so necessarily limited to the elite few. In one place, Jesus remarked: "All that the Father gives me will come to me" (6:37); and in another place, "Every one who has heard and learned from the Father comes to me" (6:45). Authentic members, therefore, who are chosen by God and taught by God, are necessarily the elite few. The dropouts, who only seemed to have accepted Jesus, were ultimately shown to be outsiders whom God did not choose. Unbelievers as well are not chosen.

Claims such as being chosen by God, being "true worshipers" (4:23-24), and being attached to the "true vine" (15:1) signal a growing elitist sense of membership. Because Christian claims deny all value and status to synagogue Jews, such claims must lead to confrontation. Energy, then, will no longer tend to flow outward in preaching to new members, but becomes channeled inward in apology and defense as hostility to these claims mounts. And as hostility mounts, one becomes more and more aware of different types of members in the Johannine group.

Membership within the Johannine group in stage two is not only smaller but more elitist. Its smallness is due in part to the emerging crisis, for some people are afraid to join (12:42) and others seem to be dropping out (6:60-65). It is now possible to rank members in the Johannine group according to their belief. This possibility did not exist when membership depended on a simpler confession of Jesus as king and prophet. Such a ranking yields five groups of people. (1) *Authentic Members* are those who publicly confess Jesus as the replacement of Israel's cultus, as the authentic, exclusive mediation of God's benefaction. Their confession will bring them into direct confrontation with the synagogue, with attendant penalties. (2) *Inauthentic members* may be Jesus' "brothers" (7:1-9), or followers of inadequate faith (8:31), but they do not truly accept Jesus (see 2:23-25). (3) *Cryptobelievers*,[41] are inclined to confess faith in Jesus, but do not do so publicly for fear of being cast out of the synagogue (see 9:22; 12:42-43). (4) *Dropouts* once confessed faith in Jesus, but do so no longer (6:60-65). They are now considered outsiders. (5) *All others*, who do not believe in Jesus, are outsiders and enemies.

The Gospel document reflects the perspective of those willing to confess Jesus as the authentic replacement of Israel's cultus, and so they see true membership in the Johannine group limited to authentic believers such as those who publicly acclaim Jesus at the risk of excommunication (see 9:17, 33-34; 12:12-17). The good shepherd has long been willing to lay down his life for his sheep (10:11, 15), but now good sheep are told that they, too, must be willing to suffer for the faith. When Philip and Andrew bring potential disciples to Jesus, he immediately catechizes them on the need for courage, comparing discipleship with a grain of wheat which must fall into the ground and die (12:24). They must "hate their lives in this world" (12:25). Authentic believers, then, are public believers; all else are pseudofollowers of Jesus.

Christology. At a later stage in the group's history, we hear of new and different confessions about Jesus. Instead of seeing Jesus as another prophet, even as the authentic leader of the covenant, he is heralded as a figure greater than the prophets and patriarchs of Israel's history, "greater than" Jacob (4:12), Abraham (8:53, 56–58), and even Moses (1:17; 3:13–15; 5:36, 46; 6:31–32). Implicit in these confessions is the claim that in Jesus a newer and better covenant is offered than Moses offered; in Jesus a newer and better covenant people is formed than was formed through Abraham; in Jesus a newer and better revelation about worship is offered than came through Jacob. It is not enough to see Jesus as the latest and best of a line of prophets and founding figures; now radical and exclusive claims are made that Jesus is superior to older prophets and leaders. In fact, he replaces them and makes their revelations obsolete. Jesus is the revealer of *new* things—a new place to worship, a new way of worship, and new rites. Jesus is confessed as the ultimate word from God who surpasses and replaces all previous words. The christological confession of this group cannot be appreciated except in the context of the experience of the confessing group. That Jesus is greater than Israel's prophets and patriarchs and that he replaces them makes sense in terms of the new claims that Christian sacraments and worship replace inferior Jewish rites. The full extent of what Jesus means at this stage of Johannine history is clear when we see that Jesus himself *is* the temple; his flesh and blood *are* life; his fluids *give* purification; confession of him *is* worship of God. No Old Testament figure could claim that his person or his teaching was purification, sacrifice, or holiness. Jesus claims that those who accept him in faith even now have eternal life, not just life such as Moses' manna might give, but eschatological life. The group's exclusive claims to have the truth, the whole truth, and nothing but the truth are tied ultimately to their claims that Jesus is in every way superior to all previous religious

135

figures. An exclusive Christology, then, corresponds with an exclusive sense of membership.

Before we analyze these data of stage two in social-science categories, it might be helpful to compare them with the data from stage one.

COMPARISON: DESCRIPTIONS OF STAGES ONE AND TWO

Stage One	*Stage Two*
ACTIVITY	
missionary propaganda, to all;	replacement propaganda, to Jews in synagogues;
object: Jesus as king and prophet	object: Jesus as true temple, cult, feast
SCRIPTURE	
Scriptures valid as prophetic of Jesus (1:45; 5:46);	Scriptures in question as Jesus replaces persons, cultus;
no scriptural halakah emphasized	halakah emphasized in replacement of rites and feasts
MEMBERSHIP	
commensurate with mission, group is inclusive and preaches to all	increasingly exclusive and elitist, as group claims absolute truth and correct rites
STRATEGY	
competitive with synagogue, in that it claims to legitimate Jesus as the prophet of reform	intensely reforming; as Jesus replaces Jewish rites, he threatens synagogue system
CHRISTOLOGY	
Jesus as latest, greatest prophet and king	Jesus as definitive replacement of all former prophets and patriarchs

As the comparison shows, the differences lie in the respective Christologies and the claims surrounding those confessions. Christians in stage one are much less reforming, challenging, and elitist than those of stage two, who see Jesus replacing all spokesmen and all cultic matters with his own person, thus challenging the foundations of the current synagogue system. Debate over the applicability of the Scriptures to Jesus characterizes the synagogue's reactions to the early missionary preaching of stage one (see 1:45–46; 7:40–43,

136

52), whereas forensic processes typify the synagogue's reactions to the replacement claims (see 3:1–21; 8:12–20; 10:22–26).[42]

Social-Science Perspective:
Strong Group / Rising Grid

Purity. Jesus' preaching ostensibly stayed within the parameters of the basic system of Judaism. Even as he embarked on a program of radical reform of the major structural and symbolic elements of the Judaism of his day, he would still claim to be within the system of Judaism, but as its only authentic or true form. The major elements of Judaism that came under his reform were the validity of the temple system and cultic observances and the centrality of circumcision and strict Sabbath observance.

The temple system expressed the major values, structures, and classifications of the Judaism of Jesus' day. But Jesus claims to replace the physical temple with a new temple, which is his body (2:19–21). Jesus' challenge to the temple constitutes a formal attack on the extensive system of structuring Israel's life according to the patterns of order and classification symbolized in the temple. Even as the temple is replaced by Jesus' body, so Jewish feasts are systematically replaced by Jesus with authentic feasts centered around his person and actions. (1) Jesus' giving of true bread is the authentic Passover bread (6:4) and his crucified body is the true Passover lamb (19:31–36). (2) Jesus' gift of true light and water replaces the objectives of the old feast of Tabernacles (7:2, 37–39; 8:12). (3) The feast of Dedication (10:22) as well as other feasts (5:1) are redefined to focus on Jesus. Even if the strategy is reform and replacement, the essentials of the system are claimed by Jesus and his followers, which was not the case in stage one.

Douglas remarks that as the major symbols of the system are challenged, fixed holy space will likewise be contested, with the result that holy space becomes fluid.[43] Jesus, of course, contests the validity of "this mountain and Jerusalem as the place of worship" (4:21), for true worshipers should worship not on a fixed mountain in some temple but "in spirit and truth" (4:23–24), which at a minimum means Jesus' own person as the temple replacement: "He spoke of the temple of his body" (2:21).

Even as Jewish sacrifices are neutralized by claims that there is no fixed sacred space at which to offer them, thus decentralizing Israel's focus on Jerusalem and its temple, Jesus offers superior means of achieving the purposes of those sacrifices. For example, at Cana his newer and better "wine" is located in "six stone jars standing there, for the Jewish rites of purification" (2:6), signaling that purification can be had with Jesus' fluids. Those fluids, moreover, are acknowledged as superior to all that went before, since the best is saved for last (2:10). Forgiveness of sins, moreover, is not confined to sin offerings in the temple or to the ceremonies of Yom Kippur, for Jesus gives the disciples the power of the Holy Spirit with which to forgive sins (20:22–23). Sacred space, then, is where Jesus is or his Spirit dwells, and where they are found, true purification is also found.[44]

Three customs, circumcision, Sabbath observance, and kosher diet, characterized Jews in Jesus' time. The Fourth Gospel records Jesus challenging the absolute importance of two of them.[45] In place of circumcision as the definitive mark of membership in the covenant, Jesus demands a birth through water and the spirit (3:5). By his frequent healing on the Sabbath (5:9–10; 7:22–23; 9:14) Jesus challenged the strict observance of the Sabbath as a symbol of orthodox membership in the covenant. Jesus' program of replacement, then, constitutes a thorough and systematic reform of the values, structures, and symbols of Judaism.[46]

Ritual.   As replacement strategy develops, there is an increase in correct rites that focus on the boundaries distinguishing insiders from outsiders. Only those who practice Jesus' authentic rites enjoy true membership in God's covenant community, as the following texts indicate:[47]

> *Unless* you are born of water and the spirit, you cannot enter the kingdom. (3:5)

> *Unless* you eat the flesh of the Son of Man, you have no life in you. (6:53)

The increasing clarity of Jesus' program of replacement of Jewish rituals constitutes a sharper boundary between insider and outsider than was the case in stage one, with a resulting limitation of membership because of the sharper criteria for membership. Evidently external behavior is not as disparaged or suspect as it was in stage one, for the performance of these material rites is essential for membership.

Douglas postulates that in this type of social situation, even as attention is focused on boundaries, there is a sense that they are under attack by an evil power. Considerable attention, then, must be given to rituals that identify the evil or pollution that has surreptitiously crossed those boundaries and now resides in the social or physical body and works its harm. As we shall see in the group's cosmology, it perceives the world peopled with devils in disguise, people claiming to be observant but whose claims mask their demonic nature. Many who reject Jesus accuse him of having a demon (7:20; 8:48–50; 10:20–21), arguing that he only claims to be pious but in fact is deceiving the crowds (7:12, 47). Comparably, Jesus accuses pseudodisciples of being in fact the spawn of the devil (8:44). This accusation of demon possession is itself a line-drawing ritual, clearly distinguishing where the accuser and the accused stand.[48]

Personal Identity. Identity remains dyadic, as individuals draw their primary identity from membership in a family or a group such as the Pharisees or the followers of Jesus. Membership in this stage, however, is not so much the voluntary association heralded in stage one, where great emphasis is put on people coming to the light (3:19) or doing the works of God (6:27); rather, as we saw above, true members are chosen and drawn by God (6:37, 45, 65). Internal roles in this society, moreover, are confused, for a fierce competition for leadership in the synagogue is under way, a contest without clear rules for succession to power or its legitimation (see 3:1–2, 10; 7:15, 25–52). It is most important at this point that distinctions are regularly made between appearances and reality, outer and inner, or exterior actions and interior motives. For example, Christian entrance rites are better than synagogue ones because they entail being born of "water and spirit" (3:5). True hearers of God's word are "spirit," not "flesh" (3:6), and so those of heaven can understand heavenly things, which is not the case with those of earth (3:12).

Body. The physical body is quite tightly controlled as is the social body, as more and more rituals prescribe proper washing (3:3, 5; 13:3–14), proper eating (6:25–59), and correct drinking (4:7–14; 7:37–39). Pious acts, such as the anointing of Jesus' feet (12:1–7), are highly praised. But in this situation what is material and external is also ambiguous. It so happens that some who ate the bread of life prove not to be true followers (6:60–65), thus calling into question the value of that ritual; and some who claim to be followers of Jesus (8:30) are proved to be the spawn of the devil (8:44). As we noted above, people perceive their rivals ambiguously, as demons disguised as observant Jews or dutiful followers. Confusion is the order of the day.

Sin. In this situation, sin has two aspects. First, if authentic Christian rituals (3:3, 5; 6:53) are essential for membership in God's covenant, then sin may be described as refusal to perform them. Sin then may be the violation of a formal norm. Such was not the case in stage one, when Jesus flaunted traditional Sabbath observance. But as the synagogue norms are challenged and replaced, sin continues to be thought of as a failure of the heart (12:40), as unbelief. This sin, moreover, is totally polluting.

Cosmology. The world, while still anthropomorphically conceived, is considerably less predictable than from the viewpoint in stage one, for one hears more and more of an evil power in the world assaulting God's creatures (12:31; 16:11). In fact, the world more and more is perceived dualistically: God's world vs. this world; God's ruler vs. ruler of this world.[49] All evil is explained as the work of the devil, who carries out his attacks through people under his power (see 6:70; 13:2, 27). Jesus' opponents consider him a demonic agent in disguise (7:20; 8:48–50; 10:20–21), just as Jesus accuses pseudobelievers of being the spawn of the devil (8:44). This is cosmos dualistically perceived which is at war; the stakes are high, the outcome questionable.

As we did with the descriptive data from stages one and two, we can compare the results of the social-science analysis of these two stages.

COMPARISON: STAGES ONE AND TWO IN SOCIAL-SCIENCE PERSPECTIVE

Stage One (strong group / low grid)	*Stage Two* (strong group / rising grid)
PURITY	
still within Jewish system, focus on Jesus' place in nontemple scheme of things	intense competition for control of major symbols of purity system: temple and cultus
RITUAL	
basic boundary-making rituals focusing on faith in Jesus	intensified boundary-making rituals, stressing new entrance ritual (3:3, 5) and tests of authentic membership (6:53)

140

A BASIC MODEL: CHRISTOLOGY AND REVOLT

Stage One	*Stage Two*
PERSONAL IDENTITY	
dyadic; people known as disciples of Moses or Jesus; emphasis on voluntary choice of membership (3:18–19)	dyadic; Jesus' disciples known as those chosen by God (6:60–65); emphasis on divine election to membership
BODY	
body controlled, but distrust of externals (7:24; 8:15) and even of Jesus' signs (4:48; 6:26)	body more strongly controlled; specific bodily rituals (washing, eating) required; less distrust of externals, as replacement of temple and cult favor Christian rituals
SIN	
sin as internal phenomenon (unbelief), which totally corrupts; sin is not a violation of norms, such as Sabbath rules (5:10; 7:21–23)	sin now means failure to perform external rituals (3:3, 5; 6:53); sin also pollutes totally
COSMOLOGY	
world anthropomorphically perceived, a fair place where one's deeds correspond to God's judgment (5:14)	world anthropomorphically perceived, but as a place of conflict between God and the devil; one's fate is not proportional to one's deeds, as evil wars on good

As this comparison indicates, grid rises in stage two, as christological claims are intensified and membership qualifications rise in a move to achieve dominance in the synagogue and within the accepted system of Judaism. Whereas Christians in stage one seemed to care little about the temple and its cultus, that neglect is reversed by the attempts of Jesus in stage two to control the values and structures of the Jewish purity system.[50] Moving away from ignoring rituals, the community proposes several as essential for covenant membership, stressing the value of external, bodily activity even as it radically devalued the rituals of the synagogue. The intensified challenge to the purity system in stage two is mirrored in the new view of a cosmos at war, as forces of good and evil battle for control of human hearts. Grid, while trying to rise in stage two, remains precariously subject to shocks as we learn of dropouts leaving the group (6:60–65) and excommunications from the synagogue. The intensified claims of stage two (i.e., rising grid) did not always meet with success.

STAGE THREE:
HIGH CHRISTOLOGY

The task of the rest of our study is the proper assessment of the stage of the Fourth Gospel which proclaimed Jesus as "equal to God." In one sense, the first four chapters of this study provide much of the data for our present analysis, a descriptive survey of the same material that will now be considered in social-science perspective. A new hypothesis emerges about this stage, that it should be described as weak group/low grid, a position characterized by revolt, not reform, and by radical distancing from previous values, structures, and classifications.[51]

Stage two involved the Johannine group in a grid-raising strategy as Jesus was heralded as the replacement of the major elements of Israel's symbol system. Yet despite the exalted claims of the Johannine group, they experienced the trauma of excommunication and the shock of dropouts abandoning the group. Grid dropped sharply after rising so dramatically. It is at this point that I would situate stage three, the period of the full articulation of Jesus as equal to God and Lord and God, the heavenly figure who is not of this world. Meeks's suggestions about an alienated Jesus make excellent sense now, as Jesus is himself lifted up from this world, even as his disciples are excommunicated from the synagogue. Far from positively engaging the world, as was the case in stage two, the Johannine community is hated by this world and finds itself in flight from it. In the next chapter, I will take up explicitly the issue of a dichotomized cosmos and its relation to the Johannine Christology, but for the present, let us sketch the cosmology of the group whose strategy of replacement was jolted by excommunication and apostasy, an experience that led it to perceive the world according to factors labeled weak group and low grid.

The following social-science description of stage three will be more fully demonstrated in the next chapters. At present, all that can be done is sketch what seems to be a totally different stage of development of the Johannine group. Following excommunication from without and apostasy from within, what was the cosmology of this group like?

Purity. In Douglas's model, the posture here is basically an "anti-" stance in which people reject the position from which they have just emerged with all its values, structures, and classifications. Revolt, not reform, becomes the strategy. In terms of the Fourth Gospel, the strong sense of an orderly system symbolized by the temple, its feasts, and cultic objects, which characterizes stage two, collapses. As we shall shortly see, the telltale evidence of this is 6:63 and 8:23, in which all value is placed not in material rites or in anything fleshly, earthly, or material, but in spirit alone: "The spirit alone gives life; the flesh is of no avail." As we saw in chapter 5, Jesus' remark occurs as a riposte to the rejection he experienced in reaction to the remarkable claims made in the bread of life Discourse, after which some find his talk stale and drop out of his group. Apostasy calls into question the value previously placed on the group's rituals, for the dropouts presumably were followers who were born of water and the spirit (3:3, 5) and who had crossed from death to life and passed beyond judgment (5:24). But as they proved *not* to have been chosen by God (6:64–65), those rites cannot automatically be said to have effected what was claimed. With apostasy, the value of things material, even the required birth ("unless . . . ," 3:3) and the demanded eating ("Unless . . . ," 6:53) lose their value and normative status as membership criteria. The purity system of the previous location is rejected and under attack; to say the least, there exists in stage three a weak group factor.

The sense of rejection of its former location can be seen also in the shift from dualism to dichotomy. With its keen sense of pervasive, cosmic dualism, the Johannine group finally took a stand, not only against the unbelieving synagogue, but against this world, which might include the apostolic churches as well. As we shall shortly see, Jesus stands above and against this world and all that is from below. In earlier stages of the Gospel, dualism, which distinguished Christians from synagogue Jews, functioned as a boundary distinguishing the two groups as light vs. darkness, true vs. false, and so forth. But with Jesus' welcome ascension to former glory, that dualism becomes a dichotomy in which what is not of this world and what is from above stand against the values, symbols, and structures of this world. The latter are completely rejected. There is no longer a claim of replacement but a proclamation of rejection of all things earthly, material, and fleshly.

The "anti-" stance against previously held values can also be observed in the way the world is treated. In stages one and two, this world was a place to be catechized, a place deserving of God's benevolent attention, and a place in which the Word seemed willing to pitch his tent. But as opposition to Jesus culminated in

143

excommunication from the synagogue, this world became a hateful place (15:18–25), a place from which one should flee (13:1–3; 17:5), a place of exile. At last, the Johannine group finds itself standing against this world, a world that once was a place of promise.

The attitude of revolt turns not only against the synagogue and its system, but against certain members of the group following Jesus. Although 6:60–65 describes dropouts who apostatized from the group, the text indicates other internal problems in which certain members of the group took a superior stand over against other followers of Jesus. An internal fight developed within the Johannine group, a fight between those willing or eager to confess Jesus publicly in ways that would lead to their excommunication and those who were not willing. For example, Peter's denial of Jesus (13:36–38; 18:17, 25–27) will have serious consequences on his standing as leader, as the restoration of him in 21:15–19 indicates. In this third stage, then, we come to sense a conflict between Johannine Christians like the beloved disciple, who follows Jesus into danger (18:15–16) and to his death (19:26–27), and the apostolic churches represented by Peter. As Johannine Christians took a consistent stand against all persons from below or of this world, both synagogue Jews and unacceptable Christians, this could only mean a progressive weakening of commitment to all former values, symbols, and structures (weak group), and so stage three may be described as revolt against the previous purity system that characterized it.

Ritual. Again Douglas suggests that the attitude to ritual will likewise be an "anti-" stand. Boundary rituals formerly emphasized material rites, which symbolized the transition from outsider to insider (3:3, 5; 6:53). But because dropouts, who had been baptized and eaten the bread of life, left the group, a new antisacramental stance emerges (6:63). It stresses different, spiritual criteria for membership: "*Unless* you believe that 'I AM' you will die in your sins" (8:24). And in the face of weak members who are afraid publicly to profess faith in Jesus, we find another criterion: "*Unless* I wash you, you have no part with me" (13:8). Footwashing, it is argued,[52] has to do with martyrdom or preparation for sacrifice, a meaning that fits the demand for public confession of Jesus even if this leads to excommunication or martyrdom (16:1–2; see 12:24). Douglas, moreover, predicts that with such a rejection of former rituals, effervescence and spontaneity will flourish, which in New Testament terms means charismatic phenomena and increased spirit activity, a point to which we shall return in the last chapter. Former material rituals, then, are rejected and replaced by spiritual and individualistic activity. This serves to distinguish one not only from the synagogue, but from weak members of the group. Boundaries must be drawn between authentic followers of Jesus and synagogue Jews and also Christians of inadequate faith, boundaries styled as both a revolt against former modes of classification and superior forms of elitist behavior.

Personal Identity. As one rejects the system from which one has been expelled (i.e., weak group), revolt will entail a rejection of one's identity as embedded in that group with a corresponding rejection of the controls of that group. Douglas describes this as the place of individualism, not dyadic personality. This is borne out by some recent studies of John 15. They suggest that according to the vine image, the Johannine community came to see itself as "an association of Christian individualists, each united to Jesus as a branch on the vine but not overly concerned with the salvific aspect of being united to one another."[53] Aliens in an alien world, they are never sure of one another (see 8:30), and so cling only to Jesus, not to the group. Evidence for this sense of individualism may be found in the criticism of the role of Peter and the authority that Peter represents in the apostolic churches. The new model of personal identity becomes the individually beloved disciple who is Jesus' intimate,[54] who has immediate access to Jesus' heart and secrets (13:25–26), who alone follows Jesus into danger (18:15; 19:26), and who quickly believes on Easter (20:8) without the material proofs that were offered to the Eleven (20:20) and to Thomas (20:26–29).[55]

Body. The "anti-" stance against former structures, which characterizes the new social body, is mirrored in the new sense of the irrelevance of the physical body. Since life is spiritual, purity concerns for controlling or guarding the body are absent. Jesus' statement in 6:63 sums up this point, as we hear of a criticism of eucharistic rites (Jesus' body!) and a celebration of spirit: "The spirit gives life; the flesh is of no avail."

If in stage two social controls were replicated in specific regulations of the physical body, in stage three, when formal social controls vanish, there is a corresponding absence of control of the physical

145

body, as is evidenced by the attack on norms based on things fleshly or material. Material rites for membership vanish (again 6:63), especially the norm of eating the flesh of the Son of man (6:53). The legitimacy of Peter, which is based on what the original apostles had seen, heard, and touched, is undercut now by spiritual leadership not normed by anything fleshly or bodily.

Sin. Grace and life no longer depend on being born of water and spirit or eating the flesh of the Son of man, but come from believing that Jesus is "I AM" and from willingness to confess Jesus publicly, even if this would bring excommunication. Correspondingly, sin no longer resides in the failure to perform the required rites of stage two, but in the failure to believe the right confession (8:24) or in cowardice to acclaim Jesus publicly (12:42). Sin, then, becomes progressively private, as one's identity becomes more individualistic, and increasingly an interior phenomenon, since external sacraments or their lack cannot indicate one's true belief in Jesus.

Cosmology. As identity becomes more individualistic and former structures are devalued, one begins to seek God directly, without the mediation provided by sacramental rites, or official leaders and spokespersons of the tradition, or even a mediating group. It is in this context that spirit becomes the vehicle for individual inspiration and personal access to all one needs to know.

Stage three, then, represents a formal posture of withdrawal from and revolt against the structures and symbols of stage two. Reform, the strategy of stage two, is replaced by revolt against the world and all that is from below, whatever that entails. In the judgment of the members of this group, things of this world include not only the synagogue and its system, but even Christian phenomena such as the material rites of baptism and eucharist as well as apostolic leadership. The saying of Jesus becomes the dominant slogan: "The spirit gives life; the flesh is of no avail" (6:63). The christological confession of stage three reflects this same posture of revolt and withdrawal. Jesus is no longer the replacement of temple, feasts, and cult but the heavenly figure who is equal to God but not of this world, as he ascends out of this world to his true place and status, to the glory he had with God before the creation of the world (17:5). The faces of Jesus and his followers are turned away from this world and from all things from below. This would imply a focus no longer turned outward toward group boundaries, precise criteria for membership, and mission. Rather the direction is now inward, as enlightened individuals who confess Jesus as an ascending heavenly figure go their own way independent of synagogue or apostolic church (see "secessionists" in 1 John). Stage three, then, may be located as weak group/low grid.

As we did with stages one and two, it may help to compare the social-science analysis of stage three with that of stage two.

COMPARISON: STAGES TWO AND THREE IN SOCIAL-SCIENCE PERSPECTIVE

Stage Two *(strong group / rising grid)*	*Stage Three* *(weak group / low grid)*
PURITY	
strong system: value found in Jesus' replacement of temple, feasts, and cultus; reform of synagogue system	weak system: no value found in rituals or anything material (6:63); revolt against former system
RITUAL	
boundary rituals, stressing entrance and membership rituals, directed against those of the synagogue; in an ambiguous cosmos, rituals needed to expose demons in disguise	anti previous rituals; celebration of spirit over matter (6:63), distinguishing superior followers from those of inadequate faith
PERSONAL IDENTITY	
dyadic personality: identity as member of Jesus' group, which is the reformed covenant community; true members chosen by God	individualistic personality: identity as beloved disciple who has immediate access to Jesus, independent of membership in group (vine and branch)
BODY	
strong bodily control, replicating strong social control; bodily rituals required (3:3; 6:53)	weak bodily control, with no prescribed bodily rituals; life is spiritual (6:63)
SIN	
sin is both a pollution that totally corrupts and a failure to perform external rituals ("unless you are born of water . . . " 3:3; "Unless you eat . . . " 6:53)	sin becomes a matter of personal and interior decision ("unless you believe . . . " 8:24; see 13:8)

147

Stage Two	*Stage Three*

COSMOLOGY

dualistic cosmos of warring forces and disguised demons; suffering can come from the devil, who attacks God's faithful ones; sense of intense conflict	superiority to former warring cosmos, as "spirit" triumphs; individuals do not need mediation of cult and system, but enjoy personal access to God and things heavenly

As this comparison indicates, the differences are dramatic and significant, for this latter group of Johannine Christians, who have been battered by excommunication from the synagogue and buffeted by apostasy from within, adopt an attitude of superiority to previously held values and structures. In Douglas's terms, the group factor, that is, the sense of an ordered and systematic cosmos, plummeted, as did grid, that is, the acceptance of the norms and values of the social group in which one finds oneself. This latter group is in high revolt against its former purity system, rituals, and required behavior. It no longer values that system (6:63), and does not depend on it for access to membership, benefits, or meaning. It comprises a loose association of individuals, each beloved of the Lord, who have no need for the structures of the former group and are suspicious of those who continue to press them. Whereas the former stage was striving to reform the major symbols of Judaism, stage three is in revolt against those and all such symbols. Whereas the former stage engaged the world as its light and salvation, stage three is detached from it as heaven is superior to earth, spirit to flesh, and things above to things below (8:23).

CONCLUSIONS AND FURTHER TASKS

This chapter began with the question of the social location of the confession of Jesus as equal to God. Only when that is determined can the important question of its function and ideological implications be posed. The solution to these questions led us into a process of mapping the development of the Johannine community according to the anthropological model of Mary Douglas for exploring diverse cosmologies. The use of Douglas's basic group/grid model indicates that the Johannine group went through several stages of development, representing three quite different world views and social contexts. Encoded in the Gospel's narrative are clues that allow us to describe the values, structures, and strategies appropriate to each stage of development and so to gain a window into their respective cosmologies. This was a necessary and useful step because the high Christology, which is located in stage three, can only be fully appreciated when seen as the ideological articulation of a weak group/low grid society and in contrast with the Christologies of the other two stages and their ideological implications. As figure 3 (p. 150) indicates, the development of the Johannine community entails a progression from strong group/low grid (stage one) to strong group/rising grid (stage two) and finally to weak group/low grid (stage three). This progress reflects a shift from initial faction formation to a program of reform of the system and finally to a revolt against the system. As we noted in passing, the Christologies of the Gospel also progressed: from establishment of the credentials of Jesus as prophet and king, to claims that Jesus replaces the major personages as well as the temple system in his own person, and finally to the articulation of Jesus as equal to God, indeed as a divine, heavenly figure who is not of this world.

Inasmuch as the basic Douglas model has been accurate and enlightening in objectively sorting out the complex data in the Fourth Gospel, it suggested fresh and precise ways of assessing the social context of the high Christology. One thing the model does, which is of great consequence to this study, is indicate the relationship of a phenomenon such as a christological confession with other aspects of the world view, how the value it encodes is replicated[56] and made redundant[57] throughout the system. This observation is the conceptual argument behind the interest in the way "equal to God" in the Fourth Gospel implies "not of this world."

As we noted, much of the social-science analysis of stage three was presented as a hypothesis, stated but not proved. Demonstration is the business of the next two chapters. First, Douglas offers still more suggestions for examining in social-science perspective the implications of "equal to God . . . not of this world" in her remarks on the anthropological implications of a spirit vs. matter dichotomy. We will find that dichotomy to be the cosmological context in which one must situate the exalted confession of Jesus. In chapter 8, Douglas's suggestions on the ideological implications of "spirit" will be used to refine the import of 6:63, 8:23, and other statements like them on the meaning and function of the high Christology as an ideology of revolt.

149

FIGURE 3
STAGES OF JOHANNINE DEVELOPMENT
IN GROUP AND GRID

GRID
high

weak
GROUP

strong
GROUP

low
GRID

STAGE TWO
(strong *group*/rising *grid*)
1. strategy: exclusive claims of reform and replacement
2. Christology: Jesus is greater
   than patriarchs and prophets;
   he replaces major symbols and
   rites with his own person

STAGE THREE
(weak *group*/low *grid*)
1. strategy: revolt against and
   withdrawal from the world
2. Christology: Jesus is equal to
   God but not of this world; he
   ascends to heaven, his true
   home

STAGE ONE
(strong *group*/low *grid*)
1. strategy: faction formation
   around Jesus, the new leader;
   challenge to the system
2. Christology: Jesus is prophet
   and king, who fulfills the
   Scripture and demonstrates his
   credentials with signs

7

CHRISTOLOGY
AND COSMOLOGY:
SPIRIT VERSUS FLESH

SPIRIT/FLESH COSMOLOGY

Mary Douglas's modeling indicates that value statements such as equal to God tend to be replicated and structured in other aspects of a group's world view. We are pursuing further the link between equal to God and not of this world, which was asserted in the last chapter to be the perspective of stage three of the development of the Fourth Gospel. In particular, it was asserted that "equal to God . . . but not of this world" represents a value and perspective replicated in 6:63, where spirit is affirmed as the only value and flesh is denied all value. Douglas's works offer further suggestions about the relationship of spirit to flesh, which can prove most useful in expanding her basic model employed to describe stage three.

The hypothesis of this chapter is that the high christological confession is expressed in such a way that it replicates the basic cosmological perspective of the Johannine group. That is, (1) the Christology replicates the viewpoint of a cosmos divided into dichotomous realms of spirit/flesh and heaven/earth, and (2) it expresses the value structure of this cosmos in which all value is given to the heavenly, spirit world, with a corresponding devaluation of the earthly, fleshly world. In short, as the high christological confession replicates the cosmological perspective of the community, it functions as an ideology.

In 1969 Douglas published an article, "Social Preconditions of Enthusiasm and Heterodoxy,"[1] the substance of which reappeared in her book *Natural Symbols*.[2] The article offered a way of assessing the relationship of an individual to society through the symbolic importance given to language patterns that express relationships between spirit/matter and mind/body. Douglas's remarks are immediately welcome for they seem to offer an adequate and fresh approach for analysis of equal to God, which was formulated precisely in terms of spirit/flesh and heaven/earth dichotomies. The one who is equal to God is also not of this world.

Against this general background we situate Douglas's remarks on the relationship of spirit/flesh and mind/body. "The anthropologist," she remarks, "can never assume that the chosen symbols of differentiation are arbitrary. If they are used to discriminate contended positions, they are also likely to express something about the social situation."[3] So if a social unit emphatically distinguishes itself from others on the basis of spirit vs. flesh or heaven vs. earth, we are advised to pay attention to these remarks as important clues to the social location of the group being studied.

Douglas's remarks on spirit/body dichotomy belong in her larger discussion of the symbolic importance of the human body. As an anthropologist, she notes that the physical body can have diverse meanings. In general, she argues that:

> The body is a model which can stand for any bounded system. Its boundaries can represent any boundaries which are threatened or precarious.[4]

Just as the social body draws boundary lines around itself, restricts admission, or expels undesirable foreigners, so this pattern is replicated and symbolized in the way the physical body is treated.[5] Showing how the group variable is replicated in the social treatment of the physical body, Douglas remarks on the varying degree of control that might be exercised over the body: "Bodily control is an expression of social control—abandonment of bodily control in ritual responds to the requirements of a social experience which is being expressed."[6] The principle is clear: "The social body constrains the way the physical body is perceived . . . the physical experience of the body sustains a particular view of society."[7] And where group is strong, one expects to find a tightly regulated physical body, especially in regard to its surface and orifices, with specifically prescribed and proscribed behavior.[8] Where group is weak, one finds little control of the physical body.[9] As structures and systems are rejected (weak group) and personal identity becomes more individualistic, there is no pressure to conform to a system that is being rejected, and so bodily control will be radically devalued. In place of a controlled body, weak group interest lies in spirit. In contradistinction to tight control of the body, weak group emphasizes effervescence and spontaneity.

Douglas's hypothesis can be more precisely stated: "The relation of spirit to matter or mind to body [can] be interpreted as exchanges of condensed statements about the relation of society to the individual."[10] Body, flesh, or matter represents society; the mind or spirit represents the individual. Turning to the relative emphasis that could be put on either one or the other, Douglas states:

> To insist on the superiority of spiritual over material elements is to insist on the liberties of the individual and to imply a political program for freeing him from social constraints. In the contrary view to declare that spirit works through matter, that spiritual values are made effective through material acts, that body and mind are separate but intimately united, all this emphasis on the necessary mingling of spirit and matter implies that the individual is by nature subordinate to society and finds his freedom within its forms.[11]

Douglas sees that a movement to exalt spirit over matter will necessarily lead one "to adopt the philosophical attitude which, following Durkheim's insight, is appropriate to detachment from or revolt against the established social forms."[12] Conversely, she remarks that "anyone whose social position is one of withdrawal from the dominant form of social control will tend to see himself in relation to society in terms of a spirit/flesh dichotomy."[13]

This mode of analysis, of course, is but a dilation and completion of her exposition of cosmologies plotted out according to her group/grid variables:

> If a scale can be established to assess the diminution from strong to weak social control, there will be a corresponding relaxation of bodily control in forms of expression. This predicts a general tendency to give up ritualism in favour of ecstatic forms as social control diminishes. Second I will argue that within any one social system, people who are relatively more withdrawn from institutional forms of control will not only conform to this trend by choosing against ritualist forms, but intellectually they will also adopt a spirit/matter dichotomy.[14]

Douglas's remarks invite us to examine once more equal to God in terms of its implied cosmological perspective, not of this world. There is ample data that the Johannine confession of Jesus as a heavenly, divine figure was expressed in cosmological terms (e.g., 8:23), an observation that indicates that it might encode the view of the cosmos expressed by the recurring dichotomies we will shortly discuss.

SPIRIT/FLESH CHRISTOLOGY

Although it is not clear that the high Christology originally developed in terms of a spirit/flesh dichotomy, it quickly became conceptualized in those terms and functioned as an ideology of revolt against nonbelievers. In two striking places the Gospel explains its high Christology in terms of spirit/flesh and heaven/earth dichotomies, 6:62–63 and 8:23–24.

The most provocative celebration of spirit over flesh comes in the denouement to the bread of life discourse (6:60–65). This passage contains reactions to the discourse, first reactions of unbelief and apostasy by former followers of Jesus and then Jesus' own reactions to them. "Many of his disciples, when they heard it, said, 'This is a hard saying'" (6:60), and so dropped out of his group.[15] Commenting on their "scandal of faith," Jesus emphasizes the differences between him and these dropouts by contrasting himself with them in terms of a heaven/earth dichotomy: "What if you were to see the Son of man ascending where he was before?" (6:62). Jesus is properly a heavenly being whose home is heaven, a statement emphasized over and over in the Gospel.[16] As we saw in chapter 5, 6:62 adds to this perspective the sense that the heavenly Jesus meets only rejection below on earth, and so is an alien in this earthly, fleshly world to which the dropouts belong. A certain view of the cosmos, then, is encoded in 6:62 which distinguishes Jesus from this world, and contrasts heaven, the place where Jesus is truly appreciated, with earth, where he finds only rejection.

At this point, Jesus makes a sweeping statement which redefines the values of the Johannine cosmos: "The spirit gives life, the flesh is of no avail" (6:63). In the context of 6:60–65, this remark cuts two ways. First, it undercuts any prior claim to authentic membership by these people, whether they were born of water and the spirit (3:5) or whether they ate the bread of life (6:53). These material rites, despite their absolute requirement by Jesus (see *"unless . . ."* 3:3, 5; 6:53), do not and cannot produce life. The unqualified remark in 6:63, moreover, reinforces the dichotomy expressed in 6:62, so that the evangelist describes a cosmos divided into recurring dichotomies of heaven/earth (6:62) and spirit/flesh (6:63). All value is placed on the side of heaven and spirit, whereas earth and flesh are completely valueless—of no avail.

The context of the remarks in 6:60–65 has a bearing on the full import of 6:62–63 as a value statement and as a redefinition of the cosmos. In 6:60–65 the conflict is between Christian and Christian, between Jesus and his former followers who have dropped out of his faction. Unlike the bread of life discourse itself (6:49, 58), 6:63 does not proclaim the superiority of one rite over another. It is, rather, a sweeping statement in which *all things material* are seen as of no avail. And in the context this would apply even to Christian rites, such as eating the bread of life. If the disputants in 6:60–65 were followers of Jesus, then it is presumed that they fulfilled the earlier criteria for membership, which at one time were material rites:

Unless one is born anew, one cannot see the kingdom of God. (3:3)

Unless one is born of water and the spirit, one cannot enter the kingdom of God. (3:5)

Unless you eat the flesh of the Son of man and drink his blood, you have no life in you. (6:53)

Being born anew and eating the flesh of the Son of man were said to have the immediate effect of giving life, even of transferring the disciple beyond judgment by passing from death to life (3:18; 5:24). But if a disciple subsequently dropped out—a disciple who was born anew, who had passed beyond judgment—then how could the required rites be correct? New criteria must be found to indicate who are authentic insiders, criteria quite different from previous ones. In this case, it is the words of Jesus, which are labeled spirit: "My words are spirit and life" (6:63). Jesus declared that flesh is untrustworthy, completely valueless, and of no avail. The only thing that counts is spirit, which in the context is a code word for special values and special confessions, things that are decidedly not fleshly.

John 6:62–63, then, suggests the following conclusions: (1) Jesus' remarks embody a series of recurring dualisms which dichotomize the cosmos into heaven/earth and spirit/flesh spheres. (2) Confession of Jesus as the one who is originally a heavenly, descending figure (6:62) but who is rejected here on earth replicates the view of the cosmos divided into contrasting spheres, spirit and flesh. (3) Jesus' remarks function to dismiss former insiders whose current faith is clearly inadequate by some new standard, which is the high Christology (see 6:33, 41–42). Christology, I suggest, replicates cosmology, just as cosmology implies Christology. On these three points 6:62–63 may be adequately interpreted according to Douglas's model as a statement of spirit/flesh dichotomy embodying a posture of revolt against former structures and rituals.

John 8:23–24 likewise expresses the same value and functions similarly. Like 6:63, 8:23–24 is addressed to followers of Jesus, at least apparent followers (see 8:30). In the context, Jesus establishes a new criterion for determining who is a genuine follower, "*Unless* you believe that 'I AM,' you will die in your sins" (8:24). It stands in stark contrast to other criteria for authentic membership, criteria which had to do with material, fleshly rites (see 3:3, 5; 6:53). We noted earlier that "I AM" is a coded phrase that contains the high christological confession of Jesus as the eternal, imperishable deity who has life in himself. According to 8:24, this spiritual confession alone is life-giving.

This confession, moreover, occurs in a context describing the cosmos in terms of recurring dualisms: "You are from below, I am from above; you are of this world, I am not of this world" (8:23). Those who confess Jesus as "I AM" belong to his world, that is, to what is from above and not of this world, whereas those who do not confess him as such are from below and of this world. Like 6:63, 8:23 places all value on the side of what is from above, while it completely devalues what is from below.

John 6:62–63 and 8:23–24, therefore, convey the same basic message. (1) Both are addressed to would-be or pseudodisciples, who had inadequate faith.[17] (2) Both emphasize that Jesus, who is equal to God, is primarily, even exclusively, a heavenly figure who is of another world, definitely not of this world. (3) Both imply that the christological emphasis on Jesus' being from above and not of this world replicates an overarching perception of the cosmos divided into dichotomous realms: heaven/earth, spirit/flesh, from above/from below, and not of this world/of this world. (4) Both function as new criteria for authentic membership, criteria that radically surpass all previous requirements, especially material rites. (5) Value is found only on the side of heaven, spirit, from above; what is from below, fleshly, and earthly is valueless. Once more, then, Christology replicates cosmology and cosmology implies Christology.

CHRISTOLOGY AND COSMOLOGY

John 6:62–63 and 8:23–24 are not isolated examples of dichotomous, cosmological patterns in the Fourth Gospel. As we try to assess more fully the ideological implications of the high christological confession, let us briefly survey Johannine patterns of redundant dualisms to get a firmer sense of the way 6:62–63 and

8:23–24 replicate the relationship of Christology and cosmology. (See figure 4 below).

Scholars have often noted dualistic patterns in the Fourth Gospel, especially contrasts between light/dark, true/false, and so forth,[18] interest in which has tended to be focused on the relationship of dualistic patterns in John and Qumran.[19] We focus, however, on the dichotomous cosmological patterns in the Gospel which appear so pervasively that they may be fittingly called "redundant" dichotomies.

As Douglas's basic model indicates, where group is strong, that is, where there is a strong purity system (e.g., stages one and two), one finds that the chief rituals of this organization are boundary making and maintenance. Johannine dualisms, then, originally appear in

FIGURE 4
REDUNDANT DICHOTOMIES IN
THE FOURTH GOSPEL

1. Spirit vs. Flesh

3:6	what is born of flesh is flesh;
	what is born of spirit is spirit
6:63	the spirit gives life;
	the flesh is of no avail
7:24	do not judge according to the flesh
8:15	do not judge according to the flesh

2. Spirit vs. Matter

2:21	physical temple vs. risen body
4:21–24	worship of God in spirit and truth

3. Heaven vs. Earth

3:12	if you do not believe earthly things
	how can I tell you heavenly things

4. Heavenly World vs. This World

8:23	you are of this world, I am *not* of this world
1:9–10	
7:7	hatred of this world for Jesus
15:18–19	because he is *not* of this world
17:15	

5. From Above vs. from Below

8:23	You are from below, I am from above

terms of boundaries drawn between followers of Jesus and the synagogue. But not all such remarks express the view of the cosmos conveyed by 6:62–63 and 8:23–24. It is important for us to survey these recurring dualisms, to see how the spirit/flesh, heaven/earth dichotomies in 6:62–63 and 8:23–24 take this characteristic Johannine mode of discourse one step further. It is my hypothesis that in the latter stages of the Johannine community's history, dichotomous patterns such as spirit/flesh and heaven/earth served a distinctive function vis-à-vis the high christological confession quite in keeping with Douglas's remarks about an ideology of revolt, with which we began this chapter. I will argue that Christology replicates cosmology and that cosmology informs Christology.

In the following discussion, the term "cosmology" is used in several senses: (1) in a strict sense, cosmology refers to the view of the world perceived as divided into mutually exclusive realms, heaven and earth; but (2) that view is replicated in the discussion of what properly belongs to heaven and what to earth, so that a dichotomous cosmological view is replicated in a wide range of things, persons, and topics;[20] and finally, (3) since a dichotomous cosmological perspective is a general value orientation, it extends to what is valued (spirit/heaven) and what is disvalued (earth/flesh).[21]

Spirit vs. Flesh

Jesus not only indicates that Nicodemus is an outsider, but why he is such: "That which is born of flesh is flesh, that which is born of spirit is spirit" (3:6). Nicodemus obviously is labeled "flesh," for he understands Jesus' remark about "being born *anothen*" in fleshly terms as a second physical birth: "Can he enter into his mother's womb and be born *deuteron* [i.e., a second time]?"[22] Because he is flesh, not spirit, he can neither understand spiritual things nor recognize heavenly figures: "If I have told you earthly things and you do not believe, how can you believe if I tell you heavenly things?" (3:12). The Johannine world, then, is dichotomized into contrasting realms—spirit vs. flesh and heaven vs. earth—with superiority clearly on the side of spirit and heaven. Yet this mode of discourse functions in terms of a replacement argument by the Johannine group that Jesus offers God's people *true* passover bread, the *authentic* place to worship, the *correct* entrance rites, and so forth.[23] The conflict is between synagogue and church. Material rites are still valued and required, the issue being the competing claims of the Johannine group to have the only valid rites, cultic objects, feasts, and so forth.

In another vein, Jesus repeatedly criticizes his critics for "judging according to the flesh" (8:15; 7:24), because they dismiss him for a material violation of the Sabbath, failing to see things in a correct way. Douglas's model suggests that in competitive, conflictive situations (when grid is low or falling), the challengers or reformers will tend to see a distinction between outer and inner, even sensing that the outer, which may look correct, is really evil in disguise, that is, hypocrisy or even witchcraft.[24] In this context, the challenger or reformer claims that truth is a matter of the heart or the interior, and so attacks what is external, outer, or formal (see Matt. 23:25–28). The urging, then, "not to judge according to the flesh" should be seen as an appropriate statement of strong group/low grid, in which the rules and norms of the day are being challenged by an appeal to what is below the surface or in the heart. Flesh is in need of reform, while truth can be found in the heart or interior. While 8:15 and 7:24 function as challenges for reform, they are not statements of revolt against the whole system. Rather, they would use what is true (what is inner, below the surface) as principles of reform.

Summing up this inquiry into spirit/flesh dichotomy, we note that the argument about true cultic rituals belongs in the period of Johannine history described in the last chapter as "replacement" (strong group/rising grid). A spirit/flesh dichotomy functions there as a principle of reform, not revolt, as better rituals replace obsolete or false ones. Likewise the criticism of "judging according to the flesh" stems from an early period when Christians objected to their claims being judged by material standards such as strict Sabbath observance, and so it functions as well as a reforming principle.

How different, however, are 6:62–63 and 8:23–24. They are directed not to the synagogue, but to Christians of inadequate faith. They describe Jesus basically as a heavenly figure who is not of this world, which confession itself now serves as the new criterion for membership and adequate faith. And they function not as reforming principles, but as firm boundary lines distinguishing true followers from all else, boundary lines which devalue even things held sacred earlier, but now seen as hopelessly inadequate. John 6:62–63 and 8:23–24 revolt against all former criteria: all things earthly, fleshly, and material are of no avail, even the group's reformed rites. These two texts, then, express a weak group/low grid perspective where dichotomous remarks signal a revolt against previously held values and positions.

Spirit vs. Body

Although in one place Jesus challenges the physical temple, implying that in the new order the new temple is his body (2:21), in the discourse with the Samaritan woman he emphatically attacks the physical localization of God's temple either on Mt. Gerizim or Mt. Zion (4:20–21). In the future true worshipers will worship "in spirit and truth" (4:23). Since "God is spirit," those who worship God must "worship in spirit and truth" (4:24). These remarks would seem to belong to a mode of discourse in the Fourth Gospel in which Jesus' rites, feasts, and so forth, replace those of Judaism (strong group/rising grid). John 2:21 and 4:20–24, then, herald reform, not revolt.

Heavenly vs. Earthly

At first glance, there is serious confusion in the Fourth Gospel about the value of the world. At one point we are told that this world is the object of God's benevolent attention: "God so loved the world that he gave his only Son. . . . God sent the Son into the world that the world might be saved" (3:16–17; see 12:47). Jesus appeared glad to "come into the world" (6:32; 11:27), for he is "the light of the world" (8:12; 9:5; 12:46) and gives "his flesh for the life of the world" (6:51). Some commentators indicate that the high-water mark of this benevolent perception of "the world" occurs in the remark in the Prologue that the Word came into the world, became flesh, and pitched his tent among us (1:14).[25]

Balancing this, however, the same Gospel contains a strong stream of remarks that view the world quite negatively. The world Jesus came to save "did not receive him" (1:9–10), which is surely an understatement, for Jesus goes on to emphasize that the world positively "hates him" (7:7) precisely because he is not of the world (15:18–19). And so we begin to be told that Jesus came into the world not for its salvation, but for its judgment (9:39). As we saw earlier, he prosecutes it as its judge (8:21–29); and after him, the Paraclete will continue the formal trial of the world and convict it of false righteousness, false judgment, and demonic leadership (16:8–11).[26]

The world, moreover, constantly hears Jesus' remarks only on a material or fleshly level. It seems incapable of understanding Jesus' true message, precisely because "my words are spirit" and the fleshly world cannot see, feel, or hear "spirit" (3:8, 12). This sense

160

of the world's hopeless obtuseness leads Jesus to remark on the irreconcilable differences between himself and the world: "You are from below, I am from above; you are of this world, I am not of this world" (8:23). This world eventually becomes an alien land for Jesus and his followers, even a battleground where one finds only "tribulation" (16:33) and hatred (15:18–25). Finally, the world is perceived to be ruled by a demon, the ruler of this world (see 12:31; 14:30; 16:11), and all in the world who are not Jesus' followers are under his sway.[27]

Even as Jesus is not of this world, his disciples are likewise not of this world: "The world has hated them because they are *not of the world,* even as I am *not of the world*" (17:14, 16). Since the disciples may be forced to sojourn in this alien land (17:11), they need special protection from the evil one who rules this world (17:15). But if they are compelled to keep sojourning in this evil world, Jesus himself is not. We begin, then, to hear of his eager departure from this world (6:62; 13:1–3). He prays to be glorified in God's presence with the glory he had with God before the world was made (17:5). As Wayne Meeks remarked,[28] the alien deity who descended into this world ascends back to his true home. His kingdom is truly not of this world (18:36–37), and there is no reason to remain in so polluted and hostile a place.

In the earliest stage, when evangelization was the dominant activity of the Johannine group, the world was a good place, worthy of being preached to. As the conflict with the synagogue intensified, the world became a hostile place which deserved to be judged, not converted. "World" here basically meant Jews who rejected the Christian message. Finally, as 8:23–24 shows, the world could encompass also pseudofollowers of Jesus, whose membership criteria and confession were inadequate by the standards of those who confessed Jesus as the divine figure, "I AM." The proof of whether one is from above or below lies in one's christological confession: those who acknowledge Jesus as "I AM," that is, as a divine figure, are on Jesus' side and so are classified as being from above and not of this world. The converse is equally true. Clearly cosmology and Christology are recurring in 8:23–24, something which was not true earlier. This stand against the world, moreover, functions as an attack on certain Christian positions that are considered inadequate. If the world in stages one and two is in need of reform (strong group/ low grid), that is not the case in stage three. For texts such as 8:23–24 and 6:62 suggest that Jesus is in revolt against the hopeless obtuseness of the world and no longer seeks to convert it or reform it, but rejects it (weak group/low grid).

Descent/Ascent

In his initial foray into the use of the social sciences for New Testament interpretation, Meeks investigated the Johannine pattern of Jesus' descent/ascent, which I would interpret as another instance of cosmological dichotomy. The sequence of descent/ascent indicates that Jesus is first and foremost a heavenly figure who merely sojourns on earth, but then returns to his proper place, heaven. Meeks joined this pattern with Jesus' "lifting up," his exaltation on the cross and his return to glory (3:13–14). In 8:28, moreover, this is linked with the high christological confession, for "when you have lifted up the Son of man, you will know that 'I AM.'" Rejected on earth by fleshly people, Jesus will overcome the death that typifies earthly people in such a way as to demonstrate that he is not of this world, of earth or flesh, but is a heavenly, divine figure in virtue of the eschatological power to "have life in himself." As Meeks observes, the pattern of descent/ascent functions to distinguish Jesus from Nicodemus as well as Jesus' disciples from the synagogue; for the pattern conveys "contrast, foreignness, division, judgment."[29]

I would supplement Meeks's analysis on several points. Whereas Meeks interprets the descent/ascent pattern in Jesus' history as a cipher for the history of the community, I would argue in addition that this same pattern is but one more instance of recurring, cosmological dichotomies in the Fourth Gospel. Focusing more on 8:28 than Meeks does, I suggest that the cosmological dichotomy of descent/ascent is linked with the high christological confession and functions not only as the norm of "judgment" against the synagogue but as a principle of revolt against Christians of inadequate faith. It comes to serve as a principle of criticism against church as well as synagogue (hence weak group/low grid). Descent/ascent, then, is another example of how Christology replicates cosmology and cosmology informs Christology.

REPLICATED COSMOLOGY:
THINGS MATERIAL

We have seen that equal to God replicates the dichotomized view of the cosmos, how Jesus is not of this world. The confession, however, is not the only topic in the Fourth Gospel that replicates that perspective. As the following survey will show, the values encoded in a dichotomous cosmology are likewise replicated in attitudes to major topics such as sacraments, Jesus' death on the cross, and community leadership. These are selected test cases. According to anthropological theory, the principle would be expected to apply across the board to a wide range of issues, as authors and cultures tend to express their values in recurring patterns and so achieve a certain cultural consonance. This investigation of things material is ultimately in the service of the main topic of this study, "equal to God . . . but *not* of this world," for if all value is placed in things spiritual and heavenly, it would affect how Jesus is viewed according to 1:14, as the Word made Flesh who sojourns here on earth. For if "the flesh is of no avail," does the Gospel ultimately devalue even the flesh of Jesus, his humanity and his earthly existence?

Sacraments

Sacramental rituals seem to rise and fall in importance in the Fourth Gospel. The standard debate over whether this Gospel is pro- or anti-sacramental seems to be a misplaced debate. The Gospel appears to have been both; and so the interesting question becomes, When and under what conditions was the Gospel pro- or anti-sacramental?[30] According to Douglas's model, in strong group society, ritual has a definite and valued place, even if rituals tend to focus on boundaries indicating who is in or out of the group. In the early stages of this community's experience, especially when replacement Christology was the dominant ideology, Christian rituals were highly regarded.

Precisely in its altercation with the synagogue, the Johannine group repeatedly affirmed the superiority of Christian sacraments and rituals over those of traditional Judaism—a posture of reform. Instances abound: (1) The bread from heaven, which is "true flesh and true blood" (6:55), is considered infinitely superior to Moses' manna: "This is the bread which came down from heaven, not such as the fathers ate and died; who eats this bread will live forever" (6:58). (2) The Christian entrance ritual, which consists of being "born of water and the spirit" (3:5), stands in stark contrast to circumcision (see 7:22–23), for only by baptismal rebirth can one see the kingdom of God and enter it (3:3–5). (3) Jesus' body is the true Passover sacrifice of which the lamb in Exodus 12 is but a prophecy awaiting fulfillment (19:33–37). (4) Sacrament-like value is put on Jesus' spittle, which forms a paste for the healing of the eyes of the man born blind (9:6–7). He washed (more physical mediation) and was healed. (5) The Jewish waters of purification are replaced at Cana in Jesus' first sign. His fluids are clearly better than the older fluids; for as the steward remarks, "The best was saved for last" (2:10).

There seems little doubt that things material were invested with power and highly valued at one stage of Johannine history, which we describe as strong group/rising grid. Yet 6:63 stands as a powerful reminder of a time when sacraments and rituals appear to have lost all value: "The flesh is of no avail"—yes, of no avail! The sacraments and things material become untrustworthy evidence of authentic membership precisely because they are fleshly, material, and of this world; and the flesh is of no avail. What counts is "spirit," or, according to 8:24, the confession of Jesus as "I AM." New, spiritual criteria for membership are proposed. They are spiritual or heavenly, even as Jesus is radically heavenly.

Jesus' Death on the Cross

Jesus' death on the cross is noteworthy in John for the piercing of Jesus' side and the flow of blood and water from it (19:34). Both from the Gospel itself and from remarks such as 1 John 5:6–8,[31] one gets a sense of importance, probably even sacramental significance, invested in this blood and water, which reflects the perspective of the group which we have located as strong group. Yet, as this study argued in the previous chapter, the death of Jesus came to have little or no beneficial significance to some Johannine Christians. Their interest in Jesus' death focused not on blood and water from his side, but on Jesus' power to lay down his life and take it again, his imperishability which God gave him in the gift of eschatological power (5:26; 10:17–18). His death, moreover, became the welcome occasion for him to resume his former glory (17:5; 13:1–3), emphasizing his experience of hostility and rejection in this world of flesh and matter. This reflects the perspective of the group that we have located as weak group/low grid. When the flesh becomes of no avail, salvation and benefit no longer come from the cross of Jesus, but from Jesus' words (6:63) or from believing that Jesus is "I AM" (8:24).

Leadership

Scholarship has dealt extensively with the figure of the beloved disciple,[32] especially as he is contrasted with Peter. It is frequently and correctly noted that figures in the Johannine narrative have a symbolic as well as historical character.[33] This suggests immediately

164

the relevance of a discussion of Peter and the beloved disciple in relation to patterns of flesh vs. spirit. It would seem safe to remark that "Peter" functions as a type of apostolic leadership based on eyewitness contact with the earthly Jesus and legitimated primarily in a commissioning of him by the same earthly Jesus—all fleshly and material criteria. The beloved disciple, however, represents a different type of leadership. It is more charismatic and dependent on performance and achievement for its legitimacy—criteria that appeal to spiritual or heavenly phenomena.[34]

As Peter is presented in the Fourth Gospel, he is always an ambiguous figure (except for his restoration in John 21), always in the process of being put in second place. For example, of Jesus' initial disciples, he is called second, not first (1:40–41). Even in that scene, Jesus' praise (1:47) as well as the best lines in the scene (1:50) go to Nathanael. Such features cloud the traditional portrait of Peter as the premier leader of Jesus' followers. Later he refuses Jesus' symbolic footwashing, often seen as related to suffering and even martyrdom,[35] further diminishing his standing from the point of view of those who praise bold public testimony and risk of excommunication for Jesus' sake (see 12:42). Apart from fleshly questions of speed and youth, Peter is definitely in second place at the Easter tomb, arriving after others and not believing (20:4, 6–9). Except for the evident restoration of Peter in John 21, he always appears as second: second to Andrew, less insightful than Nathanael, inferior in information to the beloved disciple, and less swift or believing than he at Jesus' tomb. As a type of traditional, apostolic leadership, Peter represents an ascribed leadership based on fleshly and earthly criteria.

The beloved disciple, in contrast, is a charismatic figure whose status does not depend on ascribed authority but on achieved legitimacy.[36] He is supremely in the know: he knows who the traitor is (13:25–26), and he can see and recognize the Risen Jesus (21:7). He is not only swift of foot to Jesus' tomb, but he "went in, saw and believed" (20:8). He is admirably courageous: he follows Jesus into the hostile quarters where Jesus is arraigned by Annas (18:15–17), and he stands by Jesus at his execution (19:26). At one point he functions as a good shepherd: he opens a closed door for a sheep and leads this sheep inside (compare 10:2–4 with 18:15–17). His leadership, then, rests on performance, either his ability to secure words of Jesus accessible to no one else (13:25–26) or his faithful following of Jesus to trial and death. This leadership is legitimated by Jesus himself

(19:26–27) in a situation where performance is validated as the prime criterion. And he bears the unique name that denotes him as the ultimate intimate, "beloved disciple." His leadership, I suggest, represents a spiritual or charismatic emphasis seen in the Fourth Gospel as better or higher than what Peter represents. The contrast, moreover, is developed in terms of heaven/earth and spirit/flesh dichotomies. In this case, downplaying Peter signals a rejection of what Peter stands for and implies devaluation of the traditions about the earthly Jesus and structures and roles the earthly Jesus is credited with establishing. With his special knowledge, his remarkable belief, and his extraordinary following of Jesus in crisis, the beloved disciple represents a posture above and against what Peter represents, a posture I would identify as weak group/low grid.

At one point, things material lost their value entirely. This conclusion is consonant with the celebration of spirit over matter and heaven over earth that we noted as constitutive of the high christological confession as well. Cosmological dichotomy is replicated not only in the Christology of the Johannine group but in its evaluation of all of the topics and issues with which it concerned itself. On the basis of Douglas's model we should expect to find evidence of a devaluation of Jesus' flesh and earthly existence. I argue that this devaluation is present in the total loss of importance of the sacraments, especially Jesus' own flesh and blood (6:63). The secondary character of Peter's leadership is consonant with the devaluation of what the earthly Jesus might have done or the material qualification for leadership, namely, eyewitness experience (1 John 1:1–4). In 1 John, moreover, we find a celebrated passage which seems to reflect just this devaluation of the flesh of Jesus and his earthly life.

COMPARABLE PATTERNS IN 1 JOHN

The pattern uncovered in stage three of the Fourth Gospel's development appears in the Johannine epistles, although from the perspective of an author who condemns the radical cosmological implications of a Christology that claims that the flesh is of no avail. Since this material has a bearing on the validity of the model and our confidence in its application to the Fourth Gospel, let us briefly survey the Johannine epistles in regard to the radical relationship between Christology and cosmology.

The appropriate window into the controversy is 1 John 4:1–3, where the author notes that "spirit" is an ambiguous phenomenon,

166

neither necessarily from God nor lifegiving (4:1). New criteria of discernment are urged. Spirits are to be tested by their christological confessions: "Every spirit which confesses that Jesus Christ has come in the flesh is of God" (4:2), but "every spirit which does not confess Jesus [come in the flesh] is not of God" (4:3). Comparing 2 John 7 with 1 John 4:3, it seems acceptable to say that they are equivalent statements, so that the false spirit urges a false confession that Jesus, the earthly figure, did not come in the flesh. As Raymond Brown noted, this is not a formal denial of the fact of John 1:14, nor a rejection of the belief that Jesus was born of a woman (6:42), but a denial of the value and importance of his flesh, humanity, and earthly life.[37] Although we only have the expressed viewpoint of the author of 1 John, from a mirror reading of that document we gain a rather clear and extensive grasp of the differences between those who confess different Christologies (4:1–3), differences fully in accord with two different cosmologies, one of which formally resembles the dichotomous cosmology studied earlier in this chapter.

It is beyond the scope of this book to investigate fully the relationship of the christological confessions in 1 John 4:2–3 to key issues discussed, such as Jesus' cross and death, leadership, sacraments, and so forth, but the following gives some indication of the consonance of Christology and community values.[38]

CHRISTOLOGY AND COSMOLOGY
IN 1 JOHN

Jesus Came in the Flesh	*Jesus Did Not Come in the Flesh*
1. cross and death: value given: 1:7, 9; 2:2	1. cross and death: no value given: 5:6–8
2. leadership: value in eyewitness experience: 1:1–4	2. leadership: charismatic claims criticized in 4:1–3
3. tradition: value put on what was "from the beginning"	3. tradition: —
4. sacraments: value given; as spirit, water, and blood agree 5:6–8	4. sacraments: value withdrawn; as spirit only agrees with water 5:8
5. view of the world: true believers are not of this world, 4:6	5. view of the world: false teachers have gone out into the world, 4:5

Cross and death. Those who find value in "Jesus come in the flesh" likewise give importance to his physical death on the cross:

167

"The blood of Jesus cleanses us" (1:7) and his death is "expiation for our sins" (2:2). Not so the opponents, who would value only his coming in water, presumably his baptismal epiphany in the Spirit, not his death (5:6–8).

Leadership. Those who confess "Jesus come in the flesh" find their own leadership and status linked to the earthly, physical Jesus; for their role and their preaching rests on bodily experience of Jesus, "That which we have *heard . . . seen with our eyes . . . looked upon . . . touched with our hands*" (1:1). Not so the opponents, whose role, status, and preaching do not depend on material criteria such as 1:1–4, but on spiritual claims (4:1–3) or commerce with the risen, ascended Christ.

Tradition. Those who value Jesus come in the flesh also celebrate the tradition "which was from the beginning" (1:1). They are not urging, as others do, a new commandment, but "an old commandment which you had from the beginning" (2:7).[39] The tradition of the words of the earthly Jesus is prized by those who were physical witnesses of them and whose status and role is legitimated by their reception. First John gives no indication of what the secessionist opponents thought about tradition, but it may be inferred that the words of the Risen Christ or of his Spirit would be valued over what the earthly Jesus said. We will have more to say about this in chapter 8.

Sacraments. Those who value Jesus come in the flesh would find value both in his coming in water (his baptism and infusion with the Spirit) and in his coming in blood (his expiatory death on the cross). The whole of Jesus' life, then, from baptism to death on the cross, is perceived as valuable (5:6), which correspondingly affirms rites of water and rites of blood, presumably baptismal and eucharistic rites. Unlike the secessionists, who value only Jesus' epiphany in water and Spirit, the author of 1 John sees Spirit actually agreeing with matter (water and blood), for "there are three witnesses, the Spirit, the water, and the blood; and these three agree" (5:8). The secessionists, however, claim that Jesus came "with water only" (5:6), that is, they value only his epiphany in the Spirit at the beginning of his career, and no more. In their eyes, the Spirit that inspires the confession that "Jesus did not come in the flesh" would hardly be "agreeing" with blood, either eucharistic blood or sacrificial blood from Jesus' cross.

The implications of this become clear. Those who confess Jesus come in the flesh are those whose cosmology values things material and fleshly; as cosmos, so Christ. The blood of Jesus is prized for the Spirit agrees with it. Physical contact with the earthly Jesus is valued by those who were with the fleshly Jesus from the beginning, for they are thereby constituted legitimate leaders with an authentic tradition to maintain. Those, however, who confess Jesus did not come in the flesh are those whose cosmology devalues all things earthly, fleshly, and material, Jesus' body included. Only water and Spirit have value, that is, epiphanic phenomena from and by heavenly or spiritual beings. Criteria for leadership are not linked with eyewitness experience (recall that the beloved disciple is never reported to have seen any of Jesus' signs or heard his discourses); nor are the old traditions of the earthly Jesus (1:1–4) valued. All value is placed on what is spiritual, new, and revelatory.

Without getting into the scholarly conversation on the relationship of 1 John to the Gospel, we can at least observe from the perspective of this chapter that the Johannine epistles reflect two contrasting Christologies with two corresponding cosmologies, one of which is clearly a dichotomous cosmology of the sort studied earlier in this chapter. The secessionists, who confess that Jesus did not come in the flesh, are seen by the author of 1 John also to devalue whatever is earthly, fleshly, or material, while valuing only what is spiritual or heavenly. Christology fully replicates cosmology and vice versa. The author of 1 and 2 John, on the other hand, values things fleshly and material. While dualistic in many respects, the author of 1 and 2 John sees no radical dichotomy between things spiritual and earthly, for *they agree:* "There are three witnesses, the Spirit, the water, and the blood; *and these three agree*" (5:8). First John might be said to represent a moderating perspective to the more radical stand taken by his secessionist opponents with their spiritual Christology (4:3). Christology replicates cosmology, be it a Christology that values Jesus come in the flesh or one that denies any value to his flesh. Or, in terms of Douglas's model, the author of 1 John reaffirms the basis Christian system, signifying a strong group variable, while the secessionists he has criticized are portrayed as rejecting that system, indicating a weak group situation.

SUMMARY AND CONCLUSIONS

As this survey has shown, the Fourth Gospel contains many dichotomous patterns, among which we noted the replicated cosmological contrast of heaven vs. earth, spirit vs. flesh, from above vs. from below, *not* of this world vs. of this world. These dichotomies are replicated especially in the confession of Jesus as equal to God but not of this world. We focused on these dichotomous patterns because of the attention paid to them by Douglas as anthropological clues into the social world we are investigating. In general, the dichotomies consistently function to make boundaries, that is, they define and distinguish Jesus and his followers from the synagogue and even certain apostolic Christians. A summary of the findings of this chapter follows:

FUNCTION AND STRATEGY OF
COSMOLOGICAL DICHOTOMIES

Stage One (strong group / low grid)	Stage Two (strong group / rising grid)	Stage Three (weak group / low grid)
1. period: signs	1. period: replacement	1. period: high Christology
2. spirit vs. flesh = defense of Christians' claims	2. spirit vs. flesh = true rites replace false or obsolete ones	2. spirit vs. flesh = no value in flesh, earth; value only in heaven, spirit
3. strategy: reform of criteria for leadership	3. strategy: reform of ritual	3. strategy: revolt against all former structures, criteria, systems
4. opponents: synagogue	4. opponents: synagogue	4. opponents: Christians of inadequate faith as well as the synagogue

This functioning may be more precisely described in relation to the stages of development of the Johannine community. Stages one and two, which Johannine Christians would describe in terms of their reforming intent, were periods of growing competition and conflict between the followers of Jesus and the synagogue. Douglas's model suggests that, in just such situations, people tend to note a discrepancy between outer and inner and between externals and interiors. Christians challenge the synagogue system and disparage the way it views and structures its world, that is, what is outer and external, its formal rules, its prescribed behavior, and its classifica-tions. Because of their reforming posture, these critics tend to be deeply distrustful of all externals, which they label "hypocrisy." Con-versely, they emphasize as part of their reform what is inner and in-terior, the heart over hands. In this configuration (strong group/low grid), heaven/earth and spirit/flesh dichotomies function as boundary lines that distinguish true from false, inner from outer, in-terior from exterior. But the system (i.e., group factor) is not being formally rejected, only reformed.

In fact, even when "replacement" becomes the rallying cry, mate-rial and earthly things are not disparaged at all, at least not Christian breads, waters, feasts, places of worship, and so on. When sacramen-tal rituals enjoyed their highest value, moreover, there still existed a certain spirit/flesh dualism, which served basically to distinguish au-thentic insiders from outsiders. Even here, however, a certain am-bivalence about flesh and things material continues to exist, for in that society, evil, darkness, and falsehood masquerade as goodness, light, and truth. A person's exterior does not necessarily reflect his or her interior mind, heart, and motives. For example, Jesus is sus-pect here because he does not keep external norms such as Sabbath observance, even though he claims to be God's agent. And he warns his critics not to judge him according to the flesh. The world of mat-ter and flesh, then, remains ambiguous as "deceivers" claim to be orthodox but lie and lead others astray (7:12, 47).

But this configuration of value and strategy changed with the ex-odus of dropouts (6:60–65) and the unmasking of pseudobelievers (8:31–59), even as Christians were being expelled from the syna-gogue (9:22; 12:42), which is the historical context of stage three. These events led to a genuine physical relocation of the Johannine group (out of the synagogue) and to a new cosmological location (above, not of this world), changes that expressed new values. Sym-bolizing these recurring changes of location and value are the dis-tinctive dichotomous expressions of spirit over matter, flesh, and body which we have just surveyed. The world of the Fourth Gospel is not simply a dualistic cosmos where boundaries are made between us and them by means of heaven/earth and spirit/flesh dichoto-mies. Now Johannine Christians who confess that Jesus is "equal to God" also proclaim the total superiority of "spirit" over all things fleshly, earthly, and "from below" (6:62–63; 8:23–24), namely, that Jesus is "*not* of this world." The conflict now becomes a revolt against the system itself (weak group), be it the synagogue system or the system of the apostolic churches. The Johannine group in this new posture no longer tries to reform the synagogue's obsolete or inadequate system: it revolts against all such systems, Jewish or Christian, because the flesh is of no avail. In this context, the confession that Jesus is "equal to God" shares this posture of revolt and embodies the sense of superiority over all former structures and values because he is also acclaimed not of this world. Christology replicates cosmology in terms of spatial location, value, and structural expression.

In conclusion, Douglas's remarks on spirit/flesh dichotomy would seem to have a direct bearing on how the high christological confession was understood and functioned in the Fourth Gospel. As we have seen, it is especially the third and latest stage of development (weak group/low grid) that views the world in a series of redundant dichotomies, placing *all* value in heaven/spirit and *no* value in earth/flesh. As well as Douglas has urged us to note how Christology replicates cosmology, it remains for us to examine more fully what spirit means in Douglas's anthropological model and how these remarks might aid in our interpretation of the high christological confession itself. We are not yet finished with assessing the ideological implications of the Johannine confession of Jesus.

8

CHRIST,
SPIRIT,
AND REVOLT

INTRODUCTION

This chapter builds on the previous social-science models for appreciating the social location and function of the confession of Jesus as equal to God. Chapter 6 developed Mary Douglas's basic group/grid model as it applies to the Fourth Gospel, indicating that the high Christology should be located in stage three, a social system where group is weak and grid is low, betokening a posture of revolt against previous values and structures. Because of the values encoded in christological materials such as 6:62–63 and 8:23–24, chapter 7 expanded Douglas's basic model to examine the social situation expressed in dichotomous patterns of spirit against flesh and heaven above earth, regarding Jesus who is not of this world. We saw in chapter 7 how the high Christology replicates certain patterns of dichotomous cosmology; for in stage three, all value is exclusively placed in Jesus' heavenly, divine character (equal to God), rather than in his fleshly, earthly life (*not* of this world). Yet we saw that the high Christology was associated as well with the pattern enunciated in 6:63 (see also 1 John 4:3; 2 John 7), whereby the figure who is not of this world is also linked with spirit[1] as a value totally superior to flesh and this world. Since the analysis of spirit/flesh dichotomy in the previous chapter hardly begins to treat the ideological meaning spirit may have, we attempt now to develop still more of Douglas's model to appreciate the differing perceptions of spirit vis-à-vis society. This should allow us to finish the task of describing the social location and function of Jesus. He is not only not of this world but is associated with spirit, which is completely superior to flesh. This project assumed that from an anthropological point of view, spirit statements are also statements about societal values and structures. Our attention to spirit, then, is not a distraction from the analysis of the high Christology; for it is our hypothesis that the perception of spirit in stage three will correlate closely with the articulation of Jesus as a heavenly figure who is not of this world.

The Fourth Gospel contains a number of remarks about spirit that have been exceedingly difficult for scholars to sort out and evaluate. Spirit has been perceived as the internal voice in individuals that enables personal comprehension of Jesus.[2] Spirit may also be the means of making sense of a self-veiled world which is otherwise obtuse to Jesus' revelation,[3] or the vehicle of correct interpretation of a mystery previously obscure. Spirit, then, can be construed as the phenomenon whereby insiders are distinguished from the world and see the truth which remains impervious to outsiders. In another direction, spirit may be perceived in relation to a two-stage economy of salvation, the work of Jesus and the work of the Spirit. The relationship of these two stages is a matter of critical debate, whether the spirit and its work are subordinate to Jesus, equal to him, or perhaps superior to him.[4]

More to the point, precisely in this one document, we read that the Spirit will engage in two radically different activities. For example, according to the index of spirit-in-matter/spirit-against-matter, spirit may at one point be located in sacraments, either in birth through "water and the spirit" (3:5) or in forgiveness of sins through the apostles' agency (20:22). Yet in other contexts, it can be emphatically beyond sacraments. The dialogue in 6:63 indicates that Jesus' words are spirit and life, and earthly things such as the bread of life are of no avail.

Again, according to the index whether spirit is normed/not normed, the Gospel occasionally indicates that the Holy Spirit will serve as the exegete of the words of the earthly Jesus, remembering them (correctly) to the community and uncovering their hidden meaning, thus serving the past and normed by it: "But when the Counselor comes . . . the Spirit of Truth, he will bear witness to me" (15:26; see 14:26; 16:14). Yet this same Spirit of Truth will also lead the disciples beyond the words of the earthly Jesus "into all the truth," thus pointing to a future quite independent of tradition and past norms: "When the Spirit of truth comes, he will guide you into all the truth . . . he will declare to you the things that are to come" (16:13; see 14:26). These examples, moreover, all embody a series of contrasts—contrasts of ortho-doxy/heresy, control/freedom, and institutional support/charis-matic innovation.

Any labeling of spirit phenomena will reveal the bias and ideol-ogy of the labeler. So an investigation of the spirit passages in a given document is in reality an investigation of the perspective of an author—either the evangelist or the modern exegete, who ei-ther approves or disapproves of the spirit activity that is narrated. Such a study is inherently limited, as it may indicate only the biases either of evangelist or scholar. Although attempts have been made to sort out remarks about the spirit in the Fourth Gospel on some historical scale, to ascertain which might be ear-lier or later than others.[5] the criteria and modeling for these his-torical reconstructions remain quite subjective, arbitrary, and unconvincing.[6]

What seems needed, then, is a model for understanding not only diverse perceptions of Spirit in the biblical texts but also conflicting theological attitudes of exegetes to such texts. A cross-cultural model should be sought that will allow us to un-derstand why, how, and under what circumstances spirit will be perceived either as free/controlled or beyond/bound to the Jesus tradition.

My contribution to this conversation may be stated in the form of several hypotheses for this chapter. (1) Attitudes in the Fourth Gospel toward spirit changed in the course of the group's history, analogous to shifting attitudes to sacraments, signs, leadership, and so forth.[7] What is needed is a model to sort out and inter-pret these changing and conflicting attitudes toward spirit. (2) Douglas's basic group/grid model can be adapted to this task, along with her remarks on the ideological implications of spirit. (3) According to Douglas's model, there are various cultural percep-tions of spirit in relationship to matter, flesh, and earth. John 6:62–63 indicates only one of these possible perceptions, yet it of-fers a point of view reflecting a distinctive cosmology and indicat-ing a distinctive way of living in the cosmos (weak group/low grid; individualism vs. societal control). (4) In stage three of the Fourth Gospel (weak group/low grid), there is a correlation between the way spirit is perceived as radically free from all control and the high Christology that celebrates Jesus as "equal to God" but "*not* of this world." Both express revolt against former cultural systems.

175

The Johannine group that confessed Jesus' equality with God understood his relationship to spirit in terms of its own superiority not only to the synagogue but to certain apostolic churches. Spirit, then, is a symbol of certain values replicated also in the group's cosmology and Christology. A more precise understanding of the social meaning of spirit is essential for a full appreciation of the ideology of the Johannine high Christology.

ANTHROPOLOGICAL PERCEPTIONS
OF SPIRIT

Attitudes to Spirit

Douglas explicitly took up the issue of how spirit may be perceived in different cultural locations. Under the rubric of discussing spirit possession, she noted Raymond Firth's typology of spirit possession,[8] how spirit is perceived along a spectrum ranging from spirit as dangerous to spirit as welcome:

1. Spirit possession: a human is controlled by a spirit that exercises power over him; this dangerous state is countered by friends of the possessed who try to pacify and send the spirit away.
2. Shamanism: the spirit possessing a person is to a large extent domesticated and made to do the will of the human host.
3. Spirit mediumship: an invading spirit speaks through a possessed person; this state exhibits an ambivalent attitude as the possession is not perceived as a dangerous state, but one of usefulness whereby the group tries to obtain occult information or power from the spirit.

In keeping with her penchant for describing how social groups may be plotted according to weak or strong social control (group variable), Douglas suggested a fourth type of spirit possession:

4. Positive spiritual possession: spirit possession of a human person is not regarded as dangerous or undesirable; no attempt is made to control or use the spirit or to pacify it and send it away; here the spirit possession is perceived as a positive value, a channel of benign power for all.[9]

Douglas's initial observations, then, indicate that spirit may be seen as weakly or strongly controlled, with the corollary that spirit may be perceived as correspondingly welcome or dangerous.

CONTROL			CONTROL
weak -------------------------------------- strong			
positive	spirit	shamanism	spirit
possession	mediumship		possession
welcome -------- useful ------- domesticated ----- dangerous			
ATTITUDE			ATTITUDE

When Benign? When Dangerous?

Douglas then puts forward a pivotal question: In what type of social situation is trance or spirit possession viewed as benign or dangerous? This leads us back to one of Douglas's key themes, the group variable, in which she analyzes the degree of social control in a group and what this might imply in terms of society's structures.

In describing spirit as either dangerous or benign, Douglas sorts out this degree of control/noncontrol in terms of four overlapping categories.

(1) *Formal/Informal:* Formal behavior will be valued where role structure is well defined, signifying social distance and public, insulated roles. Informality is appropriate to role confusion, familiarity, and intimacy. Formality implies appropriate bodily control and suggests that culture is valued above nature.[10]

(2) *Smooth/Shaggy:* Smooth suggests agreement with cultural norms and ideals, and points to clear role definition and authority structure.[11] Shaggy represents a strong degree of protest against resented forms of social control and indicates a weak commitment to the norms of the group.

(3) *Structure/Unstructure:* In highly structured situations there is a minimum of possible ritual responses other than the ones required by the norms of the situation. In unstructured situations, informality is valued and there is a greater tendency to abandon reason, follow crazes, and allow greater expression of bodily abandonment.[12]

(4) *Ritual/Effervescence:* Ritualism denotes articulated social structure; here interpersonal relations are subordinate to public patterns of roles, and society is highly differentiated and exalted above self. Effervescence denotes a lack of articulation in social structure and weak control of individuals; little distinction is recognized between interpersonal and public patterns of relations; finally, society is not differentiated from self. Ritualism implies a condensed symbol

system, role differentiation, and a high value on control of consciousness. Effervescence implies diffused symbols, weak rituals, and a preference for spontaneity. It places no value on control of consciousness.

In various ways, then, Douglas continually tries to express the spectrum of noncontrol and control:

Noncontrol	Control
Informality	Formality
Shaggy	Smooth
Unstructure	Structure
Effervescence	Ritualism
Weak Group	*Strong Group*

She cautiously states her hypothesis about trance and spirit possession: "We tend to find trance-like states feared as dangerous where the social dimension is highly structured, but welcomed and even deliberately induced where this is not the case."[13] She continues, "The prediction is that, as trance is a form of dissociation, it will be more approved and welcomed the weaker the structuring of society."[14] Herein lies the importance of Douglas's model, namely, in its assertion that attitudes to spirit and spirit possession reflect cultural attitudes and structures. This means that the study of spirit in the Fourth Gospel need not be predetermined by the ideology of the inquirer (I approve of this; I don't like that), but can be conducted within the context of the social systems reflected. Under what social conditions is spirit possession viewed positively or negatively? What type of social structure is expressed when spirit possession is viewed as benign or dangerous?

Spirit and Body

We need to recall from the previous chapter Douglas's remarks about the symbolic and social meanings of spirit and matter (or body), which are essential components for a full model of how spirit is perceived. As an anthropologist, Douglas does not take for granted the linguistic phenomenon that spirit is often understood in terms of its relationship with matter (or mind with body).[15] One of Douglas's great contributions is her ever-deepening appreciation of the articulation of the physical body as a cultural product. Quoting the essay of Marcel Mauss,[16] she affirms his thesis that "there is no such thing as natural behavior" in

178

regard to the physical body. Bodily movement and bodily control are transmitted by a social process of learning. And so bodily technique can and should be studied in the context of a study of symbolic systems; it is an index of what she means by the group variable. If spirit is perceived to be in tension with body, either superior to it or embedded in it, it can be studied vis-à-vis the way the body,[17] flesh, or matter are symbolically understood. The reader is referred back to Douglas's remarks in chapter 6 on the relative control exercised over the body by social groups; for there should be a correlation between the relative control of the physical body and appreciation of spirit.

In addition, we recall Douglas's observations on the possible relationships of spirit to flesh and mind to body. "If," as she contends, "they [spirit and flesh] are used to discriminate contended positions, they are also likely to express something about the social situation."[18] So if a social unit emphatically distinguishes itself from others on the basis of spirit against flesh, we are advised to pay attention to these remarks as important clues of the social location of the group being studied.

Douglas's hypothesis can be more precisely stated: "The relation of spirit to matter or mind to body can be interpreted as exchanges of condensed statements about the relation of society to the individual."[19] The body or flesh represents society; the mind or spirit represents the individual. Turning to the relative emphasis that could be put on either one or the other, Douglas states that insistence on the superiority of spiritual over material elements implies an insistence on the liberties of the individual as well as a program for freeing the individual from social constraints. Alternatively, the contrary view that spirit works through matter, that spiritual values are effective through material acts, that spirit and matter mingle, implies that an individual is by nature subordinate to society and its structures.[20]

According to her basic model, then, spirit may be perceived in weak group or strong group situations. For example, she sees that a movement to exalt spirit over matter will lead one to adopt an attitude of detachment from or revolt against established social forms (weak group).[21] Thus, Douglas clearly enunciates her hypothesis:

> If a scale can be established to assess the diminution from strong to weak social control, there will be a corresponding relaxation of bodily control in forms of expression. This predicts a general tendency to

179

give up ritualism in favour of ecstatic forms as social control diminishes. Second I will argue that within any one social system, people who are relatively more withdrawn from institutional forms of control will not only conform to this trend by choosing against ritualist forms, but intellectually they will also adopt a spirit/matter dichotomy.[22]

We may gather together the argument of this second part of Douglas's model as follows:

Noncontrol	Control
Spirit	Body
Individual is superior to group	Society is dominant over individuals
Freedom unrestrained	Freedom contextualized
Behavior is effervescent and spontaneous	Behavior is strongly ritualistic
Weak Group	Strong Group

ANTHROPOLOGICAL MODEL OF SPIRIT

Douglas's basic group/grid model provides an excellent vehicle for sorting out the diverse perceptions of spirit we have just surveyed. Douglas's model, moreover, is sufficiently flexible to allow us to adapt it to New Testament purposes by contextualizing the perception of spirit in relationship to three specific items, that is, the relationship of spirit to (1) time orientation, (2) norms, and (3) matter, as figure 5 (pp. 182–83) indicates.

Spirit as Dangerous

In general, one's social world in a strong group/high grid situation is highly structured and strongly controlled. Personality is dyadic, that is, one's identity derives from being a member of a particular family, clan, or village. Correspondingly, there will be strong pressure to conform to the group's values, structures, and classifications. Great value tends to be placed on formal rules that organize and maintain this orderly society; and ritual responses are fixed and pervasive. It is hardly surprising, then, that spirit in this cultural script will be incorporated into the system and restrained by norms consonant with the system.

Specifically, in a strongly structured social world, spirit is perceived as follows: Nature: Inasmuch as spirit suggests revolt, freedom, or newness, it is perceived in strong group cultures as dangerous, and must be either ritually controlled or limited to a group of experts. Normed: Because spirit betokens revolt or freedom, it must be normed, but by what? Time Orientation: Spirit will be normed by the past—by the group's history, traditions, rituals, and so forth. Spirit acts to remind this group of its noble past and can be measured according to that past.

Spirit and Matter: When we ask about norms for spirit, we are in fact asking about the relationship of spirit to matter, where matter represents the system that structures society in all its particularity. Spirit here will be in or with matter. Because it is inherently dangerous, spirit must be restricted to specific experts or controlled in rites or sacraments, therefore, in a context of limits and controls. Spirit-in-matter, then, functions as a code phrase proclaiming that individuals by nature are subordinate to society and find their freedom in its forms.

Spirit as Ambiguous

The dominant structure of society in a strong group/low grid situation is now being challenged by reform. One strategy here is to attack what the reformers call the formalism or legalism of the dominant system, which is strong group/high grid. Because it is construed as a validating source of reform, spirit may be genuinely helpful toward reform under the guise of spirit confronting matter (i.e., the system); for spirit betokens reformed, inner states, as opposed to decadent, outer activity. Nature: Spirit, then, may be helpful, but in all cases it is ambiguous. Ambiguity reigns here: outer does not match inner, for behavior is no sure index of what is in the heart; and it is painfully difficult to know how to evaluate the proposed reform. One even senses here that the world has become a place threatened by warring forces of evil and good. This dualistic cosmos is perceived as a battlefield, with evil spirits attempting to seduce or deceive individuals and groups. Spirit, then, is ambiguous; for, in this context, appearances are deceptive and evil tends to be disguised as good.

Normed: One must test the spirits, which means an appeal to some norm or legitimating criterion. Spirit here will be normed by matter (i.e., criteria for testing spirits), but in considerable tension with it, as the substance of the criteria for testing spirits is itself

FIGURE 5
SPIRIT IN ANTHROPOLOGICAL PERSPECTIVE

Spirit in weak GROUP / high GRID

1. *Description:* Spirit is
   a) by nature: not dangerous
   b) time orientation: in service of the present with a view to the future
   c) normed: normed only by the individual's pragmatic choice
   d) freedom: spirit frees the individual for his/her pragmatic choices (freedom from obstacles, for choice)
   e) persons: not restricted to experts, but accessible to all

2. *Spirit and Matter:* Spirit is basically above matter, but may take diverse relationships to matters, according to the pragmatic choices of individuals. Spirit may be found
   a) in individually chosen rites, norms, classifications
   b) in any forms that serve individual self-realization

3. *Strategy:* because of pragmatic individualism, spirit possession is an individual choice which could mean controlled spirit or free spirit, depending on an individual's pragmatic choice

4. *Function:* spirit-above-matter implies that individuals are superior to society, but may choose to fit into its forms by voluntary association

---

Spirit in weak GROUP / low GRID

1. *Description:* Spirit is
   a) by nature: approved, welcome
   b) time orientation: in service of the future
   c) normed: emphatically unnormed
   d) freedom: spirit frees individual from former corrupt system and is basis of constant new individualized choices
   e) persons: accessible to all individuals

2. *Spirit and Matter:* Spirit is against matter, enemy of it, superior to it and completely unnormed by it; spirit is found
   a) in personal, unmediated experience of God and grace
   b) in prophecy, whose fulfillment lies in the future
   c) in revolt against tradition, structure

3. *Strategy:* because of strong individualism and its challenge to former structures, spirit is positively valued, sought after, manipulated

4. *Function:* spirit-against-matter supports the liberties of individuals and points to a program for freeing them from social constraints

FIGURE 5
SPIRIT IN ANTHROPOLOGICAL PERSPECTIVE

Spirit in strong GROUP / high GRID

1. *Description:* Spirit is
   a) by nature: dangerous
   b) time orientation: in service of past
   c) normed: restrained and tightly controlled
   d) freedom: spirit frees so that common good might be served
   e) persons: either tightly controlled or limited to a group of experts

2. *Spirit and Matter:* Spirit must be in or with matter
   a) in sacraments, localized in fixed sacred space
   b) in service of ascribed, traditional leadership
   c) in service of interpreting history and tradition, as well as normed by them

3. *Strategy:* because of the strength of the system, an uncontrolled spirit is not allowed, but is either controlled or limited to a group of experts

4. *Function:* spirit-in-matter implies that individuals are by nature subordinate to society and find their freedom in its forms

---

Spirit in strong GROUP / low GRID

1. *Description:* Spirit is
   a) by nature: ambiguous (dangerous or necessary)
   b) time orientation: attending to the past with a view toward legitimating the present
   c) normed: in principle relatively unnormed as reform challenges the system, but normed when competing spirits need to be tested
   d) freedom: spirit (of reform) is superior to matter in need of reform, and so represents freedom from old system, but freedom for new reformed system
   e) persons: in challenge situations, not limited to experts; but when spirits need to be tested, limited to experts

2. *Spirit and Matter:* Spirit is in tension with matter, either in challenge to formalism or in situations of ambiguity where external appearances do not match inner reality. Spirit occurs
   a) in service of alternative leadership
   b) in new rites which challenge old ones
   c) as an interior phenomenon, which is valued over external rites, actions, classifications
   d) hidden in tradition, waiting to be liberated

3. *Strategy:* because of the threat of deception, spirits may be good or bad, and so must be tested; and because of the challenge made to the system, spirit may represent reform and newness vis-à-vis the formalism of STRONG GROUP/HIGH GRID, and so be helpful

4. *Function:* spirit-in-tension-with-matter implies that, while individuals are subordinate to society, they are challenging parts of it to find more satisfying forms

hotly disputed. The reformers and those they would reform will surely disagree on criteria to test the spirit of reform.

Time Orientation: Reform of the system, which is a common aim here, means a return in the future to a state that recovers the best of the past. And so the spirit is normed in part by the past, but only by those aspects of the past that challenge what stands in need of reform. Spirit serves as the agent of the present in continuity with the best of its past.

Spirit and Matter: Spirit remains in matter, but in conflict with it or with the system in need of reform. Critical of the old system (matter), reformers claim legitimation via spirit, inherently suggesting a dualism of spirit in conflict with matter. When challenged or tested, spirit (even the spirit of the reformers) is normed by some matter, some criterion, but always a criterion that is conflictive and controversial. But normed it must be! Spirit must be in matter, but remains in tension with it.

Spirit as Neutral

In this pragmatic world of weak group/high grid, individualism dominates, which means that individual members of family, clan, or nation prize their ability to choose and decide for themselves on issues of structure, ritual, identity, morality, and so forth.[23] Nature: Spirit is a neutral value here; it may be pragmatically useful (and so, welcomed) or perceived as undesirable (and so, not chosen). Normed: But no norms exist for assessing whether spirit is dangerous or not, only the pragmatic choices of individuals. Time Orientation: Depending on individual decisions, the traditions of the past may or may not be normative here, and so spirit does not necessarily look to the past. Rather, spirit is in service of the present, the current condition of the individual, with a view to the future. Spirit and Matter: Spirit is basically above matter, norms, and societal structures, corresponding to the individual's freedom from societal control. If spirit is seen to be in matter here, this is due to the individual choice to be so, not because of any constraint from the social group.

Spirit as Welcome

At this point, individualism waxes strongest. Here, in a situation of weak group/low grid, is a posture of revolt against (not reform of) former structures, rituals, norms, and so forth. Nature: Spirit, which symbolizes this revolt against matter (i.e., the old system which is rejected), is welcomed and manipulated. Normed: In this cosmos of radical individualism and revolt, spirit could never be normed or controlled, as it is the symbolic expression of protest and newness against all former norms, structures, and the like.

Time Orientation: Inasmuch as this is a cosmos in revolt against the past—its system, structures, rituals, and so forth—it looks radically to the future, to the ever-unfolding, limitless newness which can never be normed or circumscribed by the past. As the agent of freedom and ground of the future, spirit can never be normed by the past, but stands against the past as something inferior to be discarded. Spirit and Matter: Spirit is not simply above matter, but superior to it and enemy of it, since matter means structure, control, and society.

Spirit, then, is hardly a static concept or phenomenon. For, as the foregoing model suggests, spirit is perceived in quite diverse ways and can stand as a symbol of diverse cosmologies. The model of spirit established in the first half of this study, moreover, can serve as a reliable way of sorting out the varying perceptions of it in the Fourth Gospel, and so aid us in seeing if there is any correlation or replication of attitudes to spirit and Christology in that document.

As we turn to the Fourth Gospel, we are reminded that like other phenomena such as signs, leadership, rites, and so on, spirit was not statically perceived by the Johannine Christians. It changed in meaning and function in the stages of its development. My hypothesis on the application of this anthropological model to the Fourth Gospel is that there are three quite different perceptions of spirit in the Fourth Gospel, which may be accurately labeled according to Douglas's map of societies as:

Stage One:	Strong group/low grid (spirit in tension with matter)
Stage Two:	Strong group/rising grid (spirits in conflict)
Stage Three:	Weak group/low grid (spirit against matter)

THE MODEL AND JOHANNINE SPIRIT STATEMENTS

Compared with Luke-Acts or the Pauline literature, we find relatively few references to spirit in the Fourth Gospel. I propose to use the Douglas model developed above as a more precise, testable, and useful device to aid us in sorting out the spirit statements in the Fourth Gospel according to their social strategy and function. On the basis of the model, I will plot out the various spirit statements according to Douglas's variables of group and grid, yielding the summary found in Figure 6, and explained below.

Stage One: Spirit in Tension with Matter

In stage one, at the very beginning of this Gospel's narrative, Jesus is intimately linked with spirit in his legitimation as God's new leader. According to the canons of his world, Jesus' formal credentials for leadership are scant: he does not have schooling ("How is it this man has learning, when he has never studied?" 7:15), nor, according to John, is he of Davidic origin (7:41–42; cf. Matt. 1:1–17; 2:1–6), and he certainly is not of priestly stock. The descent of God's spirit, then, legitimates Jesus, "that he might be revealed to Israel" (1:31) and that he may be acclaimed "the Son of God" (1:34). This implies a reforming function for spirit, legitimating Jesus apart from and in opposition to the structures of his society.

Nature. According to strong group/high grid societies, spirit would be linked with the legitimate, ascribed leaders of the social group, its priests, kings, nobles, and so forth. In such settings, spirit tends to be bestowed in measure, as it is apportioned to a hierarchical array of roles and offices (see, e.g., 1 Cor. 12:27–30; Eph. 4:11–12).[24] Inasmuch as this Gospel presents Jesus challenging the ascribed leadership of his day, spirit is depicted as coming upon Jesus in an unmeasured way: "For he whom God sent utters the words of God, for it is not by measure that he gives the Spirit" (3:34). The spirit, moreover, "remained" on Jesus (1:32–33), suggesting that his empowerment was not a temporary phenomenon, but a permanent character trait. Furthermore, during his earthly life, Jesus does not share this authority with the disciples and so spirit is not measured and apportioned out to roles such as apostles or prophets among his followers, until Jesus' death (7:37–39; 19:31–34) and his resurrection (20:22). Jesus remains the sole source of spirit to his followers. In summary, Jesus' own legitimation in competition with the ascribed leaders of his day may be expressed as spirit in tension with matter, where spirit stands for reform and matter for the system that is challenged, especially the traditional norms of legitimating leaders.

FIGURE 6

SPIRIT IN THE FOURTH GOSPEL

GRID
high

weak
GROUP

strong
GROUP

STAGE TWO: Spirit Disguised in
Matter

Positive Spirit
1. reformed rites, cult, etc. (3:5;
   4:23–24; 7:37–39; 20:22)

Negative Spirit
1. deceptive spirits (6:70; 13:27–
   29)
2. spirits at war (7:20; 8:48;
   10:20)
3. testing spirits (7:20; 10:19–20)

STAGE THREE: Spirit against
Matter

1. a dichotomized world (6:63;
   8:23; 3:6, 12)
2. spirit in revolt against world
   (16:7–11)
3. giver of new, unnormed wisdom (14:26b; 16:12–13)

STAGE ONE: Spirit in Tension
with Matter

1. legitimation of reformer (1:31–
   34)
2. recoverer of past, hidden
   meanings (14:26a; 15:26;
   16:14)

low
GRID

187

Time Orientation. As spirit is linked with Jesus in terms of legitimation, so it is linked with a time orientation in the Johannine propaganda about Jesus. Early disciples argue on Jesus' behalf from the Scriptures that he is the one "of whom Moses wrote and also the prophets" (1:45). Yet the Scriptures are hardly self-evident on this point (see 7:26–27, 42, 52); and so what is needed is a special power enabling one to perceive the hidden, inner meaning. Spirit allows insiders to grasp the past truth, hidden in the words of God, which remains impervious to outsiders.[25] In a way, everything in the Johannine cosmos remains opaque, even Jesus' own words and deeds, which his disciples consistently find difficult to interpret correctly. Hence, Jesus empowers them to recall his past words and gain their hidden, inner truth: "The Counselor, the Holy Spirit . . . he will bring to your remembrance all that I have said to you" (14:26; see 2:22), and "When the Counselor comes, whom I will send to you from the Father, even the Spirit of Truth, he will bear witness to me" (15:26). In view of the relationship of spirit to time, then, spirit serves the past with a view to the future. For it recovers from the ideal past the hidden, perhaps lost, meaning of both Scripture and Jesus' words, and makes this available to future generations.

Normed. The spirit Jesus promises is normed in the sense that it is sent by Jesus to serve Jesus, and so can be measured by the words and deeds of the earthly Jesus,[26] a point tied to the interpretation of "another Paraclete" in 14:16. This passage has been a perennial *crux interpretum.*[27] Raymond Brown's suggestion that the spirit in John 14–16 parallels Jesus is not only a wise interpretation of 14:16 but has bearing on the present discussion of spirit normed or measured by Jesus. Brown pointed out that in the Fourth Gospel we find parallel descriptions of movements of Jesus and the Spirit (identical *comings* into the world, *sendings* from the Father, and *being given* by God). Also parallel are the identities of Jesus and the Spirit: if the Paraclete is the Spirit of Truth, Jesus is truth itself; if the Paraclete is the Holy Spirit, Jesus is the Holy One of God. Still parallel is the relationship of the disciples to Jesus and the Spirit (they will *know* him, as they *know* Jesus; he will *dwell* in them as Jesus makes his *dwelling* in them; he will *teach* them, as Jesus *taught* them and *guided* them along the *way,* as Jesus is the *way*).[28] According to this data, the spirit is normed by the pattern of Jesus and his relationship with the disciples. Spirit, then, is normed; it does not go beyond Jesus, a pattern we shall shortly notice to be contradicted by other data on the spirit in the

Fourth Gospel. The spirit, then, is a bridge of continuity, linking the earthly Jesus, whose deeds and words have lasting, normative value, with the contemporary Jesus, who is still the Lord of this covenant group. The spirit is Jesus' agent and servant, normed by him.

Spirit and Matter. Spirit, however, remains a basically ambiguous phenomenon in this social context. This ambiguity allows Jesus' enemies and rivals to contest his claims and those of his followers. Jesus' spiritual legitimacy is regularly challenged by synagogue leaders who argue that he cannot have a good spirit, for he violates the Sabbath (5:16; 7:23; 9:16). Christian propaganda is likewise challenged, for the Scriptures clearly say that the Christ must be descended from David and come from Bethlehem (7:42), which would clearly disqualify Jesus' claims. And so, in terms of certain matter (i.e., cultural norms), Jesus' spirit fails and is negatively judged. Johannine Christians, of course, would object to their spirit being normed by this matter (see 9:30–33), even as they would protest to a literal interpretation of Jesus' words and claims. They dismiss all such rebuttals by the synagogue with the explanation that the world is made up of two classes, spirit and flesh: Jesus and his followers represent true spirit, whereas their opponents correspond to flesh. And because they are spirit, it is ridiculous to suppose that they could be normed by matter. "What is born of flesh is flesh; and what is born of spirit is spirit. . . . If I have told you earthly things and you do not believe, how can you believe if I tell you heavenly things?" (3:6, 12). Claims of legitimacy, then, rest on having spirit, but these claims remain ambiguous and hotly contested in their world, for no common norms or criteria exist for norming Jesus' spirit. In this context, spirit remains in great tension with matter.

In summary, in stage one of Johannine history (strong group/low grid), Jesus and spirit are linked in terms of reform and challenge to the system (i.e., matter) under the rubric of his legitimation for leadership and his propaganda from the Scriptures. The focus is on Israel's ideal past with a view to its reformed future. Yet spirit remains ambiguous, for it is useful in challenging the old system in need of reform, but remains constantly subject to scrutiny and testing by the old system. While it resists being normed by the old system, it is internally normed in the Johannine circle by the memory and deeds of Jesus, who is the sole authentic possessor and dispenser of spirit.

Stage Two: Spirits in Conflict

Stage two is characterized by an intensification of claims and challenges, hence the description of this stage as rising grid. In this stage we discover that spirit functions in two different but complementary ways: positively as the legitimation of new rites that replace the old ones, and negatively as the alleged demon who possesses people.

Positive Spirit The Johannine Jesus intensifies his program of reform by urging the replacement[29] of obsolete and inadequate rites with new cultic objects, feasts, and so forth, whose legitimacy lies precisely in the spirit they have. It is one thing to claim that Jesus fulfills the Scriptures, but quite another to claim that he invalidates all former rituals, feasts, cultic objects, and so forth, replacing those obsolete and ineffective things with himself. The intensity of these new claims (rising grid) drew an equally intense reaction.

The Fourth Gospel presents a systematic Christian claim that in Jesus all former rites, cult objects, places of worship, feasts, and so forth, are replaced by reformed ones that have spirit or that facilitate worship in spirit. The list would include:

1. Purificatory fluids (2:1–11; 7:37–39; 19:34)
2. Place of worship (2:13–22; 4:19–24)
3. Feasts (2:13; 5:1; 6:4; 7:2; 10:22); and cultic objects associated with feasts, such as Passover manna (6:31–59) or lamb (19:32–37), as well as the objects prayed for at feasts, such as rain (7:37–39) and sunlight (8:12) at Tabernacles
4. Rites (3:1–12)

These objects are true or authentic, which in the context implies that the synagogue cult, feasts, and so forth are obsolete and imperfect. Thus Christian claims of replacement should be seen as a more intensified claim of reform, which is the shibboleth of strong group/low grid.

Nature. In this replacement mode, spirit may be positively helpful in a reform agenda, even as it is ambiguous and contested. Christian claims that Jesus is the replacement of Jewish cult and piety rest on assertions that what Jesus offers as a replacement is better than the old materials precisely because Jesus' have spirit. For example, instead of covenant membership through circumcision, true entrance into God's kingdom comes through baptism, which is birth

190

by water and spirit (3:5). While circumcision is merely a material rite, the Christian initiatory rite is legitimated because it has and gives spirit. Instead of this or that mountain as the locus of God's presence, Jesus' risen body becomes the new temple, for "true worshipers must worship in spirit and truth," since God is spirit (4:23–24). Any material temple building, either in Samaria or Jerusalem, is simply inadequate to localize the deity and serve as an official place to worship God, who is spirit. By nature, then, spirit may be positively evaluated, but it remains in conflict with matter, and so ambiguous.

Time, norming. The claims of replacement look back to the past in that the great moments (feasts), great objects (manna, rain, light), and great places (temple) are elements of Israel's history. They are things of the past which are not to be discarded for they retain a future value, but not in their present form, which is considered ineffectual and unauthentic. Yet these past objects are normative for the way any true Israelite would think about covenant relationship with Israel's God. The past, then, serves as a norm for the present, and therefore for the correct localization of spirit.

Spirit and Matter. Even as Christians claim that their reformed rites are superior to those of the synagogue because they have spirit, these claims imply that spirit is still found in matter. Yet even if found in matter, spirit remains in considerable tension with it. Although not found in old matter (i.e., the old system of rites, places, feasts, etc.), it is found in new matter (i.e., the new Christian system of rites, places, feasts, etc.), and so, in some sense, is normed by this new matter. But Christian claims to have spiritual rites are open to dispute by the synagogue. For according to it, the authenticity of its own circumcision ritual and of the system centered around the Jerusalem temple rests on God's will expressed in the Scriptures, an indication that Christian spirit, when measured and tested by scriptural matter, would appear to the synagogue as false spirit. Christians point to the superior results of their spirit rites (3:3, 5; 4:13–14; 6:49–50, 58; 7:37–39) as the matter or norm according to which their spirit is authentic. But in either case, some matter or criterion is urged as a norm for testing spirit. In this stage of development, then, spirit is necessarily in matter, but in conflict with it. There is no agreement on what constitutes the valid matter for norming spirit.

According to the narrative of the Fourth Gospel, at an early stage of the community's history the followers of Jesus heralded him to others in missionary speeches and propaganda, a posture in which the Johannine group looked outwardly and benignly at the world. But this same narrative describes a time of intense conflict, which apparently developed as a result of Christian preaching and claims. The Johannine followers of Jesus looked to their flanks, which were under severe attack, effectively turning from missionary discourse to forensic defense of Jesus and the Christian claims about him. On the literary level, this represents a shift from missionary to forensic discourse; on the level of social dynamics, this represents a shift from modest claims about Jesus (prophet, Son of God, even king) to exalted claims (greater than Jacob, greater than Abraham). In Douglas's terms, this represents a shift in grid, which rises in proportion to intensified claims.

The intensified christological claims are found primarily in the competing claims of Jesus in comparison to other leaders. Jesus is not merely the one of whom Moses wrote and the prophets, but the one who is "greater than Jacob" (4:12) and "greater than Abraham" (8:53). When fully assessed, such claims imply that Jesus has replaced all of Israel's patriarchs and prophets, all of its foundational figures, even Moses (1:17; 3:13).

Negative Spirit These claims, however, are dealt with in the narrative in terms of spirit, as Jesus, his disciples, and the Jews categorize each other in terms of the good or bad spirit they possess. As we saw above in regard to stage one, strong group/weak grid describes a world that is fundamentally ambiguous, where truth lies hidden and where evil masquerades as good, a cosmos of deceptive and disguised spirits. That perception continues in stage two. It matters little whether we describe how Christians view outsiders or how the synagogue views Christians—this is a world of cosmic deception by disguised demons. In this regard we note two aspects of this phenomenon as it relates to spirit. First, it is important to notice the frequent mutual accusations that Jesus or his enemies have evil spirits or demons, as the following list indicates:

1. Jesus is accused of demon possession: 7:20; 8:48, 52; 10:19–21
2. Jesus accuses others of demon possession: 8:44
3. Jesus accuses Judas of demon possession: 6:70 (see also 13:2, 27)
4. This world is demon possessed: 12:31; 14:30; 16:11; 17:15

Second, given the perception of a cosmos peopled with disguised evil spirits, some matter or norm is needed to test spirits or to read hearts, so as to discern good and evil spirits within people (see 1 John 4:1–3).

Nature. To say the very least, in this situation spirit is highly ambiguous, life-threatening, and in intense conflict. And this is true from the perspective of the accused as well as that of the accuser. Regarding the accusation of having an evil spirit,[30] from a Christian point of view we learn that Judas, who in the eyes of the world appears to be Jesus' chosen disciple, is in fact an evil spirit: "Did I not choose you, the twelve, and one of you is a devil" (6:70). Judas eats at Jesus' table, a sign of ideological unity, but in fact he is plotting Jesus' betrayal. Even Judas's departure to work his harm is ambiguously understood by onlookers. Jesus, who is adept at reading hearts, knows of his possession by Satan and tells him, "What you are going to do, do quickly" (13:27). But to all intents and purposes, it appeared to others that "Jesus was telling him 'Buy what we need for the feast' or that he should give something to the poor" (13:29). People, however, are not what they seem, for Judas went out to work Jesus' arrest and death, precisely as an agent of Satan. Evil spirits can be disguised as good.

From the synagogue's point of view, Jesus himself is a demon in disguise. Although Jesus claims to seek God's glory, he does not keep the Sabbath, and so the synagogue judges him to be a deceiving demon (7:20). Jesus claims to reveal God's revelation, but the crux of his revelation in John 8 is a condemnation of the Jews who judge him to be a Samaritan, a pseudocovenant member who has a demon (8:48). Despite all of Jesus' claims to be the authentic and noble shepherd, elements of his audience see only lies in his words and so conclude that "he has a demon" (10:20). What you see is not what you get! Things are not what they appear to be! In this social location, spirit is in increasing conflict with matter, because matter (or external norms, tradition, or the system) proves ambiguous. Evil spirits appear and claim to be orthodox, but they are really disguised to conceal their true nature. Spirits are confused and spectators cannot easily tell who is who.

Spirits, moreover, are at war. Satan is attacking Jesus through the agency of Judas,[31] and only death and destruction will settle the issue. For his part, Jesus sees Satan's offspring doing what their father did, that is, murder: "He was a murderer from the beginning" (8:44), which is the hidden meaning of their repeated seeking of Jesus.[32]

Jesus sees the "ruler of the world" (12:31; 16:11) attacking his disciples (17:15) and so sends a forensic expert, the good spirit, to prosecute him (16:7–11). This, then, is a dualistic cosmos of warring spirits of good and evil. Spirits are not only confused but engaged in intense, mortal conflict.

Normed.   What is needed, then, is a testing of spirits, a way of norming them by some matter to see whether they are good or bad. Synagogue Jews test Jesus' spirit, either according to the norms of their tradition and so find him wanting, or according to the new credentials of his power and so approve him. But they put Jesus to the test.

There was a division among the Jews because of these words: "Many of them said 'He has a demon; he is mad; why listen to him?' Others said, 'These are not the sayings of one who has a demon. Can a demon open they eyes of the blind?'" (10:19–21). This testing of spirits echoes the conversation between the Pharisees and the formerly blind man. Certain Jews judge Jesus according to their tradition and dismiss him as a sinner: "This man is not from God, for he does not keep the Sabbath" (9:16; see v. 25). The cured man and others, however, test Jesus' spirit according to the measure of the great healing miracle and acclaim him "a prophet" (9:17): "If this man were not from God he could do nothing" (9:33; see 10:20). The Jews, therefore, measure the spirit of Jesus against some material norm, whether Sabbath observance or healing miracles.

For his part, Jesus tests the spirits of would-be followers. In the course of the forensic examination in 8:31–46, Jesus is able to discern that his hearers, who publicly claim to be sons of Abraham as well as sons of God, are offspring neither of the patriarch nor of God, but are sons of the devil. First, all claims to the contrary, they are proved not to be Abraham's descendants because, when tested, (1) they are not free, (2) they do not remain in the house, (3) nor do they do what their father did (8:32–41). Second, when their claims to be God's children are tested, they are exposed here also, for "if God were your Father, you would love me, for I proceeded and came forth from God" (8:42). Rather, Jesus shows that "you are of your father the devil" (8:44a); for their desire is to do their father's will, namely, murder and lying (8:44b). Jesus measures their spirit by certain criteria of his own and exposes a deceiving, evil spirit. Again, the spirit is measured in some way by matter.

194

Time. People in this cosmos look to the past for guidance and norms for the present. In this stage, what counts is the ability of someone to know what was going on from the beginning, that is, the ability not to be deceived by present disguises, but to have known all along what was what. The past, then, is normative for the present. For example, in this world of masquerade, one would expect to find certain persons skilled in penetrating disguises, in short, capable of reading human hearts. This reader of hearts, moreover, presumably has norms and criteria with which to measure and discern true and false spirits. Spirit is again in some sense normed by matter, although one expects a continual conflict over valid norms. It is no accident that Jesus is credited with this skill to a high degree. For example, after an apparently successful first visit to Jerusalem, many are said to believe in Jesus (2:23), yet he "does not trust himself to them, because he knew all men" (2:24–25).

Most important, he can read hearts, and he knows who is truly his disciple and who is not.[33] This same Jesus earlier read Nathanael's heart and so perceived that, despite Nathanael's arguments about "any good coming from Nazareth," he is "a true Israelite, in whom there is no guile" (1:47), that is, his interior spirit was good. Jesus, moreover, knew this from the beginning. One of the clearest demonstrations of Jesus' ability to read hearts comes in the context of the bread of life discourse. At the beginning, Jesus knows that those who are seeking him do so not because they believe in him, but because they have eaten their fill of his bread (6:26). From the beginning, then, Jesus knows what is in the (disguised) heart. And at the end of the discourse, when Jesus lets the dropouts depart, the editor remarks about Jesus' ability to read hearts, "For he knew *from the first* who those were that did not believe, and who it was that would betray him" (6:64). Turning to his supposed loyal disciples, he reads the heart of the traitor, proving that he is not fooled by his masquerade: "One of you is a devil" (6:70). Long before Judas plotted his treachery, Jesus was credited with knowing "from the beginning" the truth about him. Jesus, then, can test spirits, discern the human heart, and penetrate the masquerade around him. He has norms for measuring spirits,[34] norms that come from the past.

In summary, the issue in stage two is still reform, but in a more radical form of intensified claims (greater than . . .) and intensified challenges (you have a demon). The argument, moreover, remains the relationship of Jesus and spirit, but in this case which spirit, God's or Satan's? All spirit claims are subjected to testing, which means being measured by some norm. But what norm? What criteria? In this ambiguous world, matter must somehow provide norms for spirit, but the normative matter is itself hotly contested in this cosmos of hidden truth and disguised evil. Finally, we note that this spirit/matter conflict still occurs in the context of the system of the synagogue and authentic Judaism; the strategy is still its reform, not revolt from it.

Stage Three: Spirit against Matter

Stage three describes the period in the Johannine community after the followers of Jesus were excommunicated by the synagogue and after apostates dropped out of the group or showed inadequate faith. Authentic Johannine Christians stood alone in a hostile, obtuse world, not so much alienated from their surroundings as in an attitude of superiority to them. They are no longer seeking to reform obsolete synagogue rites or to inspire other Christians with their true doctrines; they are in revolt against the world, which is hopelessly blind and evil (weak group/low grid).[35]

The shift in perspective here can be grasped by recalling from the previous chapter the way in which the world is evaluated in the Fourth Gospel. At an earlier time, this world was perceived as a place worthy of God's salvific concern, as God "so loved the world that he sent his only Son" (3:16). Jesus, who is the replacement of Jewish cultic feasts and objects of prayer, proclaims himself as "the light of the world" (8:12) who desires to enlighten and benefit those in the world. Yet as the crisis deepened and the church became increasingly involved in conflict and hostility with the synagogue, culminating in its excommunication (9:22; 12:42; 16:1–2), the world came to be viewed as a place of evil (12:31), a hopelessly obtuse world (8:23) which hates Jesus and his followers (15:18–25). Jesus then becomes eager to leave this world (17:13), after which the Spirit will come to conduct a forensic proceeding against it (16:8–11). At the very least, Jesus and his Johannine followers stand apart from and against "the world." They are no longer engaged in reforming it, but are in revolt against it, even putting it on trial.

Given this new development, we are not surprised that the perception of spirit, Holy Spirit, and Spirit of Truth appears distinctively different in this weak group situation. If spirit in strong group was characterized as (1) past-oriented, (2) normed, (3) in matter, even if in tension with it, and (4) ambiguous or dangerous, that is not the case

196

in this weak group situation. Here spirit is (1) future-oriented, (2) radically unnormed, (3) superior to matter, and (4) welcome.

Nature. According to our model, we would expect that spirit (and what spirit symbolizes) would be valued above and against matter (and what matter symbolizes). This seems to be verified by certain texts in the Fourth Gospel that, while not always expressing this idea in terms of spirit, nevertheless convey it quite clearly. At this point, I suggest that we examine how aspects of the high Christology of this Gospel came to function as just such a value statement that spirit stands above and against matter. I have argued elsewhere[36] that at a certain point in the history of the Fourth Gospel community, the high christological confession of Jesus in 6:62–63 and 8:23–24 came to reflect the same tensions and polarities symbolized by the current discussion of spirit.[37] In terms of 6:62–63, even as Jesus is rejected on earth, he finds vindication in heaven. The heavenly figure who descends to earth, when he finds only hopeless obtuseness here below, cuts short criticism of himself on earth by exclaiming, "What if you were to see the Son of man ascending to where he was before?" (6:62). This implies that he experiences acceptance and worth in heaven, not here. This statement of high Christology is then joined with a remark about cosmology, the location of value and worthlessness in the cosmos: "The spirit alone gives life, the flesh is of no avail" (6:63). In 6:62, Jesus proclaims himself to be a heavenly figure whose home is in heaven, where his value is acknowledged. The earth, in contrast, is not his home, not a hospitable place, nor enlightened, and so is completely worthless. These remarks about heaven and earth are then replicated in the remarks about spirit and flesh. Earth, obviously the place of flesh, is a place of total worthlessness (no avail), while heaven, the locus of spirit (see 3:6–7, 12), contains all value.

Likewise, in 8:23–24 we have a comparable juxtaposition of Christology and cosmology. Jesus unqualifiedly declares that he is heavenly ("I am from above . . . not of this world"), but that his audience is earthly ("you are from below . . . of this world"). In the context of the Fourth Gospel, Jesus' remark functions as a sharp condemnation of his audience, for it means that they have *nothing* in common with him. What would it mean for them to join his world? "Unless you believe that 'I AM,' you will die in your sins" (8:24). That is, were they to confess the high christological confession of authentic Johannine Christians, then they would share Jesus' world;

they too would then be "from above . . . not of this world." The importance of these two texts lies in the sense communicated by them that what is below, this world of matter and flesh, is of no avail. On the contrary, all value is found in what is heavenly, spiritual, and from above.

The very Christology replicates the perspective of spirit in weak group/low grid. Spirit is against and above matter. Thus, although 6:62–63 and 8:23–24 sound like typical dualistic remarks in the Fourth Gospel, they are qualitatively different. Recalling the data presented in figure 4 (p. 157), we note that dualisms have always been a part of the Johannine landscape, functioning usually in an ideology of reform. What Jesus is, says, and does is true or authentic, in contradistinction to what the synagogue is, says, and does. Jesus is the authentic teacher of Israel, not Nicodemus; Jesus has God's word, not the word of a mere man, such as Moses; his rites of initiation are superior to those of circumcision. Dualisms function to distinguish the Johannine Jesus and his followers as true insiders from the synagogue and all others, who are outsiders. But in 6:62–63 and 8:23–24, the dualisms take on a new quality—not reform of the synagogue nor of this world, but revolt against them. In those remarks, any value whatever is denied to all things of earth, matter, and flesh, which must include even Christian rites as well, a point Brown makes regarding the position of the secessionists in 1 John 4:3; 5:6–8.[38] In context, the flesh that is of no avail would seem to apply to the point of debate between Jesus and the dropouts, his stale bread of life. Even the Christian Eucharist, which is the flesh of the Son of man and his blood (6:53), is of no avail. Granted that 6:62–63 and 8:23–24 are dualistic statements and function to affirm something, even as they devalue another thing, still they are qualitatively different from former dualisms because they proclaim a complete divorce of spirit and matter. If formerly Christian rites and objects had some value (spirit in matter), they have such no longer, when spirit alone is valued above or against matter.

Time Orientation. In this weak group situation, the Holy Spirit is said to have a new function for Jesus' group. Formerly spirit was perceived as the servant of the past, remembering Jesus' words to the group and suggesting the hidden meanings always latent there. But in this new state of revolt, the spirit begins to function as a teller of all things and of things that are to come. In former situations, the spirit was the exegete of the sayings of the earthly Jesus, in service of the past, and even normed in some way by Jesus' words and deeds, which are credited with lasting value. But in this new situation, the spirit is not bound at all to the words of the earthly Jesus; for, in the service of the future, not the past, the spirit cannot be bound by tradition, Scripture, the earthly Jesus, or any other norm.[39]

A careful examination of the spirit passages in John 14–16 indicates a strong tension, even a contradiction in them, concerning time orientation and norming. Certain passages describe the spirit as Jesus' servant, normed by the past, while others describe the spirit as a free herald of the future. For example, Jesus describes the spirit whom the Father will send in Jesus' name as the figure who "will bring to your remembrance all that I have said to you" (14:26b). This resembles what is said of the spirit in 15:26, "He will bear witness to me." The spirit, then, "will glorify me [Jesus], for he will take what is mine and declare it to you" (16:14). In these passages, spirit may be described according to the profile of stages one and two, when group was strong; spirit was in service of the past and normed by it.[40]

But juxtaposed to these passages are others in which spirit seems to be explicitly free of the memory of the earthly Jesus and becomes the source of new materials about the future, materials that cannot be normed or tested by anything in the past. For example, juxtaposed to 14:26b is the remark that "the spirit will teach you all things" (14:26a), not just past things that Jesus said (see 2:22). Juxtaposed to 16:14 is another comment about how "the spirit will guide you into all truth" and how "the spirit will declare to you things that are to come" (16:13). These remarks are best associated with stage three, when group was weak and when spirit served the future, not the past, and could never be normed by anything material—the past, the words of Jesus, or anything else.

This has considerable importance for our investigation. The community that made the confession of Jesus as equal to God is simply not normed by anything material or from below, just as Jesus is not (see 1 John 4:3; 2 John 7). Even as the community began to value only spirit and what is *not* of this world, so the function of the spirit of truth was adapted in the service of what is future and heavenly. This new spirit of the heavenly Jesus becomes the source of the group's new doctrine, all things . . . things that are to come.

Spirit and Matter.   In the relationship of spirit to matter, Jesus sees irreconcilable differences between himself and the world. As he explains the situation, he lives in a dichotomized world: "That which is born of flesh is flesh; and that which is born of spirit is spirit" (3:6). And in another place he tells his audience that he is from above and they are from below, even as he is not of this world, but they are of this world (8:23). One's spatial location, moreover, affects one's ability to understand Jesus: "If I have told you earthly things and you do not believe, how can you believe if I tell you heavenly things?" (3:12). Finally, Jesus irreconcilably attacks matter, flesh, and all things earthly when he proclaims, "It is the spirit that gives life, the flesh is of no avail" (6:63). The world, then, consists of recurring dichotomies:

$$
\begin{array}{rcl}
\text{spirit} & \text{vs.} & \text{flesh} \\
\text{heaven} & \text{vs.} & \text{earth} \\
\text{from above} & \text{vs.} & \text{from below} \\
\text{not of this world} & \text{vs.} & \text{of this world}
\end{array}
$$

And in this context, spirit is in revolt against flesh, just as heaven is superior to earth. A reform of old structures simply will not do, as matter, flesh, and earth are no longer ambiguous at all but fundamentally flawed and corrupt. They have no place in the cosmos ushered in by this spirit of revolt. Spirit, then, should not be found in matter or be compatible with it.

Yet in this dichotomized cosmos, it may turn out that even the words and deeds of the earthly Jesus come to be perceived as matter, a point noted in the previous chapter. A Christology in which Jesus' heavenly or spiritual character is uniquely valued could then be heralded as superior to a Christology based on the words and deeds of a fleshly, earthly figure. At this point I shall introduce several important pieces of scholarly conversation pertinent to these issues.

New Testament scholars are quite in agreement now about the great Easter shift,[41] how the earthly Jesus, whose words were not understood during his lifetime, stands in tension with the Risen Lord, whose person, words, and deeds are quite clearly understood. The fact of a shift is not the precise issue, but rather the relationship of the Risen Lord to the earthly Jesus. Major critical questions arise: (1) How great is the shift? (2) Where is value placed, on the earlier material of the earthly Jesus or on the later, new words of the Risen One? (3) How do the two stages relate, if at all?

One stream of interpretation would argue that the Risen Lord stands in rather close continuity with the earthly Jesus. This implies that the risen Lord basically clarified the words and parables he spoke on earth: "These are my words which I spoke with you while I was still with you . . . " (Luke 24:44). The shift, then, is a narrow gorge that is easily bridged; the same figure stands at either end of the span. In this model, the spirit the Risen Lord sends upon his followers will function to remind them and explain to them the words of the earthly Jesus.

But another stream of interpretation argued for considerable discontinuity between the Risen Lord and the earthly Jesus. While the earthly Jesus deliberately spoke in parables, intentionally hid his messianic identity, and so fourth, the Risen Lord speaks openly, gives christophanies, commissions witnesses of the resurrection, and even seems to reveal new revelations (see John 20:17). The spirit this Risen Lord sends upon his followers would not be bound by the necessarily limited and inadequate ministry of the earthly Jesus, but would serve the new agenda of the Risen Lord. The Easter shift in this perspective is a wide canyon, over which a bridge is neither entirely feasible, necessary, or desirable. In this model, the spirit of the Risen Lord becomes the inspiration of the new prophetic words of the community of Jesus' followers. These two ideal positions represent the ends of a spectrum on which scholars tend to stake out moderate and radical positions, either seeing continuity in which the spirit only completed Jesus' words[42] or radical discontinuity in which the spirit became the agent of a profound reinterpretation.[43]

The modeling used in this chapter affords us a way of seeing that both positions in regard to the relationship of earthly Jesus and Risen Lord are represented in the Fourth Gospel, but at different stages of its history. These perceptions of Jesus correlate with the perception of spirit as past-oriented and normed or future-oriented and unnormed. Stages one and two, which reflect strong group situations, see spirit as servant of the earthly Jesus, normed by his past words and deeds. Stage three, on the other hand, where group was

201

weak, perceives spirit as related to the heavenly Jesus who is not of this world, and so, like him, unnormed by things material, fleshly, or earthly.

In stage three, the issue is no longer the reform of the past, but revolt against all its material rites, leadership legitimated by fleshly norms, and the like. Value is found only in spirit, which functions as a principle of discontinuity. Correspondingly the ideal spatial location is above and not of this world. Spirit, then, becomes the symbol of this revolt. Like Jesus, spirit stands against this world, inasmuch as spirit is opposed to flesh (6:63; 3:6). This, says Douglas, is a condensed code that insists on the superiority of individuals over society. In the case of the Fourth Gospel, the Johannine circle is superior to the Jewish synagogue system, as well as to certain apostolic churches.

CHRIST AND SPIRIT: A CORRELATION

Drawing together the threads of Douglas's material in relation to the Fourth Gospel, we begin to sense a strong correlation not only between Christology and cosmology (chap. 7), but between Christology and certain perceptions of spirit (chap. 8). First, Douglas's model has given us a way to understand how attitudes to spirit reflect societal values and structures, in particular, how spirit may be controlled or uncontrolled (group factor). Her material, moreover, suggests how control of spirit or its lack can be assessed in relationship to corresponding perceptions of time, matter, and norms. What we have seen is a close correlation between spirit in stages one and two and Jesus' claims for legitimation as prophet and king of Israel and for the validity of his new rites, and so forth. Here spirit functioned in matter in terms of reform of the old system, even if it remained ambiguous and in conflict with it.

In stage three, however, spirit represents Jesus' revolt against matter, that is, all former systems, those of the synagogue as well as apostolic churches. The correlation can be drawn between the Jesus who is himself beyond matter, flesh, and this world (8:23), and who is linked with spirit, which looks radically to the future and reveals "all things . . . things which are to come," things that may be in tension with previous words and deeds of the earthly Jesus. A correlation in the perception of spirit and Christology can be more clearly noted in the following comparison:

CHRIST AND SPIRIT: CORRELATION

Stages One and Two *(strong group)*	*Stage Three* *(weak group)*
1. *Christology:*	1. *Christology:*
legitimated as prophet and king by spirit at his baptism; Jesus' flesh and earthly memory have value (e.g., signs, rites)	uniquely from heaven and from above, not of this world; only his words and confession of him as divine (8:24) have value; only spirit gives life (6:63)
2. *Spirit:*	2. *Spirit:*
past-oriented in service of the earthly Jesus	future-oriented tells all truth, even things that are to come
normed in matter/flesh	unnormed superior to matter/flesh (6:63)

Finally, Douglas's modeling of spirit has enabled us to grasp the ideological role spirit has in stage three of the Gospel, when according to texts such as 6:63 (and 1 John 4:3; 2 John 7), spirit is described against matter and in revolt against whatever is earthly, material, and fleshly. This revolt can be summarized as follows, indicating more clearly what is disvalued (matter) and what is valued (spirit).

STAGE THREE: WEAK GROUP/LOW GRID

Revolt against Matter	*Celebration of Spirit*
Matter = traditional synagogue system, as well as aspects of life in apostolic churches:	Spirit = new configuration of values and structures:
1. anti-rites, sacred places, feasts, etc.	1. new revelations from Jesus, through the Spirit of Truth
2. anti-ascribed leadership (Peter)	2. new achieved leadership (beloved disciple)
3. anti-value attached to signs or physical death of Jesus	3. value only in Jesus' words or revelations or in confession of him as divine
4. anti-past traditions as normative	4. Spirit of Truth as teacher of future things to come

Spirit, then, symbolizes and replicates what was signaled in the confession of Jesus who is equal to God but not of this world.

SUMMARY AND CONCLUSIONS

In summary, this final chapter attempted to develop a cross-cultural model for appreciating shifting perceptions of spirit. The abstract model was made concrete by showing the correlation between different perceptions of spirit and the differing stages of development in the Fourth Gospel, as figure 6 illustrated. Because this book is analyzing the high christological confession of stage three, our attention was focused on the special meaning of spirit in that stage, which was described abstractly, according to weak group/low grid, as a situation of revolt, where spirit is not only superior to matter, but irreconcilable with it.

The point of developing this model of spirit was to argue that spirit in a weak group/low grid situation implies a series of values and structures that closely correlate with what we claim is the meaning and function of the high Christology that proclaims Jesus as equal to God . . . but not of this world. In other words, the values and structures represented in that view of spirit are replicated in that christological confession. As spirit is superior to flesh, so Jesus is a heavenly figure who is not of this world. This type of analysis invites us to see a redundancy of perception in the Fourth Gospel and to appreciate the consonance achieved through it. Douglas's remarks on the meaning and function of a spirit/flesh dichotomy also have a bearing on how the high christological confession functioned as an ideology of revolt against all former values and structures. Equal to God, but not of this world reflects a world view that may be more abstractly described as weak group/low grid, with all that is implied by such a statement.

This type of analysis, moreover, equips us to contribute more critically to the scholarly conversation on the Fourth Gospel and so leads to fresh conclusions about it. For purposes of discussion, let us return to the study of Wayne Meeks and compare and contrast his results with those of this study.

We are not the first to inquire into the relationship of myth and social experience in the Fourth Gospel. Meeks broke that ground a decade ago in his article "The Man from Heaven in Johannine Sectarianism," in which he studied the myth of the descent/ascent of Jesus and asked what social function it might serve. Meeks's study focused on the descent/ascent christological pattern, which was shown to reflect a specific view of the cosmos. This study extended the investigation to other christological statements with definite cosmological implications, including 8:23–24 (whereby the heavenly Jesus is "not of this world") and 6:62–63, (where the same heavenly figure is exclusively associated with spirit in revolt against flesh). The interconnection of Christology and cosmology remains the focus, although we have introduced more data into the investigation.

Meeks's analysis, furthermore, culminated in a description both of Jesus and the Johannine group in an acute state of alienation.[44] For Meeks, alienation denotes a sectarian defensive posture in a hostile world which attacks, isolates, and estranges Jesus' followers. The models used in our study both confirm and refine Meeks's intuitions. Although not using terms such as "alien" and "myth of descending/ascending Son of man," Douglas's models offer a broad base for seeing the Johannine community as a group in radical tension with its neighbors. Douglas's models, moreover, suggest that the mood in stage three is more one of revolt against discredited systems than sectarian defense from enemies. The strategy is not that of drawing the wagons into a circle so much as that of relentless criticism and attack, which is expressed in the extensive forensic processes in which the high Christology is expounded. The recurring dichotomies of spirit vs. flesh, heaven vs. earth, and so forth, are not the dualisms of a sectarian challenge, but superior claims over against a world that is rejected and condemned. The dichotomies expressed particularly in 8:23–24 and 6:62–63 symbolize a strategy of revolt and attack. For Meeks's "alienation," Douglas would substitute "rejection"; for his sense of defense, her model suggests revolt.

Meeks's next point, the social function of the group's myth, is confirmed in principle. The myth defines and vindicates the community: "It provides a symbolic universe which gave legitimacy, a theodicy, to the group's actual isolation from the larger society."[45] Douglas's careful model of the relationship of spirit and matter offers a more sound grounding for the social function of Johannine christological statements, and so her remarks can serve as a convenient summary of the strategy and ideology implied in statements that celebrate spirit against matter:

> To insist on the superiority of spiritual over material elements is to insist on the liberties of the individual and to imply a political program for freeing him from social constraints. . . . Put crudely, those who are on the side of spontaneity, freedom and the elevation of spiritual values, reject society in its established form.[46]

As Meeks pointed to the social function of myths, so Douglas alerts us to the symbolic quality of spirit/matter dichotomies as condensed statements about the relation of individuals and society, which implies that an ideology is expressed in a christological statement such as John 6:62–63 and 8:23–24. Douglas's model offers not only the suggestion that an ideology might be symbolized by such statements, but specific clues as to its shape and thrust.[47] In short, the confession of Jesus as equal to God is hardly a neutral statement, but must be appreciated in terms of the way it was perceived and functioned for the community of the Fourth Gospel. In this, Douglas's modeling has served us well.

SUMMARY,
CONCLUSIONS, AND
FURTHER QUESTIONS

Although a resume of the content of equal to God was given at the beginning of chapter 5, we summarize here the contents of the high christological confession. Of Jesus the Fourth Gospel claimed: (1) He is equal to God, because he enjoys God's two basic powers, creative power and eschatological power; (2) He is God *(Theos)* in virtue of his creative power, but Lord *(Kyrios)* because of his eschatological power; (3) He is eternal-in-the-past and imperishable-in-the-future, marks of any true deity, which correspond to his creative and eschatological powers.[1]

Unlike other studies, this volume has not focused exclusively on the classical places in the Fourth Gospel where Jesus is confessed as God and Lord and God, such as 1:1–2 and 20:28. These titles themselves are but part of the total confession of Jesus as a divine, heavenly figure. They need to be interpreted in the light of God's two powers granted to Jesus, whereby he is God (creative power) and Lord (eschatological power). In summary, whatever can be said of Israel's deity in terms of titles/names, functions, and nature can be said also of Jesus.

Furthermore, I would conclude that more attention is correspondingly given in the Fourth Gospel to Jesus' eschatological power than to his creative power. As figure 1 (p. 34) indicated, 5:21–29 functions as a topic statement about Jesus' eschatological power, whereby he is the judge who gives postmortem life and who should receive honor equal to God's. It seems that the confession of Jesus as a divine figure must handle in particular the fact that he was rejected and died on a cross. Hence the special development in the Gospel of that aspect of eschatological power whereby Jesus is said to have life in himself.

In terms of the community's own history of conflict with the synagogue and certain apostolic churches, the emphasis on the eschatological power of Jesus correlates with the intense forensic conflict that pervades the Gospel and issues in the excommunication and especially the repeated attempts on the life of Jesus (5:18; 8:59; 10:31) and his followers (16:1-2). In all of these situations, Jesus, who is equal to God, triumphs because he is the judge and because he has power to lay down his life and take it again. The eschatological power of Jesus, then, correlates closely with the conflictive history of the community.

In the first half of this book, investigation of the content of Jesus' equality with God proceeded along the lines of traditional methods of biblical criticism, which are quite well suited to that task. But further questions were asked of this material, such as the perspective of the high Christology and its function as an ideology for this confessing group. These are new questions requiring different methods of investigation. And so in the second half of this study, we had recourse to models from cultural anthropology for studying how Jesus, who is equal to God, is emphatically not of this world.

If Christology means only a study of the content of Jesus' identity, role, and status, our task, using traditional methods of exegesis, would have been complete by chapter 4. But because Christology is inevitably related both to the historical experience of the confessing group and to their perceptions of the cosmos, we needed to find and develop ways of assessing a Christology emphasizing that the figure who is equal to God is emphatically not of this world and can only be fully appreciated when seen in his proper relationship to spirit. Chapter 5 showed that the study of equal to God would remain incomplete without addressing the issue of the social location of the confessing group and examining the social function the high Christology had for them. To stop after chapter 4 would have given us only an ahistorical summary of the high Christology, which would remain incomplete according to contemporary theories of knowledge. That earlier investigation of the content of equal to God would tell us nothing about that confession as linguistic communication. It would ignore the social context of language and meaning and so prove incomplete.

The materials of cultural anthropologist Mary Douglas offered an adequate, flexible, and enlightening model for assessing how the high Christology in the Fourth Gospel replicates the social cosmology of the Johannine group and functions as an ideology for it. Douglas's basic model of group/grid allowed us to locate the high Christology in a society in revolt against its neighbors, both synagogue and Christian. Douglas's further remarks on the social agenda, which is typically encoded in dichotomous patterns of spirit over matter and mind over flesh, allowed us to see how the high Christology came to function as an ideology of revolt against and superiority over previously held values and structures, as illustrated in key passages such as 6:62–63 and 8:23–24. Despite the great marriage of heaven and earth supposedly heralded in 1:14, the Fourth Gospel ultimately put value only in spirit, not flesh, only in being from above, not from below, and only in being not of this world, not in being of this world. Ultimately, the Gospel argued that the flesh is of no avail. In support of this, texts such as 1 John 4:3 and 2 John 7 appear as summaries of a Christology in which Jesus is exclusively perceived as a divine heavenly figure, a perception that vigorously denies any value to flesh, matter, or earth, or even to Jesus' former involvement in things material. Finally, further investigation of the social perceptions of spirit as a code for the relative degree of systematization and control in a social group led us to see more clearly that the high Christology, which valued the heavenly, spiritual Jesus as superior to anything earthly and material, functioned as an ideology of revolt against the past and all previous controls, structures, and classifications. Thus, the figure who is equal to God is also not of this world.

This modeling was most helpful in unpacking the radical ideology encoded in the high Christology, both as a strategy of revolt and as a replication of the group's cosmology. The high Christology, which was always an aggressive claim vis-à-vis the synagogue, became a code for revolt against the synagogue in particular as well as against all formal structures, including Christians considered to have inadequate faith. With Jesus as the chief paradigm, all value was found in individualism rather than group membership, in spirit rather than flesh, and in heaven, not earth. The flesh is of no avail means that all things earthly are denied value, either flesh of the earthly Jesus, his signs, his death on the cross, or the apostolic tradition of eyewitness leadership and sacramental rituals. A high christological confession does not imply per se such a strategy of revolt—witness the Catholic, Anglican, and Lutheran churches today. Only when that Christology is perceived in terms such as 6:62–63 or 8:23–24, where value is placed only in what is heavenly and spiritual, might one suspect it of signaling a revolt against all that is earthly, fleshly, and material. But the Johannine high Christology did embody such a value configuration and functioned as an ideology of revolt.

After summarizing what the models have taught us, it is appropriate to raise some questions about what Douglas's models can and cannot do for biblical interpretation. Anthropological models are not intended to replace traditional methods of exegesis, but to complement them. Our study would be incomplete without its initial chapters, where the content of the confession was examined according to the historical-critical method. But neither is the task finished when that method has done its work. In a sense, then, the analysis of a culture, or in our case, a text, is never exhausted by the approach of a single analysis, method, or model. Because other questions can be asked of a text, different models and materials are thereby needed for that new task, in this case, Douglas's cross-cultural models.

Because Douglas aims at cross-cultural analysis, her models necessarily work at a rather high level of abstraction. To them should be added studies of Eastern Mediterranean culture and analyses of Semitic and Arabic society, which would give added insight into the specific values and social dynamics particular to those cultures that produced the texts we study. This is increasingly being done.[2]

Douglas's modeling, moreover, cannot reconstruct history, for it is a static photograph of a society and does not yield the particularity of experience that constitutes data for the writing of history. It gives, rather, the abstract cosmology of a group, that is, its perception of the world. Yet these models are not without value in appreciating particular social groups at given points in their history, much the way photographs of vapor trails indicate the mass and velocity of atomic particles. Douglas's basic group/grid model can show us the coherence and redundancy of values, structures, and classifications of a particular social system.

And so, we sorted out the development of thought and value in the Fourth Gospel with a view to perceiving the high Christology as accurately as possible. We indicated that the text reflects three stages of development, each with a distinctive cosmology and social agenda. Douglas's group/grid model proved to be quite helpful in describing each stage of this development, indicating how the

Johannine community moved (1) from a reform posture, in which Jesus' legitimacy vis-à-vis competing leaders in the synagogue was argued (strong group/weak grid), (2) to a much stronger reform posture, in which Jesus claimed that his person and his rites replaced Israel's patriarchs and prophets as well as its feasts, rituals, and so forth (strong group/rising grid), and finally (3) to a posture of revolt against the synagogue that expelled the Johannine group and against certain apostolic Christians whose faith was deemed inadequate by this group (weak group/low grid). While group/grid cannot predict history nor explain the whys and wherefores of its progress, it can give a penetrating view of the values, structures, and classifications of a social group, thus offering a coherent picture of its cosmology and the recurrence of its perceptions.

In this perspective, then, the confession of Jesus as equal to God came to full articulation in the context of intense conflict (low grid). Any hint of the Christian confession of Jesus' heavenly status is quickly sniffed out by the synagogue and roundly condemned (5:17–18; 10:31–33), but that hardly deterred the Johannine Christians from making clearer and bolder claims. On the contrary, one gets a sense of bold claims made in the name of reform of the system. These claims provoke increasing hostility from the system, and this hostility leads to even stronger claims.

The high Christology not only developed in a situation of conflict but was in turn shaped by the mounting conflict it provoked. The synagogue could never tolerate claims such as were made about Jesus. Claims for his equality with God immediately provoked prosecution—"This was why the Jews sought all the more to kill him . . ." (5:18), for the synagogue judged such claims as blasphemy, "because you being a man make yourself God" (10:33). The evidence for excommunication of Johannine Christians from the synagogue is compelling (9:22; 12:42; 16:1–2). If calling Jesus "messiah" could provoke such a reaction, a fortiori would confession of him as equal to God. At this point, Meeks's remark on the dialectical spiral of confession and hostility seems appropriate:

> The Johannine dialogues suggest quite clearly that the order of development must have been dialectical: the christological claims of the Johannine Christians resulted in their becoming alienated, and finally expelled from the synagogue; that alienation in turn is "explained" by a further development of the christological motifs (i.e., the fate of the community projected onto the story of Jesus); these developed christological motifs in turn drive the group into further isolation. It is a case

of continual, harmonic reinforcement between social experience and ideology.[3]

As Meeks has shown, reactions to the Johannine christological claims, which were initially offputting to the synagogue, have a way of proving the truth of the claims, namely, that Jesus is definitely not of this world or from below. For if he were of this world, it would love him (see 15:19). But as it is, he is not, and so this world hates him.

In conclusion, the confession of Jesus' equality with God can only be fully appreciated when perceived in conjunction with his claims that he is radically not of this world, and that his "spirit" alone gives life, for the flesh is of no avail whatever—1:14 notwithstanding.

1

BACKGROUND
OF THE NAME
"I AM"

The assertions that the Johannine "I AM" statements refer to past eternity and future imperishability can be supported by investigation into both the popular interpretations of the divine name from Exod. 3:14 in tradition and midrash and speculation about God's being, which is found in key passages from Isaiah and Revelation.

EXODUS 3:14

It is generally agreed that the absolute use of "I AM" in the Fourth Gospel refers in some way to the divine name.[1] In John 17, moreover, reference is made repeatedly to "thy name," the special name God gave to Jesus and which Jesus manifests to the world:[2]

> I have manifested thy name to men whom you gave me out of the world. (17:6)

> Holy Father, keep them in thy name which you have given me. (17:11)

> While I was with them, I kept them in thy name which you gave me. (17:12)

> I have made known to them thy name and I will make it known. (17:26)

This name is not *theos* or *kyrios*, but rather the particular name of God given to Moses in Exod. 3:14, "I AM WHO I AM." It has been argued, moreover, that in the LXX of Isaiah "I AM" *(ego eimi)* has become a condensed form of this divine name. In particular, several passages are regularly cited by scholars in support of this assertion:

Isa. 43:25 (MT)	*Isa. 43:25 (LXX)*
I, I am He, who blots out transgressions	I am "I AM," who blots out transgression

Isa. 51:12 (MT)	*Isa. 51:12 (LXX)*
I, I am He, who comforts you	I am "I AM," who comforts you

Isa. 52:6 (MT)	*Isa. 52:6 (LXX)*
Therefore my people shall know my name; therefore in that day they shall know that it is I who speaks	Therefore my people shall know my name; therefore in that day they shall know that "I AM" is the one who speaks

These four points suggest the following conclusions. First, "I AM" in the Johannine text is a condensed form, even a code for God's special name, as it was in the LXX. Second, this condensed form of the divine name, which is here traced through the LXX of Isaiah, ultimately refers back to the special name given Moses at the burning bush (Exod. 3:14).

It is not enough to link the Johannine "I AM" with the divine name in either Isaiah LXX or Exod. 3:14. What did the name signify? How was it understood in postbiblical Judaism?[3] We have some evidence of this from the various translations in the LXX, Philo, and the targums. Our earliest evidence, the LXX of Exod. 3:14, gives a fresh twist to the Hebrew text:

Exod. 3:14 (MT)	*Exod. 3:14 (LXX)*
God said to Moses: "I AM WHO I AM."	God said to Moses: "I AM THE EXISTENT ONE (*ego eimi ho on*)."
And he said: "Say this to the children of Israel, 'I AM has sent me to you.'"	And he said: "Say this to the children of Israel, 'THE EXISTENT ONE (*ho on*) has sent me to you.'"

If it is permissible to read *ho on* as He Who Is, the Existent One, then the LXX contains an explicit note about God's being or existence.[4] This interpretation is picked up and expanded in traditions that are later reflected in Philo's exposition of Exod. 3:14.[5] Philo, while reluctant to assign a personal name to God, is constrained by Scripture, and so he says:

> No personal name can be properly assigned to the Existent One. Note that when the prophet desires to know what he must answer to those who ask about His name, He says: "I am He that is" [*ego eimi ho on*, Exod. 3:14 LXX], which is equivalent to "My nature is 'to be,' not to be spoken." (*Mut.* 11)

Building on the LXX, Philo regularly calls God the Existent One (*ho on*),[6] and this name for him is clearly a statement about God's eternal being:

> Among the virtues, that of God is, actually existing, inasmuch as God alone has veritable being. This is why Moses will say of Him as best he may in human speech "I am He that is" [*ego eimi ho on*, Exod. 3:14], implying that others lesser than He have not being, as being indeed is, but exist in semblance only, and are conventionally said to exist. (*Det.* 160)

God's being (*ho on*) implies a transtemporal quality, because it is not contingent like that of created beings; it *is* eternally. On just these contrasts of noncontingent against contingent being and eternal against temporal, Philo is very much in line with the targumic traditions of Exod. 3:14.

As figure 7 (p. 216) indicates, *Tg. Yer. I, II,* and *Neof.* gl 1 all translate[7] "I AM" in such a way as to bring out two points: (1) God's eternity and (2) God's noncontingency as creator of the world. God, of course, already was in the past, when God created the world; and God will be in the future to sustain creation or make a new creation—hence, God is eternally. God's creative action, moreover, serves in this context to distinguish God from the created or contingent world. God is sourceless and uncreated, by which he differs from the world that came to be and that corrupts. God's noncontingency, then, implies imperishability. The targums, moreover, consider the formula "I AM" to contain this coded statement about God's eternity and imperishability. By comparison with Philo's exegesis of Exod. 3:14, the tradition of this interpretation of the divine name can be said to have existed already by the first century.

WHO WAS, IS, AND WILL BE

Apart from explicit translations of Exod. 3:14, we can find indications of the content of this divine name in diverse postbiblical

FIGURE 7

"I AM" IN TARGUM AND MIDRASH

Exod. 3:14 (MT)	Tg. Yer I	Tg. Yer II Polyglots / Tg. Yer II Paris	Neofiti	Neofiti gl 1
(a) God said to Moses,	(a) And the Lord said to Moses:	(a) And the Memra of the Lord said to Moses:	(a) And the Lord said to Moses:	(a) And the Lord said to Moses:
(b) "I AM WHO I AM"	(b) "He who spoke and the world was; who spoke and all things were"	(b) "He who said to the world Bel and it was; and who shall yet say to it Bel and it will be"	(b) "I AM WHO I AM"	(b) "I have existed before the world was created; and I have existed after the world was created; I am he who was your support during the captivity of Egypt; and I am he who will be your support during all generations
(c) And he said: "Say this to the children of Israel:	(c) And he said: "Thus shall you say to the children of Israel:	(c) And he said to him:	(c) And he said to him: "Thus shall you say to the children of Israel:	(c) And he said: "Thus shall you say to the children of Israel:
(d) 'I AM has sent me to you'"	(d) 'I AM HE WHO IS AND WHO WILL BE has sent me to you'"	(d) "I AM"	(d) 'He who spoke and the world was from the beginning and shall say again to it Bel and it shall be. He has sent me to you'"	(d) 'I AM has sent me to you'"

writings. It is often claimed that certain passages in Revelation contain a paraphrase of the divine name based on Exod. 3:14.[8]

1:4	*1:8*	*4:8*	*11:17*
Grace and peace to you from Him	I am the Alpha and Omega	Holy, holy, holy is the Lord God Almighty	We give thee thanks, Lord God, Almighty
who is and who was and who is to come	who is and who was and who is to come, the Almighty	— who was and who is to come	thou who is and was — O Holy One

Whatever action is ascribed to God or whatever situation God's followers are in, God's eternity and imperishability are proclaimed in the confession that God is "who was, is, and will be." This formula, of course, did not originate with the author of Revelation, but goes back to the LXX and to Jewish reflections about God. In a context of judgment, the prophet records God speaking:

Isa. 48:12 (MT)	*Isa. 48:12 (LXX)*
Hearken to me, O Jacob, and Israel, whom I called! I am He, I am the first and I am the last	Hearken to me, O Jacob, and Israel, whom I called! I AM first and I AM to the age

The LXX of Isaiah contains an allusion in 48:12 to God's past deeds (and existence), a point continued in the reference to creation in 48:13, "My hand laid the foundation of the earth and my right hand spread out the heavens." God's eternity[9] from of old is reflected here: God is "[the] first" (*protos*); God is he "who was." Yet the Speaker identifies himself as "I AM" (*ego eimi*), which at least refers to God's present existence, as he "who is." "I am the last" (LXX = "I AM to [the end of] the age") speaks of God's imperishability in the future, as he "who will be" (see Isa. 41:4).

Whether or not "I AM" occurs in these passages from Isaiah, the sense of God's past and future eternity is clearly articulated. It is linked with creative actions in the past and with executive or eschatological actions in the future. The early dating of the LXX and the first-century dating of Revelation assure us that consideration of God's eternity and imperishability was current at the time of John's Gospel.

ETERNAL AND IMPERISHABLE

The background of "I AM" shows that in postbiblical Judaism God's special name (Exod. 3:14) was increasingly perceived in supratemporal terms, as he who was, is, and will be, and as eternal (in the past) and imperishable (in the future). Because the supratemporal character of God was also a regular feature of Hellenistic thought, our investigation of the Johannine understanding of the "I AM" statements can be confirmed if we view them in the light of Hellenistic god-talk. There are three aspects of God's supratemporality that have a bearing on our project: (1) the triplex designation of god as "who was, is, and will be," (2) the formula that god is "eternal *(aidios)* and imperishable *(aphthartos),*" and (3) a *topos* which contrasts true, eternal gods with temporal hero-mortals.

In the pre-Socratics, God's eternity is articulated in the triple-termed formula: "Who was always and is and will be."[10] According to Plato, "God, as the old tradition declares, holds in his hands the beginning, middle and end of all that is" (*Laws* 715e; see *Tim.* 37b). The inscription on a statue of Eon erected at Eleusis in the time of Augustus described the deity as having "no beginning, middle, or end."[11] According to Plutarch, a statue of Athena-Isis bore the following inscription: "I am all that has been and is and will be."[12] It belongs to god alone, therefore, to be supratemporal: who was, is, and will be.

Besides the triple-termed description of god as who was, is, and will be, it was popular to speak of god in two terms, eternal and imperishable. At one point, the Stoic Zeno affirmed that there are two principles in the universe, the active and the passive principle. God is the active principle for "he is everlasting *(aidion)* and is the artificer of each thing throughout the whole extent of matter." God, moreover, is a principle, not an element; it belongs to principles to be "without generation *(agenetous)* or destruction *(aphthartous),*" whereas elements "are destroyed when all things are resolved into fire."[13] And so, god must be eternal as to generation and imperishable as to terminus.[14]

This expression of god's being becomes formulaic in the course of time. Sextus Empiricus, among others, describes the common, popular idea of god as "eternal *(aidion)* and imperishable *(aphtharton)* and perfect in happiness."[15] Philo describes an apocryphal scene of Joseph addressing his brothers to reassure them of his good will out of respect for their "father," that is, God. Jacob's benevolence rests on the image of "the uncreated *(ageneton)* Father, the Imperishable *(ton aph-tharton)*, the Eternal *(ton aidion)*."[16] Over time, divine supratemporal-ity and its refinement as god's eternity and imperishability became a *topos* or commonplace in ancient god-talk.[17] Plutarch, for example, wrote that Apollo Tegyraeus should be classified as a true god, not a heroized mortal, distinguishing true gods from heroized mortals:

> My native tradition removes this god from among those deities who were changed from mortals into immortals. Like Heracles and Dionysus, whose virtues enabled them to cast off mortality and suffering; but he is one of those deities who are unbegotten *(agennēton)* and eternal *(aidion)*, if we may judge by what the most ancient and wisest men have said on such matters.[18]

Finally, in Diodorus of Sicily, this distinction becomes a formal *topos* for talking critically about god. In the fragmentary Sixth Book, he draws upon the writings of Euhemerus of Messene, in what proves to be a convenient *topos* on two kinds of gods:

> As regards the gods, men of ancient times have handed down to later generations two different conceptions: Certain of the gods, they say, are eternal and imperishable *(aidious kai aphthartous)* . . . for each of these genesis and duration are from everlasting to everlasting. But the other gods, we are told, were terrestrial beings who attained to im-mortal honor and fame because of their benefactions to mankind, such as Heracles, Dionysus, Aristaeus, and the others who were like them.[19]

From Plutarch and Diodorus, we can distill a schema for distin-guishing true gods from mere heroic mortals, a schema built on an elaborate series of contrasts:

True Gods	*Heroized Mortals*
1. ancient	1. recent, new
2. celestial	2. terrestrial
3. without a beginning and ungenerated	3. came into being and born in time
4. imperishable	4. translated in death
5. eternal	5. made immortal

In summary, supratemporality, which assumed the status of a unique, distinguishing mark of authentic deity, was understood to refer to God's antiquity and ungeneratedness, that is, past eternity, and God's deathlessness and permanence, that is, future imperisha-bility. Whereas in postbiblical Judaism we found an emphasis on God's eternity from of old and God's endurance to the end of time,

Hellenistic writers speak of God's uncreated eternity and imperishability.

This typology is important for New Testament Christology. C. H. Talbert[20] argued that the second model, that of the hero who is made immortal *(athanatos)* because of his benefactions to humanity, was influential in the creation of the gospel genre and so of the confession of Jesus. This is not without persuasion, as we note that Jesus was apotheosized in and because of his death. But the claims in the Johannine Gospel go so much further than is allowed in the second model. As we noted, Jesus is formally called God and Lord (1:1; 20:28); he is said to be "equal to God" (5:18; 10:33). The structure of the first model would seem to be in some way operative in the conception and articulation in the Fourth Gospel of Jesus as a divine figure, who is eternal in the past and imperishable in the future.

INTERPRETATION
OF PSALM 82:6

The charge that a man makes himself God is not new in biblical literature. Isaiah 14:13–14, after recording the boast of a foreign king to rival and replace Israel's God, refutes the claim that any mortal man could make himself god by specifically noting the death of the claimant: "You will be brought to Sheol, to the depths of the Pit. All the kings of the nations lie in glory, each in his own tomb, but you are cast out. . . . You go down to the Pit like a dead body trodden under foot" (Isa. 14:15–19). Death, especially a dishonorable death, silences any claims of mortals to be god. Jesus' claim, however, surpasses the naive claims of a foreign king found in Isaiah. His death, even a death on the cross, will not refute his assertion that he is equal to God, because he has already claimed to have power over death *after death,* both the death of his followers and especially his own death.

Yet the Hebrew Scriptures contain a number of passages in which a mortal is called god, apparently without disturbance or qualification. This phenomenon may be observed in Ps. 82:6 as well as several other places in the Scriptures:

I make you [Moses] as god to Pharaoh. (Exod. 7:1)

For a child is born to us, a son is given to us . . . and his name shall be called "Wonderful Counselor, Mighty God, Everlasting Father, and Prince of Peace." (Isa. 9:6)

I say, "You are gods, all of you sons of the Most High." (Ps. 82:6)

For those who say the Shema thrice daily, these texts might be disturbing. How is it that mortals are called god? According to Philo, Moses is god[1] because he is ruler and king,[2] so that his god-ness rests in his sharing of God's executive power, at least on earth (*Sac.* 9).[3]

The royal heir described in Isaiah is called god for the same reason, that is, his share in God's kingship over Israel (see also Zech. 12:8). Psalm 82:6, however, offers no clear explanation for the proclamation, "I say 'You are gods.'" It has been argued,[4] however, that those addressed in the psalm are Israel's judges, who share in God's power (see Deut. 1:17), but this is not the way the psalm was understood in the midrashim or in the Fourth Gospel.[5]

The midrashim frequently historicized Ps. 82:6 to refer to the giving of the Torah on Sinai. From an early midrash we find a fragmentary version of the interpretation of the psalm:

> God spoke to the Angel of Death: "I have not ordained you for my children, for I have made them gods. I say you are gods [Ps. 82:6]. When he came to give them the Ten Commandments, he spoke to them: Hear, my people. God, your God am I [Ps. 50:7].[6]

While this may be our earliest extant witness to a complex legend utilizing Ps. 82:6, it is not thereby the most complete example, for much is presupposed here. At least it can be noted that the passage historicizes Ps. 82:6, putting it in the context of the giving of the Torah to Israel on Sinai. In that context, the author understands the reference to "gods" in Ps. 82:6 to have specific content. God's restraint of the angel of death probably refers to God's gift of deathlessness to Israel. Yet why deathlessness? Somehow it is presumed that in the giving of the Torah, God restored to Israel a gift of godlikeness which was originally Adam's (Gen. 1:26), but was lost because of sin (Gen. 2:17; 3:19). Implicit in this midrash is a link between a restoration of holiness to Israel though the gift of Torah and a consequent restoration of deathlessness. Sinai was a second creation! Yet, because the fact that mortals are called god remains disturbing, the citation of Ps. 82:6 is balanced with a passage from Ps. 50:7 in which God alone is properly called God ("Hear . . . your God am I"). Strict monotheism, then, is maintained.

In a second instance of the legend, more of Psalm 82 is historicized, filling out the basic legendary interpretation:

> If it were possible to do away with the Angel of Death I would. But the decree has long ago been decreed. R. Jose says: It was upon this condition that the Israelites stood up before Mount Sinai, on condition that the Angel of Death should have no power over them. For it is said: "I said: Ye are godlike beings" [Ps. 82:6]. But you have corrupted your conduct. "Surely ye shall die like men" [Ps. 82:7].[7]

Again, the occasion of the psalm is Sinai, and Israel is called "god" because God made it deathless by restraining the Angel of Death. But more of the psalm is cited: Israel will die, "Surely ye shall die like men" (82:7), because of its new sin ("You corrupted your conduct"), which probably refers to the worship of the golden calf. And so, godness is related to deathlessness, just as death is linked with sin.

The midrashim we are examining all presuppose a complex yet traditional explanation of the source of death. Good biblical doctrine states that God created Adam in a state of holiness. This first person, moreover, was created in God's "image and likeness," which Wisdom 2:23 explains as a state of deathlessness: "God made man for incorruption (*eph' aphtharsiai*) and made him in the image of his own eternity (*aidiotetos*)." Deathlessness (or eternity), then, was conditioned upon holiness. Second, God explicitly warned Adam that should he sin, he would die: "For in the day that you eat it you shall die" (Gen. 2:17; 3:3). The tempter assured Eve that if she broke God's commandment "You will *not* die" (3:5), which was a lie; for of the sinful Adam God later said: "You are dust and to dust you shall return" (3:19).[8]

The *Mekilta* passage just discussed sees a clear parallel between the situations of Adam in Paradise and Israel at Sinai:

Adam in Paradise	*Israel on Sinai*
1. created in holiness,	1. reconstituted in holiness,
2. and so deathless,	2. and so deathless,
3. yet sinned (ate fruit),	3. yet sinned (worshiped calf),
4. and so died	4. and so died

Israel was re-created in holiness by the reception of God's word on Sinai. In accepting the Torah, Israel became obedient to God, that is, holy on a scale that matched Adam's original holiness and obedience. Sinai, therefore, was interpreted as a second chance for Israel, an undoing of the slavery to sin and death through the new gift of God's Torah. Having the Law, Israel was once more made holy, and because of this sinlessness it was restored to deathlessness.

Other examples of the midrashic understanding of Ps. 82:6 only confirm the direction of the interpretation just sketched.[9] In summary, then, the full historicized interpretation of Ps. 82:6–7 contains the following four points: (1) Israel arrived at Sinai sinful, liable to death and fearful to hear God's word "lest we die" (Exod.

20:19); (2) God gave Israel God's word, the Torah, on Sinai, which made Israel sinless once more; (3) God restrained the Angel of Death, making Israel deathless; and so God calls the Israelites "gods" (Ps. 82:6); (4) But Israel sinned by adoring the golden calf; for this reason Israel will "die like a man," according to Ps. 82:7. Always implied in this legend is some understanding of the relationship between holiness and deathlessness as well as that between sin and death. Implied also is the understanding that Sinai was a new creation for Israel, a restoration of the image of Adam in the likeness of God and a reaffirmation of Adam's privileges springing from that likeness.[10] In this context, "You are gods" exclusively refers to Israel's deathlessness, its sharing in God's special imperishability. I claim that this midrashic understanding of Ps. 82:6 is operative in the Johannine use of that psalm in 10:34–36.

ABBREVIATIONS

AB	Anchor Bible
ABQ	*American Baptist Quarterly*
AnBib	Analecta biblica
Bib	*Biblica*
BibLeb	*Bibel und Leben*
BJRL	*Bulletin of the John Rylands Library*
BR	*Biblical Research*
BTB	*Biblical Theology Bulletin*
BZ	*Biblische Zeitschrift*
CBQ	*Catholic Biblical Quarterly*
CTM	*Concordia Theological Monthly*
CurTM	*Currents in Theology and Mission*
DR	*Downside Review*
EvT	*Evangelische Theologie*
ExpTim	*Expository Times*
HNT	Handbuch zum Neuen Testament
HR	*History of Religions*
HTR	*Harvard Theological Review*
Int	*Interpretation*
JAAR	*Journal of the American Academy of Religion*
JBL	*Journal of Biblical Literature*
JQR	*Jewish Quarterly Review*
JSJ	*Journal for the Study of Judaism*
JSNT	*Journal for the Study of the New Testament*
JTS	*Journal of Theological Studies*
LTP	*Laval théologique et philosophique*
NovTSup	Novum Testamentum, Supplements
NT	*Novum Testamentum*

NTS	*New Testament Studies*
RB	*Revue Biblique*
RSR	*Religious Studies Review*
SBLASP	Society of Biblical Literature Abstracts and Seminar Papers
SBLDS	Society of Biblical Literature Dissertation Series
SBT	Studies in Biblical Theology
SJT	*Scottish Journal of Theology*
SNTSMS	Society for New Testament Studies Monograph Series
ST	*Studia Theologica*
Str.B.	[H. Strack and] P. Billerbeck, *Kommentar zum Neuen Testament*
TDNT	*Theological Dictionary of the New Testament*
TS	*Theological Studies*
TTZ	*Trierer theologische Zeitschrift*
TZ	*Theologische Zeitschrift*
USQR	*Union Seminary Quarterly Review*
VC	*Virgiliae Christianae*
ZNW	*Zeitschrift für die neutestamentliche Wissenschaft*
ZTK	*Zeitschrift für Theologie und Kirche*

NOTES

INTRODUCTION

1. E.g., J. R. Harris, *The Origin of the Prologue of St. John* (Cambridge: Cambridge University Press, 1907); Rudolf Schnackenburg, "Logos-Hymnus und johanneischer Prolog," *BZ* 1 (1957): 69–109; Ernst Käsemann, "The Structure and Purpose of the Prologue to John's Gospel," in *New Testament Questions of Today* (London: SCM Press, 1969), 138–67; and Peder Borgen, "Observations on the Targumic Character of the Prologue of John," *NTS* 16 (1970): 288–95.

2. See Robert Kysar, "Christology and Controversy: The Contributions of the Prologue of the Gospel of John to New Testament Christology and Their Historical Setting," *CurTM* 5 (1978): 348–64; and R. A. Culpepper, "The Pivot of John's Prologue," *NTS* 27 (1980): 1–31.

3. See Fred B. Craddock, *The Pre-Existence of Christ in the New Testament* (Nashville: Abingdon Press, 1968). I will not use the term preexistence in discussing high Christology. Rather, I will speak of Jesus as eternally existing, both in the past and in the future, a mode of expression more in keeping with notions of true deity in ancient times (see chap. 2).

4. See the recent debate in *The Myth of God Incarnate*, ed. J. Hick (London: SCM Press, 1977), and responses to it in *Incarnation and Myth: The Debate Continued*, ed. Michael Goulder (Grand Rapids: Wm. B. Eerdmans, 1979).

5. See Raymond E. Brown, *Jesus: God and Man* (Milwaukee: Bruce Publishing, 1967), 1–38; see also B. A. Mastin, "A Neglected Feature of the Christology of the Fourth Gospel," *NTS* 22 (1975): 32–51.

6. Mary Douglas's works will be discussed in part 2. On the use of her materials for biblical interpretation, see *Semeia* 35 (1986); and Bruce Malina, *Christian Origins and Cultural Anthropology* (Atlanta: John Knox Press, 1986).

7. Mary Douglas, *Forms of Symbolic Action*, Proceedings of the 1969 Annual Spring Meeting of the American Ethnological Society, ed. R. F. Spenser (Seattle: University of Washington Press, 1969), 69–80.

8. J. Louis Martyn, "Glimpses into the History of the Johannine Community," in *The Gospel of John in Christian History* (Paramus, N.J.: Paulist/ Newman Press, 1978), 90–121.

9. Raymond E. Brown, *The Community of the Beloved Disciple* (Paramus, N.J.: Paulist/Newman Press, 1979), 14–16; 88–91.

10. Ernst Käsemann, *The Testament of Jesus according to John 17* (Philadelphia: Fortress Press, 1966), 4–26.

11. Wayne Meeks, "The Man from Heaven in Johannine Sectarianism," *JBL* 91 (1972): 44–72.

12. For an overview of the situation of the Johannine community, see D. Moody Smith, "Johannine Christianity: Some Reflections on Its Character and Delineation," *NTS* 21 (1976): 222–48, reprinted in his *Johannine Christianity* (Columbia, S.C.: University of South Carolina Press, 1984), 1–36.

13. Meeks, "Man from Heaven," 70–71.

14. Peter Berger and Thomas Luckmann, *The Social Construction of Reality* (Garden City, N.Y.: Doubleday & Co., 1966); and Peter Berger, *The Sacred Canopy* (Garden City, N.Y.: Doubleday & Co., 1967).

15. See Mary Douglas, *Essays in the Sociology of Perception* (London: Routledge & Kegan Paul, 1982), esp. 1–30.

16. As Clifford Geertz points out in "Ideology as Cultural System," in *Ideology and Discontent*, ed. D. E. Apter (New York: Free Press of Glencoe, 1964), 47–49, ideology need not imply a destructive bias; it can be studied in a more neutral way as a clue to the operative cultural system.

17. See Edward Shils and Harry Johnson, "Ideology," in *International Encyclopedia of the Social Sciences*, ed. D. Sills (New York: Macmillan Co. and Free Press of Glencoe, 1968), 4:66–85; and *Ideology and Discontent*, ed. D. E. Apter.

18. Geertz, "Ideology as Cultural System," 59.

19. Geertz's term; see ibid., 47.

20. This refers to the subtitle of Mary Douglas's book, *Natural Symbols: Explorations in Cosmology* (New York: Pantheon Books, 1982), by which she means "symbolic structures," vii.

CHAPTER 1
JESUS, EQUAL TO GOD—JOHN 5

1. Interest in the forensic aspects of the Fourth Gospel has grown steadily over the past decades. See Rudolf Bultmann, *The Gospel of John* (Philadelphia: Westminster Press, 1971), 50, 84–97, 145, 172, 237–84, 552; Theo Preiss, *Life in Christ*, SBT 13 (Naperville, Ill.: Alec R. Allenson, 1954), 13–27; Wayne A. Meeks, *The Prophet-King*, NovTSup 14 (Leiden: E. J. Brill, 1967), 61–67, 305–7; Allison A. Trites, *The New Testament Concept of Witness*, SNTSMS 31 (Cambridge: Cambridge University Press, 1977), 78–124; J. Louis Martyn, *History and Tradition in the Fourth Gospel*, rev. & enl. (Nashville: Abingdon Press, 1979), chaps. 3–4; and my article "John III—A Debate over Johannine Epistemology and Christology," *NT* 23

(1981): 117–18. For general studies in forensic processes and the New Testament, see J. D. Derrett, *Law in the New Testament* (London: Darton, Longman & Todd, 1970), 389–406; A. N. Sherwin-White, *Roman Society and Roman Law in the New Testament* (Oxford: Clarendon Press, 1963), 48–70; A. A. Trites, "The Importance of Legal Scenes and Language in the Book of Acts," *NT* 15 (1974): 278–84; and my article "The Forensic Defense Speech and Paul's Trial Speeches in Acts 22—26: Form and Function," in *Luke-Acts: New Perspectives from the SBL Seminar* (New York: Crossroad, 1984), 210–24.

2. See Robert Fortna, *The Gospel of Signs*, SNTSMS 11 (Cambridge: Cambridge University Press, 1970), 48–54; W. Nicol, *The Semeia in the Fourth Gospel*, NovTSup 32 (Leiden: E. J. Brill, 1972), 15–16; and Rudolf Schnackenburg, *The Gospel according to St. John* (New York: Crossroad, 1980), 2:96.

3. Nicol, *Semeia in the Fourth Gospel*, 15–16.

4. Ibid., 23–24.

5. See Mary Smallwood, *The Jews under Roman Rule* (Leiden: E. J. Brill, 1976), 123; more recently, see Marcus Borg, *Conflict, Holiness and Politics in the Teachings of Jesus* (New York: Edwin Mellen Press, 1984), 145–62.

6. See my article, "Jacob Traditions and the Interpretation of John 4:10–26," *CBQ* 41 (1979): 419–37.

7. A. E. Harvey, *Jesus on Trial* (Atlanta: John Knox Press, 1976).

8. Yet see John 5:10–15; 9:13–15, 18–21.

9. Harvey, *Jesus on Trial*, 46–47; regarding this Harvey pointed out in the case of Daniel, Susanna, and the two elders that Daniel's sole task in the forensic proceedings was to discredit the two witnesses to Susanna's alleged adultery. He does not produce new facts in her favor but destroys the witnesses for the prosecution (pp. 20–21). On the admissibility of witnesses, see my study of Acts 4:13 in *The Passion according to Luke* (Paramus, N.J.: Paulist/Newman Press, 1985), 92, 99, 106; and my "The Forensic Defense Speech and Paul's Trial Speeches in Acts 22–26," 211–13.

10. See W. Bauer, *Das Johannesevangelium*, HNT 6 (Tübingen: J. C. B. Mohr [Paul Siebeck], 1933), 88; Str. B. II.522.

11. See Severino Pancaro, *The Law in the Fourth Gospel*, NovTSup 42 (Leiden: E. J. Brill, 1975), 208–31.

12. M. E. Boismard, "Les traditions johannique concernant le Baptiste," *RB* 70 (1963): 5–42; T. F. Glasson, "John the Baptist in the Fourth Gospel," *ExpTim* 67 (1955): 245–46; W. Wink, *John the Baptist in the Gospel Tradition*, SNTSMS 7 (Cambridge: Cambridge University Press, 1968); and Fortna, *Gospel of Signs*, 167–78.

13. On this characteristic of John the Baptizer in the Fourth Gospel, see Bultmann, *The Gospel of John*, 84; Harvey, *Jesus on Trial*, 23–30; Schnackenburg, *Gospel according to St. John*, 1:222; and Trites, *The New Testament Concept of Witness*, 91–92.

14. See Schnackenburg, *Gospel according to St. John* 1:518–25; E. Bammel, "John Did No Miracle," *Miracles*, ed. C. F. D. Moule (London: A. R. Mowbray,

1965), 181–202; Peter Riga, "Signs of Glory: The Use of 'Sēmeion' in St. John's Gospel," *Int* 17 (1963): 402–10; and Harvey, *Jesus on Trial*, 95–100. For a survey of the current discussion on the function of signs in John's Gospel, see Robert Kysar, *The Fourth Evangelist and His Gospel* (Minneapolis: Augsburg Publishing House, 1975), 225–30.

15. See C. K. Barrett, *The Gospel according to St. John*, 2d ed. (Philadelphia: Westminster Press, 1978), 266–67; and Schnackenburg, *Gospel according to St. John*, 2:124.

16. See Meeks, *Prophet-King*, 299–301.

17. C. H. Dodd, in *The Interpretation of the Fourth Gospel* (Cambridge: Cambridge University Press, 1968), 266–67, distinguishes between *phonē* and *logos* in 5:37–38, arguing that the Jews may have the *words* of God's Scripture in mind but not the *logos* they embody; Dodd then goes on to stress the relationship of *logos theos* in John 17:14, 17 with the *logos* of the Gospel Prologue.

18. See U. C. Von Wahlde, "The Witnesses to Jesus in John 5:31–40 and Belief in the Fourth Gospel," *CBQ* 43 (1981): 390–93.

19. See Trites, *New Testament Concept of Witness*, 101–2; and J. M. Boice, *Witness and Revelation in the Gospel of John* (Grand Rapids: Zondervan, 1970).

20. See Johannes Beutler, *Martyria* (Frankfurt am Main: Joseph Knecht, 1972), 126, 262–63; and Harvey, *Jesus on Trial*, 100.

21. It is important to contrast the Jews who resist the Christian interpretation of the Scriptures with Nathanael, who overcomes the difficulties proposed by the synagogue regarding this type of exegesis and perseveres in coming to Jesus; see R. F. Collins, "The Representative Figures of the Fourth Gospel," *DR* 94 (1976): 34–36.

22. See Harvey, *Jesus on Trial*, 57–58.

23. This is a typical pattern in John; see Preiss, *Life in Christ*, 14–22; Meeks, *Prophet-King*, 65 n. 1; and C. F. D. Moule, "From Defendant to Judge—and Deliverer: An Enquiry into the Use and Limitations of the Theme of Vindication in the New Testament," *Studiorum Novi Testamenti Societas*, Bulletin 3 (1952): 40–52.

24. See my treatment of this judgmental material in "John III—A Debate over Johannine Epistemology and Christology," 115–28; and my *Passion according to Luke*, 83–84, 89–98.

25. Meeks, *Prophet-King*, 118, 125, 137, 159–61, 200–204, 254–56; see also Nils Johannson, *Parakletoi* (Lund: Gleerupska Universitetsbokhandeln, 1940), 5–11.

26. See Martyn, *History and Theology in the Fourth Gospel*, 64–89.

27. There is critical disagreement over what is being argued or defended in 5:30–47; e.g., Raymond E. Brown, in *The Gospel according to John*, AB 29 (Garden City, N.Y.: Doubleday & Co., 1966), 216–17, sees the eschatology as defensive of the Sabbath violation in the sense that it belongs to Jesus to "vindicate the good" on the Sabbath; in contrast, Bultmann, in *Gospel of John*, 247–62, excludes the defense of the Sabbath from vv. 19–30 and concentrates on the Johannine presentation of Jesus as "the Revealer as Eschatological Judge."

28. Bultmann, *Gospel of John,* 244.

29. E. Lohse, "Jesu Worte über den Sabbat," in *Judentum, Urchristentum, Kirche* (Berlin: Töpelmann, 1960), 79–89; Louise Schottroff and Wolfgang Stegemann, "The Sabbath Was Made for Man: The Interpretation of Mark 2:23–28," in *God of the Lowly,* ed. W. Schottroff and W. Stegemann (Maryknoll, N.Y.: Orbis Books, 1984), 118–27.

30. This Jewish material has been conveniently collected by Barrett, *Gospel according to St. John,* 256; and Dodd, *Interpretation of the Fourth Gospel,* 320–21.

31. Bultmann, *Gospel of John,* 244; C. H. Dodd, "The Portrait of Jesus in John and the Synoptics," in *Christian History and Interpretation: Studies Presented to John Knox,* ed. W. R. Farmer and C. F. D. Moule (Cambridge: Cambridge University Press, 1967), 185.

32. H. Odeberg, in *The Fourth Gospel* (Uppsala: Almquist & Wiksells, 1929), 203, calls our attention to the implications of the charge, which to a rabbinic ear would be equivalent to "he makes himself independent of God," implying some degree of rebellion against God; see also Schnackenburg, *Gospel according to St. John,* 2:102; Str. B. II.465.

33. See John 5:30; 7:17, 18, 28; 8:28, 42; 14:10.

34. Schnackenburg, in *Gospel according to St. John,* 2:103, links this figure with the *logos* in the Prologue; C. H. Dodd, "A Hidden Parable in the Fourth Gospel," in *More New Testament Essays* (Manchester: University Press, 1968), 30–40, has examined the background of 5:19–20 as a primitive parable, but his article did not address the function of this material in the argument in John 5.

35. Several commentators have suggested that God's powers are ascribed to Jesus in 5:19–29; Dodd (*Interpretation of the Fourth Gospel,* 322–23) suggested that in 5:19–29 there was an allusion to the two supreme powers of God, but he distinguished *zōopoiein* from *krinein,* claiming that the two powers were salvation and judgment; Schnackenburg (*Gospel according to St. John,* 2:106) identified the two powers as "to give life" and "to judge"—both eschatological powers. I am suggesting that a distinction be made between vv. 19–20 (creative power) and 21–29 (eschatological power).

36. See *Gen. R.* 11.10; *Ex. R.* 30.6; *Pesiq. R.* 23.

37. *Leg. All.* II.68; *Cher.* 27–28; *Sac.* 59; *Plant.* 86–87; *Heres* 166; *Fuga* 95, 100; *Somn.* I.159, 160, 162–63; *Abr.* 124–25; *Mos.* II.99; *Leg.* 4, 6; *Q. Ex.* II.62, 64, 65, 66, 68.

38. See Harry A. Wolfson, *Philo* (Cambridge: Harvard University Press, 1948), 1:218–25; and Erwin R. Goodenough, *By Light, Light* (New Haven: Yale University Press, 1935), 24–29.

39. For other places in Philo where the two powers of God are called by God's two names, see *Plant.* 86–87; *Abr.* 124–25; *Somn.* I.160, 163; *Q. Ex.* II.62.

40. See A. Marmorstein, *The Old Rabbinic Doctrine of God* (New York: KTAV, 1968), 41–53; and E. E. Urbach, *The Sages* (Jerusalem: Magnes Press, 1975), 448–61.

41. The study by Alan Segal and Nils Dahl, "Philo and the Rabbis on the

Names of God," *JSJ* 9 (1978): 1–28, presents a contemporary discussion of this material; see also A. Marmorstein, "Philo and the Names of God," *JQR* 22 (1931–32): 295–306.

42. For a useful summary of the differences between Philo and the rabbis, see Segal and Dahl, "Philo and the Rabbis on the Names of God," 1–3.

43. Describing the faith of Abraham, the model believer, Paul noted that Abraham believed in God according to the two powers: "In the presence of the God in whom he believed, who gives life to the dead and calls into existence the things that do not exist" (Rom. 4:17); on this text, see Halvor Moxnes, *Theology in Conflict: Studies in Paul's Understanding of God in Romans*, NovTSup 53 (Leiden: E. J. Brill, 1980), 231–82.

44. In associating the name *theos* with creation, Philo is reflecting the ancient etymological tradition of deriving *theos* from *tithēmi;* see *Mos.* II.99, *Abr.* 121, *Conf.* 137, *Mut.* 29.

45. Bultmann, *Gospel of John,* 695 n. 1.

46. Both Bultmann (*Gospel of John,* 695 n. 2) and Brown (*The Gospel according to John,* 1046–47) see the two titles as reinforcing each other without attention to their possible different meanings; their focus was on the affinities of *kyrios theos* with Greco-Roman literature.

47. Following up the important study of Collins ("Representative Figures in the Fourth Gospel," 124–26), Thomas can be seen to be uniquely associated in the Gospel with death and resurrection (see 11:11, 16; 14:5; 20:24–29). There is a thematic unity to the figure of Thomas in the Gospel: (1) He is closely linked with Jesus' death, either in his ignorant willingness to die with Jesus (11:16) or his misunderstanding of his "going" (14:5). (2) More important, Thomas becomes in the Fourth Gospel the premier witness to the resurrection, either Lazarus's or Jesus' own (20:24–29; 21:2–14). Thus his confession that Jesus is Lord should be seen as an acknowledgment of Jesus' eschatological power over death.

48. Contemporary studies of New Testament Christology have stressed various aspects of the title Lord. They note that Jesus is proclaimed Lord in virtue of his resurrection (see Phil. 2:6–11; Rom. 10:9; Acts 2:36; and the use of Psalm 110 regarding the resurrection); in another vein, Jesus is acclaimed Lord in terms of the Maranatha confession, stressing his function as judge at the Parousia. In general, it can be said that Lord refers to the Risen Jesus in his role of eschatological pantocrator; see Reginald Fuller, *The Foundations of New Testament Christology* (New York: Charles Scribner's Sons, 1965), 184–86; Oscar Cullmann, *The Christology of the New Testament* (Philadelphia: Westminster Press, 1963), 216–33.

49. See Brown, *Gospel according to John,* 219–21; and A. C. Sundberg, "*Isos To Theo* Christology in John 5.17–30," *BR* 15 (1970): 19–31.

50. See Pancaro, *Law in the Fourth Gospel,* 234–39.

51. The sense of a summary of eschatological materials has been noted, e.g., by Josef Blank, *Krisis: Untersuchungen zur johanneischen Christologie und Eschatologie* (Freiburg: Lambertus Verlag, 1964), 120–34.

52. This resembles the summary of the "deeds of the Christ" in the Q

tradition in Matt. 11:2–5: "The blind will receive their sight . . . and the dead are raised up."

53. See Blank, *Krisis*, 164–82; Dodd, "The Portrait of Jesus in John and the Synoptics," 186–94; and Schnackenburg, *Gospel according to St. John*, 2:114–15.

54. E.g., see C. K. Barrett, "Unsolved New Testament Problems: The Place of Eschatology in the Fourth Gospel," *ExpTim* 59 (1948): 302–3; and Paolo Ricca, *Die Eschatologie des Vierten Evangeliums* (Zürich: Gotthelf Verlag, 1966).

55. See Bultmann, *Gospel of John*, 247–62; D. M. Smith, *The Composition and Order of the Fourth Gospel* (New Haven: Yale University Press, 1965), 214–15; and Robert Kysar, "The Eschatology of the Fourth Gospel—A Correction of Bultmann's Redactional Hypothesis," *Perspective* 13 (1972): 23–26; and idem, *Fourth Evangelist and His Gospel*, 207–14.

56. My remarks should be seen alongside Kysar's comment regarding the present state of research into Johannine eschatology: "The advancement of contemporary scholarship on this point is found in the fact that there is no appeal to a post-johannine redactor theory in order to account for the presence of future resurrection texts in the gospel" (*Fourth Evangelist and His Gospel*, 213).

57. Martyn, *History and Theology in the Fourth Gospel*, 72.

58. See Wayne Meeks, "Social Function of Apocalyptic Language in Pauline Christianity," in *Apocalypticism in the Mediterranean and the Near East*, ed. David Hellholm (Tübingen: J. C. B. Mohr, 1983), 687–705.

CHAPTER 2
JESUS' ESCHATOLOGICAL POWER—JOHN 8

1. Examples of this abound in the Fourth Gospel: 3:2; 5:18b; 6:31; 14:1–4; 16:1–4. See Peder Borgen's classic study of this, *Bread from Heaven*, NovTSup 10 (Leiden: E. J. Brill, 1965); and his article, "Observations on the Midrashic Character of John 6," *ZNW* 54 (1963): 232–40; see also my article "John III—A Debate over Johannine Epistemology and Christology," *NT* 23 (1981): 115–16.

2. The Gospel insists that he does not judge in 3:17 and 12:47, yet see the affirmative remarks in 5:22, 27; 9:39; see Raymond E. Brown, *The Gospel according to John*, AB 29 (Garden City, N.Y.: Doubleday & Co., 1966), 345.

3. See Brown, *Gospel according to John*, 343; Rudolf Schnackenburg, *The Gospel according to St. John* (New York: Crossroad, 1982), 2:187.

4. On forensic procedure in John, see chap. 1 n. 1 above; the best study of this aspect of John's Gospel is still that of A. E. Harvey, *Jesus on Trial* (Atlanta: John Knox Press, 1976).

5. See my article, "The Forensic Defense Speech and Paul's Trial Speeches in Acts 22–26: Form and Function," in *Luke-Acts: New Perspectives from the Society of Biblical Literature Seminar*, ed. C. H. Talbert (New York: Crossroad, 1984), 216–18.

6. See Jouette Bassler, *Divine Impartiality: Paul and a Theological Axiom,* SBLDS 59 (Chico, Calif.: Scholars Press, 1981), 7–27.

7. Peder Borgen, "God's Agent in the Fourth Gospel," in *Religions in Antiquity,* ed. Jacob Neusner (Leiden: E. J. Brill, 1968), 137–48; and more recently, George W. Buchanan, "Apostolic Christology," SBLASP 1986, 172–82.

8. An earlier attempt to outline the structure of John 8 is that of Walter Kern, "Der symmetrische Gesamtaufbau von JO 8, 12–58," *ZTK* 78 (1956): 451–54. While picking out many key words and indicating an *inclusio,* Kern did not engage in a formal study of the text, its logic, and its Johannine patterns.

9. See Earl Richard, "Expressions of Double Meaning and Their Function in the Gospel of John," *NTS* 31 (1985): 96–112.

10. On this Johannine form, see Herbert Leroy, *Rätsel und Missverständnis* (Bonn: Peter Hanstein, 1968), 45–47, 53–67. Norman Perrin, *What Is Redaction Criticism?* (Philadelphia: Fortress Press, 1969), 40–57, observed that Mark 8:31—10:45 is structured around a triple repetition of a comparable pattern:

Passion Prediction:	8:31	9:31	10:32–34
Misunderstanding:	8:32	9:32	10:35–40
Clarifying Remarks:	8:33—9:29	9:33—10:31	10:41–45

11. Other examples of this pattern in John are:

statement:	11:23	12:27	13:27	14:4	16:25–28
misunderstanding:	11:24	12:29	13:29	14:5	16:29–30
explanation:	11:25–26	12:30	13:31–35	14:6	16:31–33

12. E.g., C. H. Dodd, "Behind a Johannine Dialogue," in *More New Testament Studies* (Manchester: Manchester University Press, 1968), 42–43; Brown, *Gospel according to John,* 354–55.

13. The ambiguity rests also in the remark that these alleged believers are "Jews" (8:31), a term with multiple meanings in John; see Wayne A. Meeks, "Am I a Jew? Johannine Christianity and Judaism," in *Christianity, Judaism and Other Greco-Roman Cults: Studies for Morton Smith at 60,* ed. Jacob Neusner (Leiden: E. J. Brill, 1975), 1:180–83; J. Louis Martyn, *History and Theology in the Fourth Gospel,* rev. ed. (Nashville: Abingdon Press, 1979), 86–89.

14. See my article "Jesus the Judge: Forensic Process in John 8:21–59," *Bib* 68 (1987): 509–42.

15. On the forensic procedure, *cognitio,* see A. N. Sherwin-White, *Roman Society and Roman Law in the New Testament* (Oxford: Clarendon Press, 1963), 13–19, 28; and my *The Passion according to Luke* (New York: Paulist/Newman Press, 1985), 76–77, 81.

16. Although it is a commonplace to speak of Abraham's "faith" (Hab. 2:4//Gal. 3:11; Gen. 15:6//Rom. 4:3), he was also known for his hospitality; see 1 Clem. 10:6–8 and Test. Abr. 17.

17. On the midrash in 8:44, see Nils A. Dahl, "Der Erstgeborene Satans und der Vater des Teufels," in *Apophoreta,* ed. W. Eltester (Berlin: Töpelmann, 1964), 70–84.

18. They are descendants of Ishmael, not Isaac, for Isaac "remained" in Abraham's tent, whereas Ishmael did not (Gen. 21:10–14).

19. A similar occurrence of this phenomenon takes place with Nicodemus in 3:4, 9; see my article "John III—A Debate on Johannine Epistemology and Christology," 119–20.

20. Rudolf Bultmann, *The Gospel of John* (Philadelphia: Westminster Press, 1971), 348, remarked that "I AM" in 8:24 has the force of a title or name, so that the question in 8:25 is an appropriate response.

21. It is a Johannine motif that the judged One becomes the judge and the judges are judged; see my article "John III—A Debate over Johannine Epistemology and Christology," 117, 122–23.

22. See Quintilian, *Inst. Orat.* V.vii.15–18; regarding the New Testament, see Luke 19:22.

23. See A. F. Segal, "Ruler of This World: Attitudes about Mediator Figures and the Importance of Sociology for Self-Definition," in *Jewish and Christian Self-Definition,* ed. E. P. Sanders (Philadelphia: Fortress Press, 1981), 245–68.

24. See Harvey, *Jesus on Trial,* 18–20.

25. Barnabas Lindars, *The Gospel of John* (Grand Rapids: Wm. B. Eerdmans, 1972), 225, suggests that power to make alive looks backward to creation and forward to resurrection.

26. Brown (*Gospel according to John,* 6) clearly sets forth two ways of punctuating 1:3–4:

(1) And apart from him
   not a thing came to be.

(2) And apart from him
   there came to be
   not a thing which came to be.
   In him was life.

That which came to be
in him was life.

For poetic reasons, Brown favors (1); for thematic reasons, I am drawn to (2).

27. See Ps. 90:2LXX for just such a distinction; see also Brown, *Gospel according to John,* 56.

28. See Brown, *Gospel according to John,* 4; and Schnackenburg, *Gospel according to St. John,* 1:233.

29. See Friedrich Büchsel, *"eimi,"* TDNT 2:398–99; see Edwin Freed, "Who or What Was before Abraham in John 8:58?" *JSNT* 17 (1983): 52–59.

30. E.g., Schnackenburg, *Gospel according to St. John,* 2:108; and Lindars, *Gospel of John,* 223.

31. See Borgen, "God's Agent in the Fourth Gospel," 138–39. Important new studies on honor/shame in Mediterranean culture have a bearing on this perspective; see Bruce Malina, *The New Testament World: Insights from Cultural Anthropology* (Atlanta: John Knox Press, 1981), 25–50.

32. C. K. Barrett, *The Gospel according to St. John,* 2d ed. (Philadelphia: Westminster Press, 1978), 429; on the issue of Jesus' divine glory, see Ernst Käsemann, *The Testament of Jesus* (Philadelphia: Fortress Press, 1968), 4–26.

33. See Deut. 32:39 and 2 Kings 5:7.

34. See C. H. Dodd, *The Interpretation of the Fourth Gospel* (Cambridge: Cambridge University Press, 1968), 324.

35. Barrett, *Gospel according to St. John*, 216; see also Lindars, *Gospel of John*, 222.

CHAPTER 3
JESUS' POWER OVER DEATH—JOHN 10

1. Rudolf Schnackenburg, *The Gospel according to St. John* (New York: Crossroad, 1982), 2:276–78; see also Mark Appold, *The Oneness Motif in the Fourth Gospel* (Tübingen: J. C. B. Mohr, 1976), 246–57.

2. Odo Kiefer, *Die Hirtenrede: Analyse und Deutung von Joh 10, 1–18,* Stuttgarter Bibelstudium 23 (Stuttgart: Katholisches Bibelwerk, 1967).

3. J. Terence Forestell, *The Word of the Cross*, AnBib 57 (Rome: Biblical Institute Press, 1974), 74.

4. See Raymond E. Brown's review of Kiefer's book in *Bib* 31 (1969): 98–100.

5. Kiefer, *Hirtenrede*, 25.

6. Ibid., 58–60; 75–80.

7. Ibid., 76–78.

8. See Forestell, *Word of the Cross*, 74–75; and Schnackenburg, *Gospel according to St. John*, 300–301.

9. E.g., Raymond E. Brown, *The Gospel according to John*, AB 29 (Garden City, N.Y.: Doubleday & Co., 1966), 399; C. K. Barrett, *The Gospel according to St. John* (London: SPCK, 1965), 313.

10. Forestell, *Word of the Cross*, 9.

11. See ibid., 61–74; see also Rudolf Bultmann, *Theology of the New Testament* (New York: Charles Scribner's Sons, 1955), 2:53; and J. L. Martyn, "Source Criticism and *Religionsgeschichte* in the Fourth Gospel," *Perspective* 11 (1970): 266–67.

12. See Max Wilcox, "'Upon the Tree'—Deut. 21:22–23 in the New Testament," *JBL* 96 (1977): 85–99.

13. See Bultmann, *Theology of the New Testament*, 2:52–53; and Forestell, *Word of the Cross*, 101.

14. Forestell, *Word of the Cross*, 75–76; see Georg Richter, "Die Deutung des Kreuzestodes Jesu in der Leidensgeschichte des Johannesevangeliums (Joh 13–19)," *BibLeb* 9 (1968): 21–36.

15. See F. W. Danker, *Benefactor* (St. Louis: Clayton Publishing House, 1982), 321–23; and idem, "The Endangered Benefactor in Luke-Acts," SBLASP 1981, 41–43.

16. See the model developed by C. H. Talbert, *What Is a Gospel?* (Philadelphia: Fortress Press, 1977), 26–52.

17. See Brown, *Gospel according to John*, 404–5; and Schnackenburg, *Gospel according to St. John*, 2:303–4.

18. Brown, *Gospel according to John*, 404.

19. See J. D. M. Derrett, "The Good Shepherd: St. John's Use of Jewish Halakah and Haggadah," *ST* 27 (1973): 25–50; R. H. Lightfoot, *St. John's*

Gospel (Oxford: Clarendon Press, 1956), 205–7; see also Wayne A. Meeks, *The Prophet-King* (Leiden: E. J. Brill, 1967), 309–12.

20. E.g., see Brown, *Gospel according to John*, 405; Schnackenburg, *Gospel according to St. John*, 306; and Paul Winter, "Luke xxii 66b–71," *ST* 9 (1955): 112–15.

21. See J. Duncan Derrett, *Law in the New Testament* (London: Darton, Longman & Todd, 1970), 389–406.

22. See my *The Passion according to Luke* (New York: Paulist/Newman Press, 1985), 83–84, 89–98.

23. Schnackenburg, *Gospel according to St. John*, 306–7.

24. The importance and difficulty of 10:30 in early christological discussions may be surveyed in T. E. Pollard, "The Exegesis of John x.30 in the Early Trinitarian Controversies," *NTS* 3 (1956–57): 334–49. The range of interpretation was: (1) moral unity or unity of wills, (2) unity of substance, and (3) unity of operations.

25. See Edwyn C. Hoskyns, *The Fourth Gospel* (London: Faber & Faber, 1947), 389–390.

26. J. Bernard, *A Critical and Exegetical Commentary on the Gospel according to St. John* (Edinburgh: T & T Clark, 1926), 366.

27. Schnackenburg, *Gospel according to St. John*, 317.

28. J. Birdsall, "John X.29," *JTS* 11 (1960): 342–44; and J. Whittaker, "A Hellenistic Context for John 10,29," *VC* 24 (1970): 241–44.

29. Whittaker, "A Hellenistic Context for John 10,29," 245–58.

30. Ibid., 257–58.

31. See Kiefer, *Hirtenrede*, 78–79.

32. Albrecht Oepke, in *"apollymi,"* *TDNT* 1:395–96, draws a distinction between merely "dying" *(apothneskein)* and "perishing" *(apollymi);* he sees its use in the New Testament as the antithesis of being saved and eternal life: "In contrast to *sōizesthai* or to *zōē aiōnios, apollymi* is definitive destruction not merely in the sense of the extinction of physical existence but rather of an eternal plunge into Hades or a hopeless destiny of death."

33. See Richard Jungkuntz, "An Approach to the Exegesis of John 10:34–36," *CTM* 35 (1964): 556–58.

34. Bultmann, *Gospel of John*, 390.

35. See *b. Ta'an* 2a, *b. Sanh.* 113a, *Midr. Ps.* 78.5; and Barrett, *Gospel according to St. John*, 260.

36. For another view, see Wayne Meeks, "The Divine Agent and Its Counterfeit in Philo and the Fourth Gospel," in *Aspects of Religious Propaganda in Judaism and Early Christianity*, ed. Elizabeth Schüssler Fiorenza (Notre Dame, Ind.: University of Notre Dame Press, 1976), 56–57.

37. I am indebted to J. Ramsey Michaels's suggestion at the 1986 Society of Biblical Literature convention that "greater works" in 5:20 refers to the works of eschatological power mentioned in 5:21–29.

38. E.g., Barrett, *Gospel according to St. John*, 321; and Schnackenburg, *Gospel according to St. John*, 312–13.

39. C. H. Dodd, *The Interpretation of the Fourth Gospel* (Cambridge: Cambridge University Press, 1968), 257.

CHAPTER 4
JESUS' RESURRECTION—JOHN 11

1. C. H. Dodd, *The Interpretation of the Fourth Gospel* (Cambridge: Cambridge University Press, 1968), 257.

2. E. Hoskyns, *The Fourth Gospel* (London: Faber & Faber, 1947), 402.

3. B. Lindars, *The Gospel of John* (Grand Rapids: Wm. B. Eerdmans, 1972), 395.

4. Rudolf Schnackenburg, *The Gospel according to St. John* (New York: Crossroad, 1982), 2:322, 330.

5. Robert Fortna, *The Gospel of Signs* (Cambridge: Cambridge University Press, 1970), 74–87; W. Wilkens, "Die Erweckung des Lazarus," *TZ* 15 (1959): 22–39; W. Stenger, "Die Auferweckung des Lazarus (John 11, 1–45)," *TTZ* 83 (1974): 17–19; and W. Nichol, *The Sēmeia Source in the Fourth Gospel*, NovTSup 32 (Leiden: E. J. Brill, 1972), 37–39, 109–10.

6. Fortna, *Gospel of Signs*, 74–87; Stenger, "Auferweckung des Lazarus," 17–32; and Schnackenburg, *Gospel according to St. John*, 2:318–21.

7. Stenger, "Auferweckung des Lazarus," 22.

8. Ibid., 29–31.

9. James P. Martin, "History and Eschatology in the Lazarus Narrative: John 11.1–44," *SJT* 17 (1964): 335–37.

10. For a similar instance of Christian belief in an overly realized eschatology, see 2 Tim. 2:17–18; in this vein, see also discussions of the Corinthian pneumatics (1 Cor. 4:8); Richard Horsley, "'How can some of you say that there is no resurrection of the dead?' Spiritual Elitism in Corinth," *NT* 29 (1978): 303–31; and A. C. Thiselton, "Realized Eschatology at Corinth," *NTS* 24 (1978): 510–26.

11. Raymond E. Brown, *The Gospel according to John*, AB 29 (Garden City, N.Y.: Doubleday & Co., 1966), 431.

12. See Rudolf Bultmann, *The Gospel of John* (Philadelphia: Westminster Press, 1971), 402; and Dodd, *Interpretation of the Fourth Gospel*, 364.

13. The reader has already been schooled to accept Jesus' claim that his dead followers do not perish forever (10:28), a key aspect of Jesus' eschatological power argued in chap. 3.

14. Comparably, Jesus can claim to be "I AM," that is, imperishable, but this does not exclude his death on the cross; for his power lies in being able to lay down his life and take it back again (10:17–18), a point in which the reader of the Fourth Gospel was carefully schooled in the preceding chapter.

15. Fortna, *Gospel of Signs*, 197–99.

16. Ibid., 75.

17. Brown, *Gospel according to John*, 534.

18. Stenger, "Auferweckung des Lazarus," 32–34.

19. Schnackenburg, *Gospel according to St. John*, 2:322.

20. Stenger, "Auferweckung des Lazarus," 35.

21. Martin, "History and Eschatology in the Lazarus Narrative," 342.

CHAPTER 5
EQUAL TO GOD, BUT NOT OF THIS WORLD

1. Wayne Meeks, "The Man from Heaven in Johannine Sectarianism," *JBL* 91 (1972): 44–72. Godfrey Nicholson, in his *Death as Departure,* SBLDS 63 (Chico, Calif.: Scholars Press, 1983), examined the same descent/ascent motif, but unfortunately made no attempt to deal with it vis-à-vis Johannine high Christology or to assess its ideological implications for the Gospel.

2. See my study of this in "Jacob Allusions in John 1:51," *CBQ* 44 (1982): 586–605.

3. Alan Segal, *Two Powers in Heaven* (Leiden: E. J. Brill, 1977).

4. E.g., see G. G. Strousma, "Form(s) of God: Some Notes on Metatron and Christ," *HTR* 76 (1983): 269–88.

5. See Wayne Meeks, *The Prophet-King* (Leiden: E. J. Brill, 1967); and idem, "Moses as God and King," in *Religions in Antiquity,* ed. Jacob Neusner (Leiden: E. J. Brill, 1968), 354–71.

6. Rudolf Schnackenburg, *The Gospel according to St. John* (New York: Herder & Herder, 1968), 1:221–81.

7. See Nils Dahl, "The One God of Jews and Gentiles," in *Studies in Paul* (Minneapolis: Augsburg Publishing House, 1977), 178–90; and S. Dean McBride, "The Yoke of the Kingdom," *Int* 27 (1973): 273–306.

8. On the importance of establishing the point of view or perspective of a Gospel narrative, see Norman Peterson, "'Point of View' in Mark's Narrative," *Semeia* 12 (1978): 97–121; David Rhoads and Donald Michie, *Mark as Story* (Philadelphia: Fortress Press, 1982), 35–62, 147 n. 10. These authors depend on important studies in the field of rhetoric and literary criticism, such as Boris Uspensky, *Poetics of Composition* (Berkeley and Los Angeles: University of California Press, 1973); Seymour Chatman, *Story and Discourse* (Ithaca, N.Y.: Cornell University Press, 1978), 151–58; Norman Friedman, "Point of View in Fiction: The Development of a Critical Concept," in *Approaches to the Novel,* ed. Robert Scholes (Corte Madera, Calif.: Chandler & Sharp, 1961), 113–42; and Robert Weimann, "Narrative Perspective: Point of View Reconsidered," in *Structure and Society in Literary History* (Charlottesville, Va.: University Press of Virginia, 1976), 234–66.

9. One should remember that biblical documents enjoyed multiple redactions, a fact true of the Pentateuch, the Prophets, and the Psalms; even in the New Testament, Matthew reflects not only the sectarian viewpoint of the Q document, but also the more liberal perspective of Mark; see my *Christ Is Community* (Wilmington, Del.: Michael Glazier, 1985), 65–104.

10. See the analysis of Mary Douglas in "Social Preconditions of Enthusiasm and Heterodoxy," in *Forms of Symbolic Action,* Proceedings of the 1969 Annual Spring Meeting of the American Ethnological Society, ed. Robert Spenser (Seattle: University of Washington Press, 1969), 69–80.

11. See Raymond E. Brown, *The Johannine Epistles*, AB 30 (Garden City, N.Y.: Doubleday & Co., 1982), 50–54, 73–79.

12. A treatment of the structural implications of a Christology that devalues the flesh of Jesus may be found in my *Christ Is Community*, 183–92.

13. Meeks, "Man from Heaven," 50–57, 60–61.

14. Representative of these is Alan Culpepper, "The Pivot of John's Prologue," *NTS* 27 (1980): 1–31.

15. Jesus, of course, claims that he and God are "one" (10:30) and that God is in him and he is in God, but the formula equal to God, is not found on his lips. Yet the implications of the formula, that he has God's two powers and is rightly called by the names corresponding to these powers, are found on the lips of Jesus and his disciples.

16. The Johannine Gospel at times seems to defend traditional monotheism quite consciously. It is always argued that Jesus does not replace God, that is, *"make himself* God." In one place, Jesus himself would seem to be endorsing traditional monotheism, echoing the Shema (Deut. 6:4–5), when he prays to Israel's deity, "This is eternal life, that they know Thee, *the only true God . . .* " (17:3). Yet the Johannine community is also calling Jesus god, seemingly having it both ways and enjoying the difficulty their remarks create.

17. See Jürgen Becker, "Aufbau, Schichtung und theologiegeschichtliche Stellung des Gebetes in Johannes 17," *ZNW* 60 (1969): 56–83; and Schnackenburg, *Gospel according to St. John,* 3:167–69.

18. E.g., see Raymond E. Brown, *The Gospel according to John,* AB 29A (Garden City, N.Y.: Doubleday & Co., 1970), 742, 772.

19. Brown, *Gospel according to John,* 754–56.

20. John 17:15 states that Jesus does not pray that God take the disciples out of the world, but that remark stands in tension with 17:24, which indicates that Jesus desires them with him, to see his glory, which God gave him before the creation of the world. The inconsistency between 17:15 and 24 suggests to me that the prayer of Jesus has gone through considerable development, including addition of high christological materials.

21. Ernst Käsemann, *The Testament of Jesus* (Philadelphia: Fortress Press, 1969); for critiques, see that of Wayne Meeks in *USQR* 24 (1969): 414–20; and Gunther Bornkamm, "Zur Interpretation des Johannes-Evangeliums," *EvT* 28 (1968): 8–25.

22. The Johannine epistles, for example, indicate that another view of Jesus was present alongside the perspective of 1 John 4:3 and 2 John 7, which was rejected.

CHAPTER 6
A BASIC MODEL: CHRISTOLOGY AND REVOLT

1. Wayne A. Meeks, "The Man from Heaven in Johannine Sectarianism," *JBL* 91 (1972): 48.

2. Ibid., 61.

3. Ibid., 68.

4. Ibid., 70.

5. Ibid., 48–49, 70.

6. Ibid., 71.

7. Besides Meeks, see John Bogart, *Orthodox and Heretical Perfectionism in the Johannine Community as Evident in the First Epistle of John*, SBLDS 33 (Missoula, Mont.: Scholars Press, 1977), 137–38; Fernando Segovia, *Love Relationships in the Johannine Tradition*, SBLDS 58 (Chico, Calif., Scholars Press, 1982), 3–14, 204–13; and D. Bruce Woll, *Johannine Christianity in Conflict: Authority, Rank, and Succession in the First Farewell Discourse*, SBLDS 60 (Chico, Calif.: Scholars Press, 1981), 112–20.

8. Rudolf Bultmann, in *The Gospel of John* (Philadelphia: Westminster Press, 1971), set the agenda for Johannine scholarship with his description of the development of the Fourth Gospel according to his source theory; more recent advances in this direction can be found summarized in Raymond E. Brown, *The Community of the Beloved Disciple* (New York: Paulist/Newman Press, 1979), esp. 171–82; see also Robert Kysar, *The Fourth Evangelist and His Gospel* (Minneapolis: Augsburg Publishing House, 1975), 10–54.

9. Although many theories have been put forth on the relationship of the Johannine epistles to the Fourth Gospel, the most cogent and productive argument seems to be that of Raymond E. Brown, *The Epistles of John*, AB 30 (Garden City, N.Y.: Doubleday & Co., 1982), 86–102.

10. I find quite persuasive the first chapter of Bruce Malina, *The New Testament World: Insights from Cultural Anthropology* (Atlanta: John Knox Press, 1981), 1–24; see also idem, "Why Interpret the Bible with Social Sciences," *ABQ* 2 (1983): 119–33; and idem, "The Social Sciences and Biblical Interpretation," in *The Bible and Liberation*, ed. N. Gottwald (Maryknoll, N.Y.: Orbis Books, 1983), 11–25. See also L. E. Keck, "On the Ethos of Early Christianity," *JAAR* 42 (1974): 435–54; and J. Z. Smith, "The Social Description of Early Christianity," *RSR* 1 (1975): 19–25.

11. E.g., John Gager, *Kingdom and Community* (Englewood Cliffs, N.J.: Prentice-Hall, 1975); the reviews of this book are quite significant in assessing its importance: see *Zygon* 13 (1978): 109–35, esp. the article by J. Z. Smith, "Too Much Kingdom and Too Little Community," 123–30.

12. See Bruce Malina, "Normative Dissonance and Christian Origins," *Semeia* 35 (1986): 35–59.

13. See Bruce Malina, "Jesus as Charismatic Leader?" *BTB* 14 (1984): 55–62; Kojiro Miyahara, "Charisma: From Weber to Contemporary Sociology," *Sociological Inquiry* 53 (1983): 368–88.

14. See Jacob Neusner, *The Idea of Purity in Ancient Judaism* (Leiden: E. J. Brill, 1973); idem, "The Idea of Purity in Ancient Judaism," *JAAR* 43 (1975): 15–26; and Sheldon Isenberg, "Mary Douglas and Hellenistic Religions: The Case of Qumran," SBLASP 1975, 179–85.

15. E.g., Bruce Malina, "The Social World Implied in the Letters of the Christian Bishop-Martyr (Named Ignatius of Antioch)," SBLASP 1978, 71–119; see also John Pilch, "Biblical Leprosy and Body Symbolism," *BTB* 11 (1981): 108–13; see my essays "The Idea of Purity in Mark's Gospel"

and "Body Language in 1 Corinthians: The Use of Anthropological Models for Understanding Paul and His Opponents," *Semeia* 35 (1986): 91–170.

16. Shelden Isenberg and Dennis Owens, "Bodies Natural and Contrived: The Work of Mary Douglas," *RSR* 3 (1977): 1–16; see Robert Wuthnow et al., "The Cultural Anthropology of Mary Douglas," in *Cultural Analysis* (London: Routledge & Kegan Paul, 1984), 77–132.

17. Most recently, Bruce Malina, *Christian Origins and Cultural Anthropology: Practical Models for Biblical Interpretation* (Atlanta: John Knox Press, 1986).

18. The original presentation of group and grid can be found in Mary Douglas, *Natural Symbols* (New York: Pantheon Books, 1982), 54–64; see also idem, "Cultural Bias," in *In the Active Voice* (London: Routledge & Kegan Paul, 1982), 183–253; and idem, *Essays on the Sociology of Perception* (London: Routledge & Kegan Paul, 1982), 1–13. I find the exposition by Malina, *Christian Origins and Cultural Anthropology*, 13–20, a useful, enriched way of understanding these variables in relation to this project.

19. See Isenberg and Owens, "Bodies Natural and Contrived," 7–8; and Malina, *Christian Origins and Cultural Anthropology*, 20–27.

20. I attempted to distinguish the stages of Johannine development according to more theological categories in *Christ Is Community* (Wilmington, Del.: Michael Glazier, 1985), 142–83.

21. This Christology is similar to that found in the Synoptic Gospels. Jesus goes about doing miracles, healing the sick, multiplying food, and raising the dead. And the crowds interpret these deeds correctly, saying that he is "Elijah or one of the prophets" (Mark 8:28). The disciples themselves conclude that his miracles warrant calling him God's .Christ (Mark 8:29), for he does "deeds of the Christ" (Matt. 11:2).

22. See Mary Douglas, *Purity and Danger* (London: Routledge & Kegan Paul, 1966), 34–41; see my article, "The Idea of Purity in Mark's Gospel," 91–105.

23. See Mark 12:29; Rom. 3:30; 1 Cor. 8:4, 6; Gal. 3:20; Eph. 4:4–6; 1 Tim. 2:5; James 2:19; see Norman Gottwald, *The Tribes of Yahweh* (Maryknoll, N.Y.: Orbis Books, 1981), 591–649; and Nils Dahl, *Studies in Paul* (Minneapolis: Augsburg Publishing House, 1977), 178–91.

24. See Jean Soler, "The Dietary Prohibitions of the Hebrews," *The New York Review of Books*, 14 June 1979, 24–30; Jacob Neusner, "Map without Territory: Mishnah's System of Sacrifice and Sanctuary," *HR* 19 (1979): 103–27; and my article "The Idea of Purity in Mark's Gospel," 93–104.

25. See Marcel Simon, *Jewish Sects in the Time of Jesus* (Philadelphia: Fortress Press, 1967); see Josephus, *B.J.* II.119–166 and *Ant.* XVIII.11–25.

26. Gerd Theissen, in his *Sociology of Early Palestinian Christianity* (Philadelphia: Fortress Press, 1977), 77–95, consistently describes Jesus and his rivals as "renewal" movements.

27. See Douglas, *Natural Symbols*, 1–18; and Malina, *Christian Origins and Cultural Anthropology*, 21–22, 139–47.

28. In this regard, one is reminded of Paul's remark in 1 Cor. 11:19 on the need for factions *(haireseis)* to recognize those in the church who are genuine.

29. On this aspect, see Malina, *New Testament World,* 51–60; and idem, *Christian Origins and Cultural Anthropology,* 19–20.

30. On "disciple" in John, see 2:2, 11–12; 3:22; 6:3; 9:2; etc.; see also Ernst Käsemann, *The Testament of Jesus* (Philadelphia: Fortress Press, 1968), 28–32.

31. See Douglas, *Purity and Danger,* 114–16; idem, *Natural Symbols,* 65, 70–75; and see my "Body Language in 1 Corinthians," 131–38.

32. See Pilch, "Biblical Leprosy and Body Symbolism," 109–11.

33. See Douglas, *Natural Symbols,* 28–36.

34. Ibid., 103–14.

35. See Aileen Goulding, *The Fourth Gospel and Jewish Worship* (New York: Oxford University Press, 1960), 58–68, 154–66; and my article "The Jacob Traditions and the Interpretation of John 4:10–26," *CBQ* 41 (1979), esp. 436–37.

36. The list is from Raymond E. Brown, *The Gospel according to John,* AB 29 (Garden City, N.Y.: Doubleday & Co., 1966), 534.

37. See my "Jacob Traditions and the Interpretation of John 4:10–26," 424–25.

38. E.g., Abel over Cain, Isaac over Ishmael, Joseph over his brethren, Ephraim over Menasseh, David over his siblings, and Solomon over David's other sons; this pattern was later employed by Paul to gentile Christians vis-à-vis the Jews (Rom. 9:6–13). See R. N. Whybray, *The Succession Narrative* (London: SPCK, 1968), 10–55.

39. Philo calls Jacob *pternistes,* that is, "the Supplanter," *Cher* 67; *L.A.* I.61; II.89; III.15, 93, 180; *Mut.* 81; *Q.G.* IV.163; *Somn.* I.171.

40. Authentic purification remains a thematic concern in 3:25; 13:10–11; 15:3.

41. See Brown, *Community of the Beloved Disciple,* 71–81.

42. See my article "John III—A Debate over Johannine Epistemology and Christology," *NT* 23 (1981): 117–18, 126–27.

43. See J. Z. Smith, "Native Cults in the Hellenistic Period," *HR* 11 (1971): 236–39; and idem, *Map Is Not Territory* (Leiden: E. J. Brill, 1978), 147–66.

44. See Jack Lightstone, *The Commerce of the Sacred* (Chico, Calif.: Scholars Press, 1984), 1–16.

45. See Mary Smallwood, *The Jews under Roman Rule* (Leiden: E. J. Brill, 1976), 123; and J. Z. Smith, *Imagining Religion* (Chicago: University of Chicago Press, 1982), 8–14.

46. See my article "Idea of Purity in Mark's Gospel," 122–23.

47. See my article "John III—A Debate over Johannine Epistemology and Christology," 117.

48. See my article "Witchcraft Accusations in 2 Cor. 10–13: Paul in Social-Science Perspective," *Listening* 21 (1986): 160–70; the same model has been

used regarding Matthew 12 in my *Calling Jesus Names* (Sonoma, Calif.: Polebridge Press, 1988).

49. On dualism, see James H. Charlesworth, "A Critical Comparison of the Dualism in 1QS 3:13—4:26 and the 'Dualism' Contained in the Gospel of John," *NTS* 15 (1968–69): 389–418; see also A. F. Segal, "Ruler of This World: Attitudes About Mediator Figures and the Importance of Sociology for Self-Definition," in *Jewish and Christian Self-Definition*, vol. 2, *Aspects of Judaism in the Graeco-Roman Period*, ed. E. P. Sanders (Philadelphia: Fortress Press, 1981), 245–68.

50. On the importance of the temple within the system of Judaism, see my article "Idea of Purity in Mark's Gospel," 93–102, 115–19.

51. Using a different approach through an examination of the Johannine radical use of language, Bruce Malina in his article "The Gospel of John in Sociolinguistic Perspective," *Center for Hermeneutical Studies*, Colloquy 48 (Berkeley: Center for Hermeneutical Studies, 1985), 1–23, also classified the data I am studying as weak group/low grid.

52. See Herold Weiss, "Foot Washing in the Johannine Community," *NT* 21 (1979): 300–325.

53. Brown, *Community of the Beloved Disciple*, 14; see also John F. O'Grady, "Individualism and the Johannine Ecclesiology," *BTB* 5 (1975): 235–45; see also C. F. D. Moule, "The Individualism of the Fourth Gospel," *NT* 5 (1962): 171–90; and Ernst Käsemann, *Testament of Jesus*, 28–32, 40, 44, 66.

54. See Rudolf Schnackenburg, *The Gospel according to St. John* (New York: Crossroad, 1982), 3:376–80; David J. Hawkin, "The Function of the Beloved Disciple Motif in the Johannine Redaction," *LTP* 33 (1977): 135–50; and M. de Jonge, "The Beloved Disciple and the Date of the Gospel of John," in *Text and Interpretation*, ed. E. Best (New York: Cambridge University Press, 1979), 99–114.

55. Included among these "beloved disciples" must be Martha, Mary, and their brother Lazarus (11:3, 5, 11), and probably Mary Magdalene (20:11–18).

56. On "replication," see Bruce Malina, *Christian Origins and Cultural Anthropology*, 112–15.

57. On "redundancy," see Edmund Leach, *Myth and Cosmos*, ed. John Middleton (Garden City, N.Y.: Natural History Press, 1967), 1–13.

CHAPTER 7
CHRISTOLOGY AND COSMOLOGY: SPIRIT VERSUS FLESH

1. Mary Douglas, "The Social Preconditions of Enthusiasm and Heterodoxy," in *Forms of Symbolic Action*, Proceedings of the 1969 Annual Spring Meeting of the American Ethnological Society, ed. Robert F. Spenser (Seattle: University of Washington Press, 1969), 69–80.

2. Mary Douglas, *Natural Symbols* (New York: Pantheon Books, 1982), 65–81; 156–67.

3. Douglas, "Social Preconditions of Enthusiasm," 70; or idem, *Natural Symbols*, 162.

4. Mary Douglas, *Purity and Danger* (London: Routledge & Kegan Paul, 1966), 115.

5. An extensive illustration of how Douglas's remarks on purity are clues to a given social system can be found in my article "The Idea of Purity in Mark," *Semeia* 35 (1986): 92–123.

6. Douglas, *Natural Symbols*, 70–71.

7. Ibid., 65.

8. The relationship of social control and bodily discipline according to Douglas's model is illustrated extensively in my article "Body Language and 1 Corinthians: The Use of Anthropological Models for Understanding Paul and His Opponents," *Semeia* 35 (1986): 129–70.

9. A qualification is in order here. In weak group situations the individual ego is very strong and may choose rigorous bodily control, such as a strict diet and celibacy; but the bodily control here is not the imposition of society (strong group), but the individual, voluntary choice of such control.

10. Douglas, "Social Preconditions of Enthusiasm," 69; and idem, *Natural Symbols*, 162.

11. Douglas, "Social Preconditions of Enthusiasm," 69; and idem, *Natural Symbols*, 162.

12. Douglas, "Social Preconditions of Enthusiasm," 70; and idem, *Natural Symbols*, 163.

13. Douglas, "Social Preconditions of Enthusiasm," 70–71; see idem, *Natural Symbols*, 161–62.

14. Douglas, "Social Preconditions of Enthusiasm," 72; see idem, *Natural Symbols*, 70–74.

15. I have been strongly influenced on this point by Kikuo Matsunaga, "Is John's Gospel Anti-Sacramental? A New Solution in the Light of the Evangelist's Milieu," *NTS* 27 (1981): 516–24.

16. See 17:5; 13:1–3; 14:1–2; 18:36.

17. The phrase "Christians of inadequate faith" was coined by Raymond E. Brown, *The Community of the Beloved Disciple* (New York: Paulist/Newman Press, 1979), 73–81; I am extending its use to problems relating to the high christological confession, which Brown did not do.

18. A convenient survey of recent discussion may be found in Robert Kysar, *The Fourth Evangelist and His Gospel* (Minneapolis: Augsburg Publishing House, 1975), 131–37; and more recently in idem, "The Fourth Gospel: A Report on Recent Research," in *Aufsteig und Niedergand der Römischer Welt*, 25:3, 2451–52.

19. E.g., Herbert Braun, *Qumran und das Neue Testament* (Tübingen: J. C. B. Mohr, 1966), 2: 119–32; and James Charlesworth, "A Critical Comparison of the Dualism in 1 QS 3:13—4:26 and the 'Dualism' Contained in the Gospel of John," in *John and Qumran* (London: Geoffrey Chapman, 1972), 76–106.

20. To see how christological confessions may function as value statements affecting the perception of other objects in the cosmos, see my *Christ Is Community* (Wilmington, Del.: Michael Glazier, 1985), 186–91; 263–66.

21. The subtitle of Douglas's *Natural Symbols* is appropriately "Explorations in Cosmology," by which she means a typology of perception of the workings and values of the world according to her variables group and grid; see *Natural Symbols*, 103–6.

22. See my article "John III—A Debate over Johannine Epistemology and Christology," *NT* 23 (1981): 118–21.

23. On this theme of replacement in the Fourth Gospel, see my article "Jacob Traditions and the Interpretation of John 4:10–26," *CBQ* 41 (1979): 436–37.

24. I have explored this motif in greater detail in "Jesus the Witch," in *Calling Jesus Names* (Sonoma, Calif.: Polebridge Press, 1988); and in my "Witchcraft Accusations in 2 Cor. 10–13: Paul in Social Science Perspective," *Listening* 21 (1986): 166–67.

25. The reader is reminded of our discussion of this passage in chap. 5.

26. See D. A. Carson, "The Function of the Paraclete in John 16:7–11," *JBL* 98 (1979): 558–66.

27. See Alan Segal, "Ruler of This World: Attitudes about Mediator Figures and the Importance of Sociology for Self-Definition," *Jewish and Christian Self-Definition*, vol. 2, *Aspects of Judaism in the Graeco-Roman Period*, ed. E. P. Sanders (Philadelphia: Fortress Press, 1981), 245–68.

28. Wayne Meeks, "The Man from Heaven in Johannine Sectarianism," *JBL* 91 (1972): 44–72.

29. Ibid., 67.

30. On John and sacraments, see Raymond E. Brown, *New Testament Essays* (Garden City, N.Y.: Doubleday & Co., 1968), 77–107; see also Matsunaga, "Is John's Gospel Anti-Sacramental?" 516–24.

31. J. Massingberd Ford, in "'Mingled Blood' from the Side of Christ (John XIX.34)" *NTS* 15 (1968/69): 337–38, indicated how this text argues that Jesus is a kosher Passover lamb and so can cleanse us from sin; see also Raymond E. Brown, *The Epistles of John*, AB 30 (Garden City, N.Y.: Doubleday & Co., 1982), 573–603.

32. E.g., Rudolf Schnackenburg, *The Gospel according to St. John* (New York: Crossroad, 1982), 3:341–88.

33. See R. F. Collins, "Representative Figures in the Fourth Gospel," *DR* 94 (1976): 26–46, 118–32; see also E. Krafft, "Die Personen im Johannesevangelium," *EvT* 16 (1956): 18–32; J. Roloff, "Der johanneische 'Lieblingsjünger' und der Lehrer der Gerechtigkeit," *NTS* 15 (1968–69): 141; and T. Lorenzen, *Der Lieblingsjünger im Johannesevangelium* (Stuttgart: Katholisches Bibelwerk, 1971), 80–82.

34. I have developed these patterns in greater detail in chaps. 6 and 7 of *The Resurrection Stories* (Wilmington, Del.: Michael Glazier, 1988).

35. See Herold Weiss, "Foot Washing in the Johannine Community," *NT* 21 (1979): 298–325.

36. See Bruce Malina, *Christian Origins and Cultural Anthropology* (Atlanta: John Knox Press, 1986), 30–33, 107–9.

37. Brown, *Epistles of John*, 53–54, 75–79, 494–96.

38. For a fuller exposition of this argument, see my *Christ Is Community,* 183–92.

39. See also 1 John 2:24; 3:11; and 2 John 5, 6; see Brown, *Epistles of John,* 97–98, 155–58.

CHAPTER 8
CHRIST, SPIRIT, AND REVOLT

1. For an introduction to Spirit Christology, which has been of interest recently to systematic theologians, see Philip Rosato, "Spirit Christology: Ambiguity and Promise," *TS* 38 (1977): 423–49. That topic is not the emphasis of this chapter; rather, we examine what meanings attached to spirit are replicated in the particular christological perspective of the Fourth Gospel.

2. E.g., James M. Boice, *Witness and Revelation in the Gospel of John* (Grand Rapids: Zondervan, 1970), 120–22, 143–45.

3. See Heinrich Schlier, "Der Heilige Geist als Interpret nach dem Johannesevangelium," *Internationale Katholische Zeitschrift* 2 (1973): 97–103.

4. See Raymond E. Brown, *The Gospel according to John,* AB 29A (Garden City, N.Y.: Doubleday & Co., 1970), 1139–41.

5. A convenient entry into this discussion may be found in D. Bruce Woll, *Johannine Christianity in Conflict,* SBLDS 60 (Chico, Calif.: Scholars Press, 1981), 69–80.

6. Woll (ibid., 112–20) begins to introduce some social-science modeling into the discussion, but his choice of Max Weber and charismatic authority is an inadequate, incomplete, and even anachronistic model for interpretation of New Testament texts.

7. My initial attempt to plot out this development may be found in *Christ Is Community* (Wilmington, Del.: Michael Glazier, 1985), 144–83.

8. Raymond Firth, *Essays on Social Organization and Values* (London: Athlone Press, 1964), 247–56.

9. Mary Douglas, *Natural Symbols* (New York: Pantheon Books, 1982), 75.

10. Ibid., 71.

11. Ibid., 72.

12. At this point, Douglas is relying on the work of Victor Turner, "Metaphors of Anti-Structure in Religious Culture," in *Changing Perspectives in the Scientific Study of Religion,* ed. Allan Eister (New York: John Wiley & Sons, 1974), 63–84.

13. Douglas, *Natural Symbols,* 74.

14. Ibid., 74.

15. One, of course, is immediately reminded of many New Testament passages where spirit against flesh is a common theme, e.g., John 6:63; 1 John 4:2–3; Gal. 5:16–26; Rom. 8:1–14.

16. M. Mauss, "Techniques of the Body," *Economy and Society* 2 (1973): 70–88.

17. In my recent article "Body Language in 1 Corinthians: The Use of

Anthropological Models for Understanding Paul and His Opponents," *Semeia* 35 (1986): 129–70, I began to discuss the symbolic meaning of the physical body as a window into the systematic conflicts reflected in 1 Corinthians, a study presumed here.

18. Douglas, *Natural Symbols*, 160.

19. Ibid., 162.

20. Ibid., 162.

21. Ibid., 163.

22. Ibid., 162.

23. The best description of this trait is the recent book of Robert Bellah et al., *Habits of the Heart* (Berkeley and Los Angeles: University of California Press, 1985); see also Robert Bellah, "Discerning Old and New Imperatives in Theological Education," *Theological Education* 19 (1982): 7–29.

24. See my "Body Language in 1 Corinthians," 154–56.

25. In this regard, one must note the place and possible function of the reference to spirit in 7:39; the context is a formal debate about the correct interpretation of the Scriptures vis-à-vis Jesus (7:26–27, 42, 52); it is interesting to speculate whether the reference to spirit which will be given should be seen in terms of the correct reading of the Scriptures.

26. See Raymond E. Brown, "The Paraclete in the Fourth Gospel," *NTS* 13 (1966–67): 113–32; see also J. Louis Martyn, *History and Theology in the Fourth Gospel*, rev. ed. (Nashville: Abingdon Press, 1979), 144–49.

27. Some sense of the problematic nature of 14:16 may be found in Woll, *Johannine Christianity in Conflict*, 3–4, 69–96.

28. Brown, "The Paraclete in the Fourth Gospel," 126–27; see Martyn, *History and Theology in the Fourth Gospel*, 134–42.

29. See my article "Jacob Traditions and the Interpretation of John 4:10–26," *CBQ* 41 (1979): 419–37.

30. I have dealt with accusations of this sort at length elsewhere, using a model of witchcraft accusation from cultural anthropology; see "Witchcraft Accusations in 2 Cor. 10–13: Paul in Social Science Perspective," *Listening* 21 (1986): 160–70; "Jesus the Witch," in *Calling Jesus Names* (Sonoma, Calif.: Polebridge Press, 1988); and "Bewitched in Galatia," *CBQ* 50 (1988): 72–100.

31. E.g., see my *The Passion according to Luke* (New York: Paulist/Newman Press, 1985), 177–79.

32. See 7:11, 19, 25, 34, 36; 8:21, 27, 40.

33. Typically, Brown (*The Gospel according to John*, 127) explained 2:24–25 in terms of the inadequacy of sign faith, a good explanation, but one that belongs in a larger context.

34. After Jesus' departure, this function of uncovering demonic masquerades is passed on to the Paraclete; see D. A. Carson, "The Function of the Paraclete in John 16:7–11," *JBL* 98 (1979): 558–66.

35. The argument here is building on the important insights of Wayne Meeks, "The Man from Heaven in Johannine Sectarianism," *JBL* 91 (1972): 44–72.

36. See my "'My Lord and My God': The Divinity of Jesus in John's Gospel," SBLASP 1986, 152–71.

37. In this regard, my analysis of the high Christology is in full agreement with that of Meeks ("Man from Heaven in Johannine Sectarianism"), and remarkably similar to that of Ernst Käsemann, *The Testament of Jesus* (Philadelphia: Fortress Press, 1968).

38. See Raymond E. Brown, *The Epistles of John*, AB 30 (Garden City, N.Y.: Doubleday & Co., 1982), ad loc.

39. Once again, Woll (*Johannine Christianity in Conflict*, 109–28) presents evidence for a strategy similar to that described here as spirit-against-matter, but he argues that this represents the earliest strata of the Johannine community, which he describes as "charismatic in origins." See D. Moody Smith, *Johannine Christianity: Essays on Its Setting, Sources, and Theology* (Columbia, S.C.: University of South Carolina Press, 1984), 15–16, 24–25.

40. This sense of control of spirit or continuity with the past is often cited in the literature on the role of the Spirit in the Fourth Gospel; see, e.g., J. Ramsey Michaels, "The Johannine Words of Jesus and Christian Prophecy," SBLASP 1975, 240, 249; Smith, *Johannine Christianity*, 30–31.

41. E.g., M. Eugene Boring, *Sayings of the Risen Jesus* (Cambridge: Cambridge University Press, 1982), 1–14; and James M. Robinson, "On the *Gattung* of Mark (and John)," *Perspective* 11 (1970): 107–15.

42. E.g., M. Eugene Boring, "The Influence of Christian Prophecy on the Johannine Portrayal of the Paraclete and Jesus," *NTS* 25 (1978): 118.

43. See Brown, *Gospel according to John*, 1142.

44. Meeks, "Man from Heaven," 69–71.

45. Ibid., 70.

46. Mary Douglas, "The Social Preconditions of Enthusiasm and Heterodoxy," in *Forms of Symbolic Action*, Proceedings of the 1969 Annual Spring Meeting of the American Ethnological Society, ed. Robert F. Spenser (Seattle: University of Washington Press, 1969), 69.

47. Arguments about the ideological implications of religious doctrines are hardly new in biblical studies; see Norman Gottwald, *The Tribes of Yahweh* (Maryknoll, N.Y.: Orbis Books, 1981), 592–650; and Wayne A. Meeks, *The First Urban Christians* (New Haven: Yale University Press, 1983), 164–92.

SUMMARY, CONCLUSIONS, AND FURTHER QUESTIONS

1. Although it was not discussed in this book, we might include one final aspect of the Johannine high Christology: how Jesus functions as the appearing deity in Israel's past and present (see my article "The Jacob Allusions in John 1:51," *CBQ:* 44 [1982]: 586–605). This argument would relate to Jesus' use of the divine name "I AM," the name of the appearing deity who is eternal in the past.

2. E.g., Bruce Malina's first book on the use of social-science models for biblical interpretation took up this issue directly; see his *The New Testament*

World: Insights from Cultural Anthropology (Atlanta: John Knox Press, 1981); and most recently, idem, "Interpreting the Bible with Anthropology: The Case of the Rich and the Poor," *Listening* 21 (1986): 148–59. On Mediterranean culture, see David D. Gilmore, "Anthropology of the Mediterranean Area," *Annual Review of Anthropology* 11 (1982): 175–205; Jeremy Boissevain, *Friends of Friends* (New York: St. Martin's Press, 1979); John Davis, *The People of the Mediterranean: An Essay in Comparative Social Anthropology* (London: Routledge & Kegan Paul, 1977); John G. Peristiany, *Honor and Shame: The Values of Mediterranean Society* (London: Weidenfeld & Nicholson, 1965); and Julian Pitt-Rivers, *The Fate of Shechem or the Politics of Sex: Essays in the Anthropology of the Mediterranean* (New York: Cambridge University Press, 1977).

3. Wayne Meeks, "The Man from Heaven in Johannine Sectarianism," *JBL* 91 (1972): 71.

APPENDIX 1
BACKGROUND OF THE NAME "I AM"

1. For a survey of issues and evidence, see Philip Harner, *The "I Am" of the Fourth Gospel* (Philadelphia: Fortress Press, 1970); see also Raymond E. Brown, *The Gospel according to John*, AB 29 (Garden City, N.Y.: Doubleday & Co., 1966), 533–38; and Rudolf Schnackenburg, *The Gospel according to St. John* (New York: Crossroad, 1982), 2:79–89.

2. See Brown, *Gospel according to John*, 756.

3. The issue here is not the meaning of Exod. 3:14 in the Hebrew Scripture and the milieu of the ancient world. For that one can conveniently consult Brevard Childs, *The Book of Exodus* (Philadelphia: Westminster Press, 1974), 60–71.

4. I am presupposing a background for the LXX understanding of God's name, e.g., Martin Hengel, "The 'Interpretatio Graeca' of Judaism," in *Judaism and Hellenism* (Philadelphia: Fortress Press, 1974), 1:255–67. On the Hellenistic background of the LXX of Exod. 3:14, see Morton Smith, "The Image of God," *BJRL* 40 (1958): 474; and Martin McNamara, *The New Testament and the Palestinian Targum to the Pentateuch*, AnBib 27 (Rome: Biblical Institute Press, 1966), 103–5.

5. Besides *Mut.* 11 and *Det.* 160, see *Somn.* I.230–31 and *Vita Mos.* I.66, 74–76.

6. See H. A. Wolfson, *Philo* (Cambridge: Harvard University Press, 1968), 210.

7. For the collection of these texts, their translation, and interpretation, I am indebted to McNamara, *New Testament and the Palestinian Targum*, 97–112.

8. R. H. Charles, *A Critical and Exegetical Commentary to Revelation of John* (Edinburgh: T & T Clark, 1920), 10; and McNamara, *New Testament and the Palestinian Targum*, 98–101.

9. See Claus Westermann, *Isaiah 40–66* (Philadelphia: Westminster Press, 1966), 65, 94.

10. These classical citations are conveniently collected in Charles, *Revelation*, 10; F. Büchsel, *"eimi"* in *TDNT*, 2:399; and McNamara, *New Testament and the Palestinian Targum*, 102.

11. See James Reese, *Hellenistic Influence on the Book of Wisdom and Its Consequences*, AnBib 41 (Rome: Biblical Institute Press, 1970).

12. Plutarch, *de Iside* 9; see also Sextus Empiricus, *Against the Physicians* I.46.

13. Diogenes Laertius, VIII.134.

14. A comparable discussion can be found in Cicero, *De Natura Deorum* I.viii.20, x.25, xii.29, xxiv.68.

15. Sextus Empiricus, *Against the Physicians* I.45.

16. Philo, *Jos.* 265.

17. Regarding the Wisdom of Solomon, James Reese (*Hellenistic Influence on the Book of Wisdom*, 65–67) noted that the terms eternity *(aidiotes)* and imperishability *(aphtharsia)* have the force of technical philosophical terms, stemming basically from Epicurean discussions of God.

18. Plutarch, *Pelopidas* 16; a lengthy discussion of this same point can be found in his *On the Malice of Herodotus* 857D, in response to Herodotus II.145–46.

19. Diodorus of Sicily, *Library of History* VI.1.2 (see also I.12, 10–13.1).

20. C. H. Talbert, *What Is a Gospel?* (Philadelphia: Fortress Press, 1977), 25–52.

APPENDIX 2
INTERPRETATION OF PSALM 82:6

1. Philo explicitly deals with Exod. 7:1 in *Leg. All.* I.40; *Sac.* 9; *Det.* 39–40, 161–62; *Migr.* 84, 169; *Mut.* 19–20, 125, 128–29; *Somn.* II.189; *Quod Omn.* 43–44; yet Moses is "god" because of his share of God's power (*Post.* 28–31; see also *Vit. Mos.* I.158).

2. See Wayne Meeks, *The Prophet-King*, NovTSup 14 (Leiden: E. J. Brill, 1967), 107–31, 234–36; this argument appeared in a more developed form in his "Moses as God and King," in *Religions in Antiquity*, ed. Jacob Neusner (Leiden: E. J. Brill, 1968), 354–71.

3. Usually it is said that God is Sovereign of the world and that Moses (or someone else) is "god" of the world below; see *Pesikta de Rab Kahana* 198b; *Debarim Rabbah* 11.4; *Midr Pss* 90.1. An interesting passage in the *Apostolic Constitutions* calls the Christian bishop "god" according to Ps. 82:6, implying that the bishop is "god" below: "He is your ruler and governor; he is your king and potentate; he is, next to God, your earthly god, who has a right to be honored by you. For concerning him, and such as he, it is that God pronounces, 'I have said, ye are gods; and ye are all children of the most high' (Ps. 82:6) and 'Ye shall not speak evil of the gods' (Exod. 22:28)."

4. Richard Jungkuntz, "An Approach to the Exegesis of John 10:34–36," *CTM* 35 (1964): 561–62.

5. For arguments against the equation of judges and gods, see James

Ackermann, "The Rabbinic Interpretation of Psalm 82 and the Gospel of John," *HTR* 59 (1966): 187–88.

6. Tanhuma B Wa'era #9, as cited in *Str.B.* II.464.

7. *Mekilta de Rabbi Ishmael,* Tractate *Bahodesh* 9, trans. Jacob Lauterbach (Philadelphia: Jewish Publication Society of America, 1933), 2:272.

8. *b. Abodah Zarah* 5a.

9. See *Pesikta Rabbati* I.2 and 33.10; *Pesikta de Rab Kahana* 4.4; see also *Pesikta Rabbati* 14.10; *Lev. R.* XI.3 and *Num. R.* XVI.24; *Exodus R.* XXXII.7.

10. See Jacob Jervell, *Imago Dei* (Göttingen: Vandenhoeck & Ruprecht, 1960), 114–19.

INDEX OF
SCRIPTURAL PASSAGES

INDEX OF
SUBJECTS